Your iPad® at Work

SECOND EDITION

Covers iOS 5.1 on iPad, iPad2 and iPad 3rd generation

Jason R. Rich

Que®

800 East 96th Street
Indianapolis, Indiana 46240 USA

YOUR iPAD® AT WORK

COPYRIGHT © 2012 BY PEARSON EDUCATION, INC.

ISBN-13: 978-0-7897-4852-2

ISBN-10: 0-7897-4852-5

Library of Congress Cataloging-in-Publication data is on file.

Printed in the United States of America

First Printing: June 2012

TRADEMARKS

WARNING AND DISCLAIMER

BULK SALES

Que Publishing offers excellent discounts on this book when ordered in quantity for bulk purchases or special sales. For more information, please contact

U.S. Corporate and Government Sales
1-800-382-3419
corpsales@pearsontechgroup.com

For sales outside the United States, please contact

International Sales
international@pearsoned.com

EDITOR-IN-CHIEF
Greg Wiegand

ACQUISITIONS EDITOR
Laura Norman

DEVELOPMENT EDITOR
Mark Renfrow

MANAGING EDITOR
Sandra Schroeder

SENIOR PROJECT EDITOR
Tonya Simpson

COPY EDITOR
Charlotte Kughen

INDEXER
Cheryl Lenser

PROOFREADER
Leslie Joseph

TECHNICAL EDITOR
Greg Kettell

PUBLISHING COORDINATOR
Cindy Teeters

BOOK DESIGNER
Anne Jones

COMPOSITOR
Bumpy Design

CONTENTS AT A GLANCE

TABLE OF CONTENTS

ABOUT THE AUTHOR

Jason R. Rich (www.JasonRich.com) is the bestselling author of more than 52 books, as well as a frequent contributor to a handful of major daily newspapers, national magazines, and popular websites. He also is an accomplished photographer and an avid Apple iPad, iPhone, and Mac user.

You can read more than 80 free feature-length "how to" articles by Jason R. Rich covering the Apple iPhone and iPad at the Que Publishing website. Visit www.iOSArticles.com and click the Articles tab. You can also follow Jason R. Rich on Twitter (@JasonRich7).

DEDICATION

This book is dedicated to the late Steve Jobs, as well as to my newborn niece, Natalie.

ACKNOWLEDGMENTS

Thanks to Laura Norman at Que Publishing for inviting me to work on this book, and for all of her guidance as I've worked on this project. My gratitude also goes out to Mark Renfrow, Greg Wiegand, Tonya Simpson, Cindy Teeters, Todd Brakke, Gregg Kettell, and Paul Boger, as well as everyone else at Que Publishing and Pearson who contributed their expertise, hard work, and creativity to the creation of *Your iPad at Work*.

Thanks to my friends and family for their ongoing support. Finally, thanks to you, the reader. I hope this book helps you take full advantage of the power and capabilities of this amazing tablet device so that you're able to fully utilize your iPad in every aspect of your life.

WE WANT TO HEAR FROM YOU!

As the reader of this book, *you* are our most important critic and commentator. We value your opinion and want to know what we're doing right, what we could do better, what areas you'd like to see us publish in, and any other words of wisdom you're willing to pass our way.

As an editor-in-chief for Que Publishing, I welcome your comments. You can email or write me directly to let me know what you did or didn't like about this book—as well as what we can do to make our books better.

Please note that I cannot help you with technical problems related to the topic of this book. We do have a User Services group, however, where I will forward specific technical questions related to the book.

When you write, please be sure to include this book's title and author as well as your name, email address, and phone number. I will carefully review your comments and share them with the author and editors who worked on the book.

Email: feedback@quepublishing.com

Mail: Greg Wiegand
Editor-in-Chief
Que Publishing
800 East 96th Street
Indianapolis, IN 46240 USA

READER SERVICES

Visit our website and register this book at quepublishing.com/register for convenient access to any updates, downloads, or errata that might be available for this book.

Introduction

When Apple announced the original iPad back in 2010, the company's iconic CEO, the late Steve Jobs (1955–2011), referred to the tablet device as "magical." That was the start of a technological revolution that has since captured the imaginations of iPad users around the world, and for Apple, it has resulted in tens of millions of iPad units sold each subsequent year.

In 2011, the original, first-generation iPad was replaced by the iPad 2. Almost exactly a year after that (March 2012), Apple launched the third-generation iPad (see Figure I.1), referred to as the *new iPad*, and demand for the tablet continues to be unprecedented.

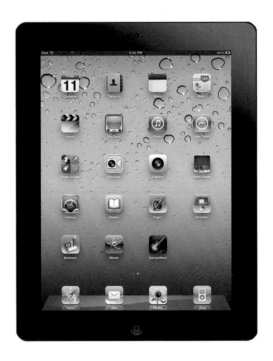

FIGURE I.1

The iPad 2 and new iPad (third-generation iPad) look almost identical on the outside, but inside, the new iPad is more advanced.

In just a few short years, the iPad has gone from being a cool, high-tech gadget to becoming an indispensible business tool used in virtually all industries. With each generation of iPad that's been released, more and more business people, entrepreneurs, consultants, freelancers, and other types of professionals have discovered firsthand that the iPad can often replace the need to carry around a larger and heavier laptop computer or netbook.

Regardless of what you do for a living, this all new edition of *Your iPad at Work* helps you quickly learn how to use your iPad 2 or new iPad. When you combine any iPad model with the right collection of apps and accessories, it becomes the perfect tool for anyone who needs advanced computing power while on the go—at a desk, by the pool, on an airplane, in the car (not while driving), or while sitting on a couch at home.

WHAT YOU CAN EXPECT FROM THIS BOOK

Your iPad at Work provides step-by-step instructions, plus hundreds of tips, strategies, and ideas for incorporating the iPad 2 or new iPad into your personal and professional life with the shortest learning curve possible—even if you don't consider yourself to be technologically savvy or adept at using the latest high-tech gadgets.

> **TIP** As you read *Your iPad at Work*, keep your eye out for the Tips, Notes, and Caution icons. Each of these icons has short tidbits of information that are particularly important and directly relevant to the chapter you're reading.

Before we start exploring all of the work-related tasks your iPad is capable of, including managing email, web surfing, word processing, managing contacts, scheduling, text messaging, video conferencing, making voice-over-IP phone calls, sending/receiving faxes, working with databases and spreadsheets, creating digital slide presentations, audio recording (dictation), managing to-do lists, facilitating project management, credit card transaction processing, taking and editing pictures, shooting and editing video, tweeting, reading eBooks, online banking, and countless other tasks, you need to learn the basics of how to interact with this cutting-edge device.

> **TIP** In addition to what you discover from this book, you can access more than 80 how-to articles by *Your iPad at Work* author Jason R. Rich, which have been published on the quepublishing.com website. Simply visit www.iOSArticles.com, and click the Articles tab.

UNBOXING YOUR iPAD

Right out of the box, your iPad 2 or new iPad (third-generation iPad) comes preinstalled with Apple's iOS 5.1 (or later) operating system and a collection of apps that are designed to handle the core tasks you'll probably be using your tablet for. With a quick visit to the App Store, however, you can greatly enhance the capabilities of your iPad by acquiring optional apps for it.

> **NOTE** You learn more about finding, acquiring and installing apps in Chapter 6, "Finding and Installing Apps from the App Store," and learn about popular business-related apps worth checking out from Chapters 10, 11, and 13.

Chances are that as soon as you take the iPad out of the box for the very first time, its battery will be close to fully charged and it'll be ready for you to activate and set up. Whether the iPad you're about to activate is your first or you're upgrading to a newer model, plan on spending at least 15 to 30 minutes getting your new tablet up and running. The specific setup process is described shortly.

> **NOTE** Just about all the information in this book applies to all iPad 2 and new iPad models. Most also applies when using an original (first-generation) iPad.
>
> If you're using a new iPad, almost anytime the iPad's virtual keyboard is displayed, the Dictation key is available. It displays a microphone icon and appears between the .?123 (or ABC) key and Spacebar key.
>
> Throughout *Your iPad at Work*, some of the screen shots were captured using an iPad 2, so the Dictation key is not always displayed. However, it might be visible on your new iPad as you're following the steps or procedures outlined within each chapter.

THE iPAD 2 VERSUS THE NEW iPAD

Currently, there are three generations of iPads. The original iPad is no longer being sold by Apple; however, you can still purchase a used or refurbished original iPad, starting at less than $200.00.

With each generation of iPads that Apple has released, the basic look and design of the tablet has remained consistent, but the technology built in to the tablet has been dramatically improved. So, if you're an original iPad user wondering whether you should upgrade to the iPad 2 or new iPad, the answer is an unequivocal yes, especially if you'll be using the tablet for work-related tasks.

However, if you're an iPad 2 user and you've already discovered that it's an indispensible communications, organizational, and productivity tool and you're wondering whether you should upgrade to the new iPad, take a look at what the new iPad (which was the third-generation iPad, released in March 2012) offers to make your decision.

NEW FEATURES OF THE NEW iPAD

From the outside, the iPad 2 and new iPad look virtually identical. It's what's on the inside that set the tablets apart. To begin, the new iPad features a state-of-the-art retina display. It's the same size as the display offered by the iPad 2, but offers a significantly higher resolution.

The new iPad also offers a faster processor, known as the Apple A5X chip. In addition, Apple's newest tablet offers an 5MP iSight camera built in, which is a significant improvement over the camera that's built in to the iPad 2.

NOTE When discussing digital cameras, a megapixel (MP) is defined as one million pixels or colored dots. Thus, a 5MP digital camera utilizes five million pixels to create each full-color digital image.

Although all iPad models can connect to the Internet via a Wi-Fi connection (which requires you be within the radius of a Wi-Fi hotspot), when it comes to surfing the Web, some models of the new iPad can also access the Internet using a 4G LTE wireless data network, which is significantly faster than the 3G networks that some models of the original iPad and iPad 2 are able to connect to.

NOTE Although some models of the new iPad offer 4G LTE wireless data network connectivity, wireless data service providers, such as AT&T Wireless and Verizon Wireless, don't yet offer 4G LTE service across the United States. If you'll be using your iPad where service hasn't yet been upgraded to 4G LTE service, your new iPad will automatically connect to a 3G wireless data network.

Also, depending on your wireless data service provider, your new iPad might be able to serve as a personal hotspot, enabling you to wirelessly connect multiple Wi-Fi–enabled devices to the Internet using the tablet's connection. (At least initially, this feature is not being offered by AT&T Wireless in the U.S.)

Another significant improvement that the new iPad offers is the Dictation mode, which works with most apps. Instead of using the iPad's virtual keyboard to compose text, when using certain apps, such as Safari, Mail, Calendar, Twitter, or Pages, for example, you can tap on the Dictation key and then speak to your iPad and have it convert your speech into text.

Both the iPad 2 and new iPad can utilize a Smart Cover, run using the iOS 5.1 (or later) operating system, and have more than 200,000 optional iPad-specific apps available for them. The iPad 2 and new iPad are also fully compatible with Apple's iCloud service and have an average battery life of about 10 hours.

So, if you're thinking about upgrading from an iPad 2 to a new iPad, or if you're buying your first iPad and can't decide which generation iPad to purchase, consider how you'll be using the tablet, and determine whether the faster processing speed, higher resolution screen, improved built-in camera, 4G LTE web surfing speed, and/or the new iPad's Dictation mode will be useful to you, and then take a look at the prices for each model.

Both the iPad 2 and new iPad come in several different system configurations. You can choose from a black or white casing for either model. You also need to decide how much internal storage space you'll want or need. Your options include 16GB, 32GB, or 64GB. Keep in mind that iPads are not upgradable in terms of internal storage space, so you must anticipate your needs before purchasing a tablet. Finally, you must choose between a Wi-Fi only model, a Wi-Fi + 3G (for iPad 2), or Wi-Fi + 4G (for new iPad) model.

NOTE A Wi-Fi only iPad can connect to the Internet from any Wi-Fi hotspot or wireless network. However, you must remain within the radius of a Wi-Fi signal to maintain the Internet connection.

A Wi-Fi + 3G (or 4G) iPad model can also connect to the wireless data network offered by a wireless data service provider. This requires paying a monthly fee, which includes a predetermined amount of wireless data use, such as 2G per month. If you go beyond your wireless data allocation, you are billed extra (per gigabyte) for use.

The following chart displays the prices of the iPad 2 and new iPad, based on the various system configurations available. These prices were accurate as of March 2012, when the new iPad was first released.

iPad Model	16GB	32GB	64GB
iPad 2 Wi-Fi Only	$399.00	N/A*	N/A*
iPad 2 Wi-Fi + 3G	$529.00	N/A*	N/A*
new iPad Wi-Fi Only	$499.00	$599.00	$699.00
new iPad Wi-Fi + 4G	$629.00	$729.00	$829.00

*Although Apple no longer sells this configuration of the iPad 2, they are still readily available on the secondary used market or available as refurbished iPads.

In addition to the price of the tablet itself, you might want to invest in an Apple Smart Cover for your tablet ($39.00 for the polyurethane edition or $69.00 for the leather edition) as well as the AppleCare+ extended warranty ($99.99 for two years of coverage). Plus, if you purchase a Wi-Fi + 3G (4G) iPad model, you must pay for a monthly wireless data plan, which costs between $14.99 and $50.00 per month depending on which wireless data service provider your iPad is registered with and which wireless data plan you select.

TIP Be sure to register your copy of *Your iPad at Work* on the Que website so you can access the two free appendixes related to this book and discover more about what your iPad can do. Appendix A demonstrates ways to help you save money when shopping for almost anything online using your iPad, including last-minute gifts. Appendix B teaches you how to have fun using your iPad by experiencing some of the most popular games available for the tablet. To access this free bonus material, visit www.quepublishing.com/title/9780789748522, and click Register Your Product.

PREINSTALLED APPS FOR ALL iPADS RUNNING iOS (5.1 OR LATER)

Both the iPad 2 and new iPad run the latest version of Apple's iOS (5.1 or later) operating system. Each tablet also comes bundled with a handful of preinstalled apps. Here's a quick rundown of each app (listed in alphabetical order) that you can begin using immediately, as soon as your iPad is activated (see Figure I.2).

FIGURE I.2

The iPad's Home screen with the preinstalled app icons displayed. This is what the Home screen looks like immediately after you activate the iPad.

- **App Store:** Find, purchase, download, and install apps directly from your iPad. To learn more, see Chapter 7.

- **Calendar:** Manage your schedule on your iPad and sync data with iCloud and other calendar/scheduling software on your Mac or PC. To learn more, see Chapter 4, "Using the Calendar, Reminders, and Notification Center Apps."

- **Camera:** Take photos or shoot high-definition videos using your iPad's built-in camera.

- **Contacts:** Manage your personal contacts database and sync it with iCloud or other contact management software on your primary computer. To learn more, see Chapter 5, "Working with the Contacts App."

- **FaceTime:** Participate in free, real-time video conferences from your iPad using a Wi-Fi Internet connection. To learn more, see Chapter 12, "Conducting Video Conferences and Virtual Meetings."
- **Game Center:** This is an interactive, online-based community for participating in multiplayer games via your iPad. You can compete against and communicate with other players from around the world and experience a variety of Game Center–compatible games.
- **iTunes:** Acquire music, TV shows, movies, and other iTunes Store content from your iPad. To learn more, see Chapter 15, "Downloading Versus Streaming Online Content."
- **Mail:** Manage one or more existing email accounts on your tablet. Send and receive emails, plus manage your message archive. For more information, see Chapter 2, "Working with Email."
- **Maps:** Use detailed onscreen maps and turn-by-turn directions from Google Maps when your iPad is connected to the Web. You also can find specific addresses of companies.
- **Messages:** Send and receive text messages for free, and communicate with other Mac, iPad, iPhone, or iPod touch users, or send/receive instant messages using a compatible service, such as AIM. For more information, see Chapter 12.
- **Music:** Listen to music, audiobooks, and other audio content.
- **Newsstand:** Acquire and read digital editions of newspapers and magazines. To learn more, see Chapter 14, "Staying Informed Using the iBooks and Newsstand Apps."
- **Notes:** Create, organize, share, and print memos with this basic text editor. It does not offer full word-processing capabilities.
- **Photo Booth:** Take and share photos on your iPad with whimsical themes.
- **Photos:** View, edit, print, and share photos stored on your iPad. For enhanced photo-editing capabilities, purchase Apple's iPhoto app for the iPad.
- **Reminders:** Manage to-do lists with this powerful app. Like many other of the iPad's preinstalled apps, it works seamlessly with iCloud for syncing data with other Macs or iOS devices. To learn more, see Chapter 4.
- **Safari:** Use this app to surf the Web. To learn more, see Chapter 3, "Surfing the Web."
- **Settings:** Use this app to customize the settings of your iPad and to personalize how it functions. More information about Settings is offered later in this introduction.

- **Videos:** Watch TV shows, movies, and other video content on your iPad. To learn more, see Chapter 15.
- **YouTube:** Stream and watch free YouTube videos. To learn more, see Chapter 15.

OPTIONAL "MUST-HAVE" iPAD APPS DEVELOPED BY APPLE

The following apps developed by Apple do not come preinstalled on the iPad 2 or new iPad, but you should seriously consider downloading them from the App Store to enhance the capabilities of your tablet:

- **Cards** (Free): Create and send custom-designed greeting cards directly from your iPad that get professionally printed on card stock by Apple and mailed to the recipient (a per-card fee applies). The result is a personalized greeting card that's as nice as anything you'd buy at the store, only your card features your own photo(s) and message.
- **Find iPhone** (Free): Take advantage of iCloud's Find My Mac, Find My iPhone, or Find My iPad feature from this app to pinpoint the exact location of your other compatible Apple equipment. This app offers an alternative to visiting www.iCloud.com/#find.
- **Find My Friends** (Free): Discover the location of friends, family or co-workers, in real time, who are using an iPhone or iPad. (The other person's permission is required.)
- **Garage Band** ($4.99): Compose and record music using your iPad and transform the tablet into a multi-track recording studio.
- **iBooks** (Free): Acquire and read eBooks from Apple's iBookstore on your tablet. To learn more, see Chapter 14.
- **iMovie** ($4.99): Edit professional-quality videos on your iPad using footage shot with the tablet's built-in camera (and the Camera app), or footage transferred into your tablet from other sources.
- **iPhoto** ($4.99): View, edit, organize, print, and share digital photos on your iPad. This app offers far more advanced image-editing features, for example, than the Photos app that comes preinstalled on the tablet.
- **Keynote** ($9.99): Part of Apple's iWork trio of apps, Keynote is a feature-packed digital slide presentation tool, similar in functionality (and compatible with) Microsoft PowerPoint.

- **Numbers** ($9.99): Also part of Apple's iWork trio of apps, Numbers is a powerful spreadsheet management application that is compatible with Microsoft Excel.

- **Pages** ($9.99): The final app in Apple's iWork trio of apps. It's a full-featured word processor compatible with Microsoft Word.

- **Twitter** (Free): Manage one or more Twitter accounts from your iPad and send tweets from within apps such as Photos or Safari. To learn more, see Chapter 3.

> NOTE   Pages, Keynote, and Numbers all seamlessly integrate with Apple's iCloud service, making it easy to automatically synchronize data, documents, and files between your tablet, Mac, and other iOS devices. To learn more about Apple's iWork for iPad apps, see Chapter 10, "Working with Pages, Numbers, and Keynote."

THE ANATOMY OF THE iPAD 2 AND NEW iPAD

The iPad weighs less than 1.5 pounds, measures 9.5" × 7.31", and is between .34" and .37" thick (depending on the model). When you look at the front of the iPad 2 or new iPad, you see the main screen. The front-facing camera is located at the top center of the tablet, and you can find the iPad's Home button at the bottom center of the iPad's front, as well as the other physical ports and buttons found on the top, bottom, and side of the iPad (shown in Figure I.3).

> NOTE   As you learn in Chapter 1, "Activating and Customizing Your iPad," the new iPad features a state-of-the-art Retina display, which is the most advanced and high-definition display offered on any mobile device. The camera that's built in to the new iPad has also been dramatically improved upon, as has the tablet's main microprocessor. It's also Bluetooth 4.0–compatible.

Aside from these few buttons and ports, you do everything while using your iPad via the tablet's touch screen. To properly navigate around your tablet via this touch screen, you need to utilize several simple finger movements.

FIGURE I.3

The front of the iPad features a 7", full-color, multi-touch screen, the Home button, and the device's front-facing camera. On the back of the iPad unit, in the upper-left corner, you see the rear-facing camera. The iPad's power button is located near the top-right corner of the tablet.

USING THE TOUCH SCREEN

From the moment you turn on your iPad 2 or new iPad (or take it out of Sleep Mode), aside from pressing the Home button to return to the Home screen at any time, virtually all of your interaction with the tablet is through the following finger movements and taps on the tablet's highly sensitive touch screen:

■ **Tapping:** Tapping an icon or link that's displayed on your iPad's screen serves the same purpose as clicking the mouse when you use your main computer. And, just as when you use a computer, you can single-tap or double-tap, which is equivalent to a single- or double-click of the mouse.

■ **Hold:** Instead of a quick tap, in some cases, it is necessary to press and hold your finger on an icon or onscreen command option. When a hold action is required, place your finger on the appropriate icon or command option and hold it there. There's never a need to press down hard on the tablet's screen.

■ **Swipe:** A swipe refers to quickly moving a finger along the screen from right to left, left to right, top to bottom, or bottom to top to scroll to the left, right, down, or up, respectively, depending on which app you're using.

■ **Pinch:** Using your thumb and index finger (the finger next to your thumb), perform a pinch motion on the touch screen to zoom out when using certain apps. Or, unpinch (move your fingers apart quickly) to zoom in on what you're looking at on the screen when using most apps.

■ **Grab:** Using all five of your fingers, start with them spread out on the tablet's screen and then quickly bring them together in a grabbing motion. This immediately returns you to the iPad's Home screen (instead of pressing the Home button).

■ **Pull-Down:** Using your index finger, swipe it quickly downward from the very top of the iPad. This causes the Notification Center window to appear, alerting you of incoming email messages, text messages, alarms, or other time-sensitive actions that you need to deal with. You can be holding the iPad in portrait or landscape mode for this to work. To make this window disappear, tap anywhere on the screen outside the Notification Center window.

■ **Four-Finger Upward Swipe:** Using all of your fingers on one hand (except your thumb), start at the very bottom of the screen and swipe upward. This reveals the iPad's multitasking mode. Or, you can quickly press the Home button twice to access multitasking mode and switch between apps.

TIP   Another way to zoom in or out when looking at the iPad's screen is to double-tap the area of the screen you want to zoom in on.

EXPLORING THE iPAD'S HOME SCREEN

The Home screen on your iPad serves as a central hub from which you can launch individual apps and use the various features and functions of your tablet. Regardless of what you're doing on your tablet or what app you're using, at any time you can return to the Home screen by pressing the Home button on the front-bottom of the tablet.

See Figure I.4 for a sample Home screen that displays a handful of preinstalled and optional third-party apps, as well as some important onscreen icons and indicators.

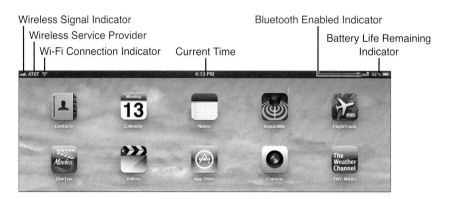

FIGURE I.4

A portion of the main Home screen.

Within the main area of the Home screen are all the icons for apps currently installed on your iPad. On the main iPad Home screen, you can simultaneously display 20 app icons (or folder icons, which are explained shortly), plus an additional 6 app icons on the very bottom of the screen. You also can have multiple Home screens with different app icons displayed on each.

> **TIP** You can choose to display up to six app icons at the very bottom of the Home screen. These icons remain constant, regardless of which Home screen you're looking at. Thus, you should select the apps you use the most and place them in these locations.

The iPad's wallpaper is displayed behind your app icons. You can also customize this from the Settings app. Customizing the Home screen's wallpaper is just one way you can personalize your iPad. How to do this is explained in Chapter 1.

ARRANGING ICONS ON THE HOME SCREEN

In addition to selecting your wallpaper graphic, you can determine the position of app icons on your Home screen. To move app icons around, hold down any onscreen app icon for two to three seconds until all the icons on the Home screen start to shake. Now place your finger on any app icon that you want to move and drag it to a new position on the Home screen. You can move one app icon at a time as long as the icons continue shaking.

During this process (shown in Figure I.5), some of the app icons display a small black-and-white X in the upper-left corner of the icon. You can delete the icons displaying the X from the iPad at any time by tapping the X and confirming your delete request. However, you cannot delete the icons for the apps that came prein-stalled on your iPad.

FIGURE I.5

When the app icons are shaking, you can delete the ones with an X icon. The icons without the X represent the apps that came preinstalled on your tablet.

When you finish moving the icons around, press the Home button to exit out of this mode and save your changes. The icons stop shaking, and you can return to the normal use of your tablet.

CREATING FOLDERS TO ORGANIZE APP ICONS

You can use folders to help organize your Home screen, group apps based on their category, and remove clutter from your Home screen by consolidating the app icons that are displayed.

To create a folder, from the Home screen press and hold down any app icon for two to three seconds. When all the app icons start to shake, pick one app icon that you want to place into a new folder. Hold your finger on that app icon, and drag it directly on top of a second app icon that you want to also include in the folder you're creating.

When the two app icons overlap, a folder is automatically created. As soon as this happens, the other app icons on the Home screen fade slightly and a window con-taining the two apps within the newly created folder appears.

At the top of this window is a text field that contains the default name of the folder. (Your iPad gives the folder an appropriate default name based on the category into which the two apps fall.) You can keep this name by tapping anywhere on the screen outside the folder window. Alternatively, you can change the name of the folder by tapping the circular X icon that's displayed to the extreme right of the folder name field.

To save your folder, tap anywhere outside the folder window. You will see the newly created folder appear among your app icons on the Home screen. In Figure I.6, the folder is labeled Photography and it contains multiple apps.

FIGURE I.6

When a folder appears on the Home screen, it displays alongside the app icons but looks slightly different. Thumbnails of the apps that are stored within the folder are shown within the folder icon.

After you initially create a folder, it contains two app icons. You can add more icons to it whenever all the app icons on the Home screen are shaking. Simply place your finger on the app icon you want to move into the folder and drag that icon on top of the folder icon.

When you're finished adding app icons to the folder, you can move the folder around on the Home screen just as you would move any app icon, or press the Home button to save your changes and return the Home screen to its normal appearance (causing the app icons to stop shaking).

To launch an app that's stored in a folder, from the Home screen tap the folder icon. When the folder window appears on the iPad's screen (as shown in Figure I.7), it displays all the app icons stored within the folder. Tap the icon for the app you want to use.

FIGURE I.7

An open folder and its folder window (which in this example contains 11 photography-related apps) on the iPad's Home screen.

To remove an app icon from within a folder, from the Home screen tap the folder icon representing the folder in which the app is stored. When the folder window appears, hold your finger on the app icon that you want to move. When the app icons start to shake, drag the app icon out of the folder window and back onto the main Home screen.

If you want to delete an app from a folder and from the iPad, when the icons are shaking tap the black-and-white X icon in the icon's upper-left corner. All apps that you acquire for your iPad are automatically stored within your free Apple iCloud account and can be reinstalled on your tablet at anytime.

> TIP   In addition to app icons and folders, you can set Safari bookmark icons to be displayed on your Home screen. Step-by-step directions for creating a Safari bookmark icon are provided in Chapter 3, "Surfing the Web."

IN THIS CHAPTER

- Setting up your iPad
- Choosing and activating a wireless data plan
- Custom configuring the pre-installed apps
- Personalizing your tablet

1

ACTIVATING AND CUSTOMIZING YOUR iPAD

Before you can begin using an iPad you've just acquired, it must first be activated. Then—in addition to choosing your tablet's Lock screen and Home screen wallpaper, and rearranging the app icons on your Home screen—you can customize your iPad, as well as individual apps, in a number of ways. Activating and customizing your iPad is the focus of this chapter.

TURNING YOUR iPAD ON OR OFF

Like any electronic device, your iPad has a Power button. It's located near the top-right corner of the tablet. To turn on the iPad when it's powered off, press the Power button for between one and three seconds. You see the Apple logo appear and the iPad boots up within about 15 seconds, causing the Lock screen to be displayed.

To turn off (power down) the iPad, press and hold the Power button for between three and five seconds, until the Slide to Power Off slider appears. Then, swipe your finger from left to right along this slider.

NOTE When your iPad is completely powered off, none of its apps continue to work in the background and the tablet is not automatically able to connect to the Internet.

PLACING YOUR iPAD INTO SLEEP MODE

In addition to being in a powered on or powered off state, your iPad can also be placed in Sleep Mode when it's not actively being used. While in Sleep Mode, various apps can continue running in the background and the tablet automatically wakes up if an alert, alarm, or notification is generated by an app that requires your attention. Also while in Sleep Mode, the iPad can automatically access the Internet to check for incoming emails or update data within a specific app, for example.

To place your iPad into Sleep Mode, press the Power button once quickly (do not hold it down for several seconds as you would when powering it off). Or simply place an Apple Smart Cover (or compatible cover) over the iPad's screen.

While in Sleep Mode, your iPad's screen is turned off. To wake up the iPad from Sleep Mode, quickly press and release either the Power button or the Home button on the tablet. Whenever you wake up the iPad, the Lock screen appears.

TIP If you'll be using a Smart Cover with your iPad 2 or new iPad, when you place the cover over the tablet's screen, it automatically goes into Sleep Mode. However, when the Smart Cover is removed, the tablet automatically wakes up and returns you to the Lock screen.

Depending on how the iPad is set up from within Settings, you can adjust the iPad's Auto Lock feature to place the tablet into Sleep Mode if the tablet is left unattended for a predetermined about of time.

ACTIVATING YOUR iPAD

When you first purchase your iPad 2 or new iPad, take it out of the box, and turn it on, you see a black screen that displays the iPad logo. Before you can begin using your tablet, you must initialize it and set it up for the first time. When prompted, swipe your finger on the onscreen slider switch to begin the setup procedure.

TIP   The wireless setup procedure that's built into iOS 5.1 is used to initially set up your iPad. To do this, your tablet needs access to a Wi-Fi network. Or, you can connect your tablet to your primary computer via the supplied USB cable and then use the iTunes software on your primary computer (PC or Mac) to initially set up your tablet. This setup procedure is mandatory, but you need to do it only once.

iPAD WIRELESS SETUP

If you're setting up a brand-new iPad that comes with iOS 5.1 (or later) installed, and you're within a Wi-Fi hotspot, you can use the wireless setup procedure.

The very first time you turn on a new tablet, you see a black screen with the word *iPad* displayed near the center of the screen (shown in Figure 1.1). Near the bottom-center of this screen is a virtual slider switch. Using your finger, move this slider from left to right.

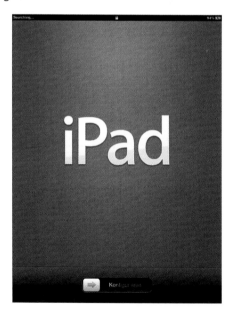

FIGURE 1.1

This is the first thing you see when you turn on your brand new iPad.

When the Welcome screen appears (shown in Figure 1.2), select your language (the default option is English), and then tap the right-pointing arrow icon that's displayed near the upper-right corner of the screen.

FIGURE 1.2

Select your language preference, and then tap the arrow icon to continue with the initial setup procedure.

Next, select your country or region. If you purchased the iPad within the United States, the default option is United States. Tap the Next icon that's displayed near the top-right corner of the screen to continue.

On the screen that displays, you can enable or disable the iPad's Location Services feature. This option allows your iPad (and the various apps running on it) to pinpoint your exact location and utilize (and sometimes share) your location information. The pros and cons of this feature are covered in more detail later in this chapter, but for now, turn On this main Location Services feature. From the Settings app, you can later decide which specific apps can utilize this feature.

From the Wi-Fi Networks screen (shown in Figure 1.3), select the Wi-Fi network your tablet should connect to. The available Wi-Fi networks are displayed on this screen. When you tap the network you want to choose, a small check mark appears next to the Wi-Fi network's name. Tap the Next icon that's displayed near the upper-right corner of the screen to continue.

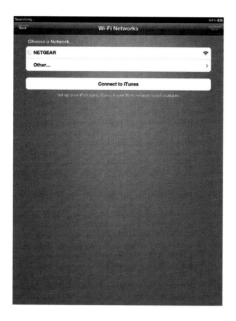

FIGURE 1.3

To continue with the wireless setup, your tablet must be within a Wi-Fi hotspot.

The Set Up iPad screen displays next. From this screen, you can set up your iPad from scratch, or restore the tablet from a previous backup. Near the bottom center of this screen are the following three options (shown in Figure 1.4):

- Set Up As new iPad
- Restore from iCloud Backup
- Restore from iTunes

If you're upgrading from an original iPad to the iPad 2, or from the iPad 2 to a new iPad, and want to load all of your apps, iPad customizations, and data, you have two choices. If your backup data is stored on iCloud, select the Restore from iCloud Backup option. Or, if the backup data from your original iPad is stored on your primary computer (because it was created using the iTunes Sync or iTunes Wireless Sync process), connect your tablet to your primary computer via the supplied USB cable, and follow the onscreen prompts.

However, if you're not upgrading, tap the Set Up As New iPad option, and then tap the Next icon that appears near the upper-right corner of the screen to continue.

FIGURE 1.4

When you activate your iPad, choose whether you want to set it up as a new device or restore your data from an older iPad.

When the Apple ID screen appears, you see a handful of enlarged app icons scrolling across the screen. Near the bottom center of this screen are two command icons:

- Sign In with an Apple ID
- Create a Free Apple ID

If you already own any other Apple computer or iOS device, chances are you already have an Apple ID account set up. Tap the Sign In with an Apple ID command icon to continue. When the next screen appears, use the iPad's virtual keyboard to enter your Apple ID and password.

By entering your existing Apple ID and password, your new iPad automatically loads app-related data stored on iCloud, including your Contacts database, Calendar data, Safari bookmarks, and iCloud-related email account information.

NOTE If you don't yet have an Apple ID, tap the Create a Free Apple ID command icon, and then follow the screen prompts to create one. After you have your Apple ID, you can continue with the setup procedure for your iPad. If you can't remember your existing Apple ID or password, visit https://appleid.apple.com.

Next, you'll be able to set up iCloud services from the Set Up iCloud screen. Near the bottom center of this screen, you can turn on or off the iCloud service. When you've made your selection, tap the Next icon that's displayed in the upper-right corner of the screen.

Setting up iCloud is free, and because many apps enable you to share data and sync files using this online-based file-sharing service, this is something you should do now. However, you have the opportunity to set up iCloud later via the Settings app.

Continue working your way through this step-by-step iPad activation procedure, which should take less than five more minutes to complete. When you're done, the Thank You screen appears.

If you're activating a new iPad, you have the option to turn on the new Dictation feature (as shown in Figure 1.5). Tap on the Use Dictation option to activate it. You learn more about this useful feature at the end of this chapter.

FIGURE 1.5

If you're activating a new iPad, you can turn on the Dictation feature. This feature is not available on the original iPad or iPad 2.

Now that your iPad has been set up, the tablet's Home screen is displayed. On the Home screen are the app icons for all the core apps that come preinstalled on your tablet.

TIP   Your iPad is now fully activated and ready to be used. However, you might want to plug it in to charge the battery. You can see the level of battery life remaining by looking at the battery icon located in the upper-right corner of the tablet's screen. You can use the iPad while it is charging. A lightning bolt graphic appears within the onscreen battery icon to indicate when the tablet is currently charging.

ACTIVATING YOUR iPAD'S DATA SERVICES

Now that you have activated your iPad, if you have an iPad 2 Wi-Fi + 3G or new iPad Wi-Fi + 4G model, you can activate a wireless data service plan. To do this, make sure your iPad is not in Airplane Mode. (If it is in Airplane Mode, see the "Switching to Airplane Mode" section later in this chapter for information on where to turn off Airplane Mode.) You should see the 3G or 4G connection signal bars and the AT&T or Verizon label in the upper-left corner of the screen. Next, tap the Safari app icon from the Home screen.

Within the U.S., before you're allowed to gain access to the wireless web via a 3G or 4G connection, you must activate an account with AT&T Wireless, Verizon Wireless, or another compatible wireless data service provider.

NOTE   This wireless data plan account setup procedure takes just a few minutes and requires a major credit card (or debit card) to activate.

When you tap the Safari icon for the first time, follow the onscreen prompts when asked if you want to set up an AT&T Wireless or Verizon Wireless account. You must choose a monthly service plan that costs between $14.99 and $50.00 per month, depending on the plan you choose. This is a month-to-month plan that you can cancel or change any time. No long-term service agreement is required, however, it is auto-renewing until you cancel it.

TIP   If you're an AT&T Wireless customer who is upgrading from one iPad model to another, and you have an unlimited wireless data plan that's no longer available and you want to keep it, visit www.att.com/ipadlanding, or call (800) 331-0500, to transfer your data plan. Do not cancel your existing data plan and then create a new one on your new iPad.

CUSTOMIZING iPAD'S SETTINGS

Along with adding apps to your iPad to customize the tablet's features and functionality, you can use the built-in Settings app to personalize a wide range of options that affect your interaction with the tablet, how it connects to the Internet, and how your apps function.

Regardless of what you use your iPad for, you will occasionally need to access the Settings app. Think of the Settings app as the control center for the tablet's operating system. For example, it's from here that you can put your tablet into Airplane Mode, find and connect to a Wi-Fi hotspot, set up your email accounts, and customize your tablet's wallpapers. In fact, there are dozens of options available from the various Settings menus and submenus that directly affect how your iPad operates.

Upon launching the Settings app on any iPad model, you can see the screen is divided into two sections. On the left are the main options offered within the Settings app, starting with the virtual Airplane Mode (On/Off) switch that's located near the top-left corner of the screen (shown in Figure 1.6)

FIGURE 1.6

The left side of the screen displays the main Settings menu. Tap on a menu option to display a relevant submenu on the right side of the iPad's screen.

On the right side of the screen are the various submenu options available to you based on the highlighted selection on the left side of the screen. If you hold your iPad vertically (in portrait mode), you can see the entire main Settings screen at once. As you can see, the General option on the left is highlighted (in blue on your screen), and the specific options you can adjust on your iPad under the General option are displayed on the right side of the screen.

To select a different Settings category, tap its menu option that's listed within the left column of the Settings screen.

SWITCHING TO AIRPLANE MODE

The first option found under the Settings heading, within the left column of the main Settings app screen, is the virtual Airplane Mode On/Off switch. This option enables you to turn off the iPad's capability to communicate with the Internet using a 3G (4G) or Wi-Fi connection. To switch Airplane Mode to the On or Off position, simply tap the virtual switch that's displayed near the upper-left corner of the main settings screen.

When Airplane Mode is turned off, and you're using an iPad with 3G (or 4G), the tablet automatically connects to the wireless data network to which you've subscribed (as long as you're not within the signal radius of a Wi-Fi hotspot). The signal bars for this wireless data connection are displayed in the upper-left corner of the screen.

If you turn on Airplane Mode, the tablet's wireless data connection shuts down and your existing Wi-Fi connection also turns off. Everything else on your tablet remains functional. Some apps, however, (such as FaceTime) do require an active Wi-Fi connection to work. When your tablet is in Airplane Mode, a small airplane-shaped icon appears in the upper-left corner of the screen.

> TIP   While Airplane Mode is turned on, you have the option to reconnect to a Wi-Fi hotspot from the Wi-Fi settings option (discussed in the following section). This is useful if you're aboard an airplane, for example, that offers Wi-Fi but does not allow you to utilize the 3G/4G capabilities of your tablet. You can also turn on Airplane Mode when you travel overseas and want to connect to the Web using only a Wi-Fi hotspot.

CONNECTING TO A WI-FI HOTSPOT

Located directly below the Airplane Mode switch is the Wi-Fi option. When you tap Wi-Fi in the left column of the main Settings screen, the right side of the screen

immediately displays the various options available to you for choosing and connecting to a Wi-Fi hotspot.

At the top, the first user-selectable option is labeled Wi-Fi. It's accompanied by a
virtual On/Off switch to its right. When the Wi-Fi option is turned on, your iPad
immediately begins looking for all Wi-Fi hotspots in the vicinity.

The available networks are displayed under the Choose a Network heading on the
right side of the screen. A lock icon to the right of any network listed in the Choose
a Network section indicates the Wi-Fi hotspot is password protected. The signal
strength of each Wi-Fi hotspot in your immediate area is also displayed to the right
of the network's name.

Tap a public hotspot that does not display a lock icon, unless you possess the
password for a locked network. Keep in mind that the network options you see
displayed under the Choose a Network heading are based on the active Wi-Fi
hotspots in your immediate vicinity.

When you select a Wi-Fi network that is password protected, an Enter Password
window displays on your screen. Using the iPad's virtual keyboard, enter the correct password to connect to the Wi-Fi network you selected. You might also have
to do this when connecting to a public Wi-Fi hotspot offered within a hotel, for
example.

In a few seconds, a check mark appears to the left of your selected Wi-Fi hotspot,
and a Wi-Fi signal indicator displays in the upper-left corner of your iPad's screen
to confirm that a Wi-Fi connection has been established.

If you leave the Wi-Fi option turned on, your iPad can automatically find and
connect to an available Wi-Fi hotspot, with or without your approval, based on
whether you have the Ask to Join Networks option turned on or off.

BENEFITS OF ACCESSING THE WEB VIA A WI-FI HOTSPOT

There are several benefits to connecting to the Internet using a Wi-Fi connection,
as opposed to a 3G or 4G connection (if you're using an iPad 2 or new iPad with
Wi-Fi + 3G or Wi-Fi + 4G capabilities). These benefits include

- A Wi-Fi connection is often much faster than a 3G or even a 4G connection;
  however, the signal strength and number of people simultaneously accessing
  the Wi-Fi network affects your connection speed.

- When connected to the Internet via Wi-Fi, you can send and receive as much
  data as you'd like, stream content from the Web, and upload or download
  large files without worrying about using up your monthly wireless data allocation that's associated with your 3G or 4G wireless data plan.

■ Using a Wi-Fi connection, you can use the FaceTime app for video conferencing, plus download movies and TV show episodes from iTunes directly onto your tablet.

NOTE   The main drawback to using Wi-Fi to connect to the Internet from your iPad is that a Wi-Fi hotspot must be accessible, and you must stay within the radius of that Wi-Fi signal to remain connected to the Internet. The signal of most Wi-Fi hotspots only extends for several hundred feet from the wireless Internet router. When you go beyond this signal radius, your Internet connection is lost.

CONFIGURING NOTIFICATIONS SETTINGS

The Notifications option, also displayed in the left column of the Settings app, enables you to globally turn Notifications on or off using a virtual switch that appears on the right side of the screen. When turned off, all sounds, alerts, and Home screen badges are disabled.

From the Notifications option within Settings, you can also customize the Notification Center, which is continuously operational when your iPad is turned on. To learn more about Notification Center, refer to Chapter 4, "Using the Calendar, Reminders, and Notification Center Apps."

SETTING LOCATION SERVICES OPTIONS

The fourth option displayed on the left side of the Settings screen is labeled Location Services. When this option is turned on, the iPad can automatically utilize the GPS functionality built in to the device in conjunction with various apps. Certain apps and services, such as Maps or Find My iPad, rely on knowing your exact location to function properly.

When Location Services is selected in the left column menu, a virtual On/Off switch that completely enables or disables this feature is displayed on the right. Below that is a listing of all apps currently installed on your iPad that can use Location Services. You can turn on the master Location Services switch, but turn off the feature in conjunction with specific apps that would otherwise utilize it.

When the Location Services option is on, your iPad can fully utilize its GPS capabilities. When the option is off, your tablet is not able to determine (or broadcast) your exact location.

Some apps automatically track your whereabouts and add that geographic information to files. For example, if Location Services is turned on, when you snap a photo using the Camera app, the exact location where the photo was shot is automatically saved.

Likewise, when posting a tweet, you can set the Twitter app to automatically display your exact location within that tweet message if Location Services is turned on. And, theoretically, your boss, spouse, or someone else who knows your Apple ID could track your whereabouts using the Find My iPad service from any computer. Or, with your permission, the Find My Friends app can be used for this purpose.

> **NOTE** If you don't want the iPad tracking your whereabouts in real time, turn off this feature. When using Maps, for example, if the feature is turned off, you must manually enter your location each time you use the app.

CONFIGURING CELLULAR DATA OPTIONS

When you select the Cellular Data option, a virtual On/Off switch appears on the right side of the screen (see Figure 1.7). The Data Roaming option also appears, and on the new iPad an Enable LTE option is also available.

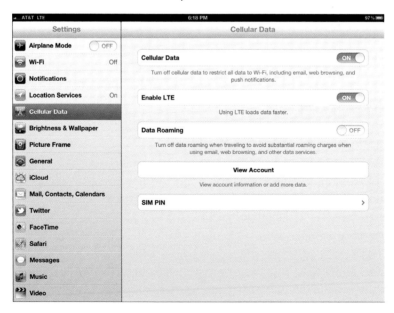

FIGURE 1.7

From the Cellular Data option, you can control whether your iPad can connect to the 3G or 4G wireless data network. You can also give your tablet the ability to roam (for an additional fee) to other networks for 3G or 4G Internet access.

NOTE This Cellular Data option only applies to original iPad Wi-Fi +3G, iPad 2 Wi-Fi + 3G, and new iPad Wi-Fi + 4G models.

When the Cellular Data option is on, your tablet can access either the 3G or 4G wireless data you subscribe to. When it's off, your iPad can access the Internet only using a Wi-Fi connection, assuming a Wi-Fi hotspot is present.

When set to on, the Data Roaming option enables your iPad to connect to a 3G (or 4G) network outside the one you subscribe to. The ability to tap into another wireless data network might be useful if you must connect to the Internet, there's no Wi-Fi hotspot present, and you're outside the coverage area of your wireless data network (such as when you're traveling abroad).

CAUTION When your iPad is permitted to roam and connect to another 3G or 4G wireless data network (such as when you're traveling abroad), you might incur hefty roaming charges, often as high as $20.00 per megabyte (MB). Refrain from using this feature unless you've secured a 3G or 4G data roaming plan in advance through your service provider, or you're prepared to pay a fortune to access the Web. See Chapter 18, "Must-Have Accessories," for more information about traveling abroad with your iPad.

You can view or modify your 3G (or 4G) wireless data plan account details by tapping the View Account option. After you log in with the username and password you created when you set up the account, you can do things such as change your credit card billing information or modify your monthly plan.

ADJUSTING THE SCREEN BRIGHTNESS

Also along the left column displayed within the Settings app is the Brightness & Wallpaper setting. When you tap this setting, the Brightness & Wallpaper options appear on the right side of the Settings screen (see Figure 1.8).

At the top of the screen is a Brightness slider. Place your finger on the white dot on the slider and drag it to the right to make the screen brighter, or drag it to the left to make the screen darker. Manually adjusting the brightness resets the "base" brightness of the Auto-Brightness option, making the screen easier to read in certain lighting conditions (based on your personal preference).

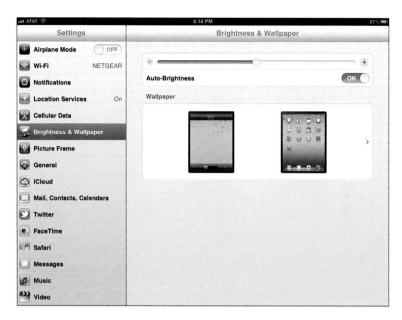

FIGURE 1.8

Use the Brightness slider to control how light or dark your iPad's screen appears. You can change this based on the external lighting conditions where you're using your iPad to make what's displayed on the screen easier to view.

The Auto-Brightness option displayed under the brightness slider has a virtual On/ Off switch associated with it. The default setting for this feature is On, which means the iPad uses its built-in ambient light sensor to automatically adjust the brightness of the screen. Leave the setting on unless you consistently have difficulty seeing what's displayed on your iPad's screen based on its brightness setting.

CUSTOMIZING THE LOCK SCREEN AND HOME SCREEN WALLPAPERS

One of the ways you can customize the appearance of your iPad is to change the wallpaper displayed on the device's Lock screen and behind your app icons on the Home screen.

CHOOSING A PREINSTALLED WALLPAPER

From the Brightness & Wallpaper option in the Settings app, you can quickly change the wallpapers that are displayed on the tablet. Your iPad has 34 preinstalled wallpaper designs, plus you can use any digital images stored on your iPad (within the Photos app) as your Lock screen or Home screen wallpaper.

Below the brightness slider is the Wallpaper option. Here, you see a thumbnail graphic of your iPad's Lock screen on the left and Home screen on the right. Tap either of these thumbnail images to change their appearance. The right side of the Settings screen changes, and two options are listed. The Wallpaper option is on top and the Camera Roll or Photos option is on bottom.

Tap the Wallpaper option to display thumbnails for the 34 preinstalled wallpaper graphics you can choose from (shown in Figure 1.9).

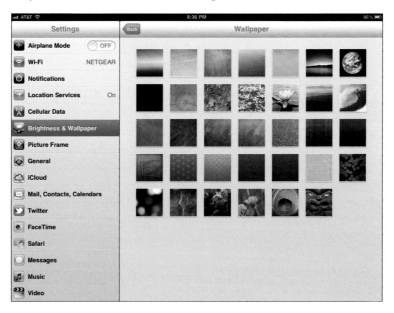

FIGURE 1.9

Choose from 34 preinstalled wallpaper graphics for your iPad's Lock screen and Home screen.

When looking at the collection of wallpaper graphics, tap the one you'd like to use, such as the planet earth graphic that's displayed on the top row. Next, the graphic you select is displayed in full-screen mode. In the upper-right corner of the screen are three command buttons. Choose one of these options by tapping its icon:

- **Set Lock Screen:** Tap this icon to change just the wallpaper graphic of your iPad's Lock screen. This is the screen you see when you first turn on your tablet or wake it from Sleep Mode.

- **Set Home Screen:** Tap this icon to change just the wallpaper graphic of your iPad's Home screen. This is the graphic that displays behind your app icons on each of your Home screen pages.

- **Set Both:** Tap this icon to use the same wallpaper graphic as both your Lock screen and your Home screen wallpapers.

After you make your selection, your newly selected wallpaper graphic is displayed when you return to the iPad's Lock screen or Home screen.

Instead of choosing one of the preinstalled wallpaper graphics, you also have the option to use any of your own digital images. This includes photos you've transferred to your iPad and have stored within the Photos app, and photos you've shot using the tablet's Camera app.

DISPLAYING A CUSTOM IMAGE AS A WALLPAPER

To select one of your own photos to use as your Lock screen or Home screen wallpaper, tap the Brightness & Wallpaper option in the Settings app.

On the right side of the screen, tap the thumbnails of your iPad's Lock screen and Home screen. Underneath the Wallpaper option, tap the folder that contains the image you want to use as your wallpaper. This might be a photo you've shot using your iPad (found within the Camera Roll folder), or a photo you've imported into the Photos app of your tablet. You could also use a photo you've saved on your iPad from your iCloud Photo Stream, a feature that is discussed later in Chapter 9, "Syncing Your iPad via iTunes or iCloud."

When the image thumbnails appear, tap on the one you want to use as your wallpaper for your Lock screen or Home screen (or both). When the photo you selected appears in full-screen mode, tap one of the three command icons that appear in the upper-right corner of the screen. Once again, your options include Set Lock Screen, Set Home Screen, or Set Both.

After you make your selection, your newly selected wallpaper graphic displays on your Lock screen and Home screen, as you can see in Figure 1.10 and Figure 1.11.

FIGURE 1.10

A newly selected Lock screen graphic, chosen from a photo stored on the iPad within the Photos app.

FIGURE 1.11

The image selected from the Settings app is displayed as your Home screen wallpaper appearing behind your app icons.

TRANSFORMING YOUR iPAD INTO A DIGITAL PICTURE FRAME

When your iPad isn't in use or on the go with you, it might sit idly on your desk. If this is the case, you could transform the device into a digital picture frame and have it display an animated slideshow of your favorite images when it's not otherwise being used. You can set up and customize an animated slideshow using the Picture Frame option of the Settings app.

GENERAL OPTIONS

Several options found under the General heading are things you'll probably never need to tinker with or adjust, such as International or Accessibility, so just leave them at their default settings. Others are things you might need to change often as you use your iPad for different tasks.

The General option of the Settings screen enables you to view and adjust the following options:

- **About:** Tap the About option to access information about your iPad, including its serial number, which version of the iOS is running, the memory capacity, and how much memory is currently available on the device. This is purely an informative screen with no options to customize or adjust.

- **Software Update:** Periodically, when Apple releases a revision to the iOS operating system, you must download and install an update. You can do it wirelessly using the Software Update feature. When you tap Software Update, your iPad checks to see whether a new version of the iOS is available and, if so, prompts you to download and install it.

- **Usage:** Tap the Usage option to decide whether to display your tablet's battery life as a numeric percentage (such as 73%) or only as a battery-shaped graphic icon. Also, from this screen you can see how much data the iPad has sent or received using the 3G/4G wireless data network to which it's connected.

  Tap the Reset Statistics option to reset the Sent and Received settings. When you add the Sent and Received numbers together, you can determine your total data usage since you last tapped the Reset Statistics icon. This feature is particularly useful to determine how much you'll be billed when you're overseas and roaming, or for making sure you don't go beyond your monthly allocated data use based on the 3G/4G wireless data plan you have.

- **Sounds:** Tap this option to adjust the overall volume of the iPad's built-in speaker (or the volume of the audio you hear through headsets), as well as to

turn on or off various audible tones and alarms your tablet is able to generate. All of these sound-related options have virtual On/Off switches associated with them.

- **Network:** This option enables you to select and connect your iPad to either a
  virtual private network (VPN) or Wi-Fi network, assuming one is present. For
  help connecting to a VPN, contact the IT department in your company.

- **Bluetooth:** If you plan to use any type of Bluetooth device with your tablet,
  such as wireless external speakers, a headset, or a wireless keyboard, you first
  need to turn on the Bluetooth feature on your iPad and then pair that device
  with your tablet. You can manage Bluetooth devices from the Bluetooth submenu within Settings.

TIP   If you're using your iPad without having a Bluetooth device connected,
you can set the Bluetooth feature to Off to avoid getting notices about Bluetooth
devices and to prolong the tablet's battery life.

When you set this feature to On, your iPad automatically seeks out any Bluetooth-
compatible devices in the vicinity. The first time you use a particular Bluetooth
device with your iPad, you must pair it. Follow the directions that came with the
device or accessory to perform this initial setup task.

- **iTunes Wi-Fi Sync:** Instead of using iCloud or the traditional iTunes Sync
  process to back up or synchronize your iPad, the iTunes Wi-Fi (Wireless) Sync
  option enables you to utilize the iTunes Sync process without directly connecting your iPad to your primary computer using the supplied USB cable.
  Instead, you can link wirelessly, as long as both the computer and iPad are
  connected to the same wireless network.

- **Spotlight Search:** Determine which apps are searched when you use the
  Spotlight Search feature built in to the iPad.

- **Auto-Lock:** Set your iPad to switch into Sleep Mode anytime it is left idle for
  a predetermined amount of time. This helps conserve battery life. From the
  Auto-Lock option, you can determine whether Sleep Mode should be activated after 2, 5, 10, or 15 minutes of nonuse. Or you can choose the Never
  option so the iPad never automatically switches into Sleep Mode, even if you
  leave it unattended for an extended period.

- **Passcode Lock:** Use this feature to set and then turn on or off the Passcode
  option built in to the iPad's operating system. To learn more about this feature, see "Keeping Your iPad Private with the Passcode Lock Feature," later in
  this chapter.

- **iPad Cover Lock/Unlock:** This feature is only applicable if you're using an optional Apple Smart Cover with your iPad. If so, when the feature is turned on, your tablet automatically goes into Sleep Mode when the Smart Cover is placed over the screen, and it wakes again as soon as the Smart Cover is removed.

- **Restrictions:** Use these features to "childproof" your tablet. You have the option to Enable Restrictions and then manually set those restrictions. For example, you can block certain apps from being used, keep the user from deleting or adding apps to the iPad, keep someone from making in-app purchases, or keep someone from accessing certain types of iTunes or app content (including TV shows, movies, music, and podcasts).

- **Use Side Switch To:** There is a tiny switch located on the right side of your iPad, just above the volume up/down button. You can determine what the primary function of this switch should be. Use it either as a Lock Rotation switch or a Mute switch.

- **Multitasking Gestures:** When the Multitasking Gestures option is set to On, several additional finger/hand motions are usable when interacting with your tablet's touch-screen. For example, you can start with your fingers spread out and perform a full-hand pinch motion while in any app to return to the Home screen. Or, you can swipe upward to reveal the multitasking bar (instead of pressing the Home button twice). You can then perform a full hand swipe to switch between apps in multitasking mode.

- **Date & Time:** Switch between a 12- or 24-hour clock and determine whether you want your iPad to automatically set the time or date (when it's connected to the Internet). To ensure the time and date are correct regardless of what time zone you travel to, leave the Set Automatically option set to On.

- **Keyboard:** You can make certain customizations from the Settings screen that affect how your virtual keyboard responds as you type. The Keyboard option gives you six customizable settings, such as Auto-Capitalization, Auto-Correction, and Check Spelling. You also have the option to turn on or off the Split Keyboard feature, plus create and edit keyboard shortcuts that are useful when typing text. A keyboard shortcut might include typing "omw," which the iPad translates into "on my way."

TIP $\quad$ If you're a new iPad user, from the Keyboard submenu screen within Settings, you can turn on or off the Dictation feature. When turned off, the microphone-shaped Dictation key is no longer displayed on the virtual keyboard

■ **International:** By default, if you purchased your iPad in the United States, the default language and keyboard options are for English. However, you can adjust these settings by tapping the International option.

■ **Accessibility:** The Accessibility options are designed to make the iPad easier to use by people with various sight or hearing difficulties, or with some type of physical limitation.

■ **Reset:** Every so often, you might run into a problem with your iPad, such as when the system crashes, or you need to reset specific settings. To restore your iPad to its factory default settings and erase everything stored on it, tap the Reset option, and then tap the Erase All Content and Settings option. In general, you should refrain from using these settings unless you're instructed to use them by an Apple Genius or technical support person.

> **CAUTION**   Before using any of the Reset options, which potentially erase important data from your iPad, be sure to perform an iTunes Sync or iCloud Backup to create a reliable backup.

KEEPING YOUR iPAD PRIVATE WITH THE PASSCODE LOCK FEATURE

There are several simple ways to protect the data stored on your iPad and keep it away from unauthorized users. If you want to keep data on your tablet private, the first thing to do is set up and activate the Passcode Lock feature that's built in to the iOS.

To set up the Passcode Lock feature, from the Settings app, tap the General setting on the left side of the screen. Next, tap the Passcode Lock option that's listed on the right side of the screen, and set the Passcode feature to On. (By default, the Passcode option is set to Off.)

When the Passcode Lock screen appears (see Figure 1.12), tap the Turn Passcode On button to activate this security feature.

When the Set Passcode window appears on the tablet's screen (see Figure 1.13), use the virtual numeric keypad to create a four-digit security passcode for your device. You must enter this code every time you turn on the tablet or wake it from Sleep Mode.

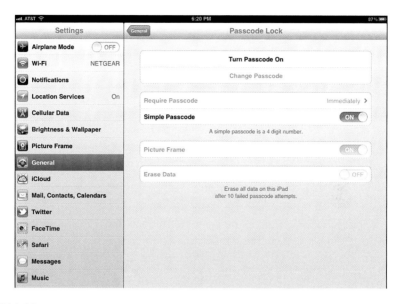

FIGURE 1.12

From the Passcode Lock screen, you can set and then activate the Passcode Lock feature built in to the iPad. Use it to keep unauthorized people from using your tablet or accessing your sensitive data.

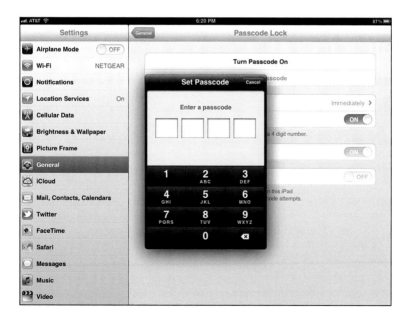

FIGURE 1.13

Create a four-digit numeric passcode for your iPad from this Set Passcode window.

You can enter any four-digit code as your passcode. When prompted, type the same code a second time. The Set Passcode window disappears and the feature becomes active.

From the Passcode Lock screen in the Settings app, you can further customize this feature. For example, tap the Require Passcode option to determine when the iPad prompts the user to enter the passcode. The default option is Immediately, meaning each time the tablet is turned on or woken up.

If you don't believe a four-digit passcode is secure enough, turn off the Simple Passcode option, which makes a Change Passcode window appear along with the iPad's full virtual keyboard. You can create a more complicated, alphanumeric passcode to protect your device from unauthorized use.

From the Passcode Lock screen, you can determine whether the Picture Frame app option is displayed on your Lock screen. This option has a virtual On/Off switch associated with it. When turned on, the Picture Frame app icon displays on the Lock screen. When turned off, you are not able to turn on the Picture Frame app from the Lock screen because the icon does not display.

Also on the Passcode Lock screen is the Erase Data option. If an unauthorized user enters the wrong passcode 10 consecutive times, the iPad automatically erases all data stored on it when the feature is turned on.

CAUTION   Activating the Erase Data feature gives you an added layer of security if your tablet falls into the wrong hands. However, to recover the data later, you must have a reliable backup created using the iTunes Sync process or iCloud Backup feature; otherwise, that data is lost forever.

CUSTOMIZING iCLOUD SETTINGS

From the left side of the Settings screen, tap the iCloud option to customize the settings associated with Apple's online file-sharing and data backup service. You learn more about this service in Chapter 9, "Syncing Your iPad via iTunes or iCloud."

From Settings, however, you can adjust what data automatically gets wirelessly backed up and/or synced with the iCloud service, including Mail, Contacts, Calendars, Reminders, (Safari) Bookmarks, Notes, and Photo Stream. You can also turn on or off the Find My iPad service. Your options are shown in Figure 1.14.

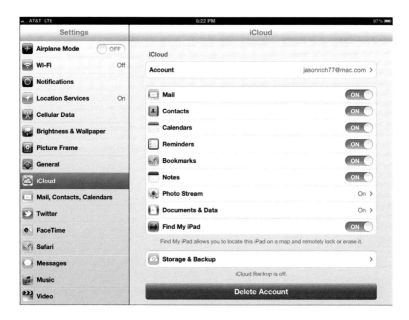

FIGURE 1.14

Being able to back up your iPad and transfer files wirelessly using Apple's iCloud service is a major enhancement to the iPad 2 or new iPad that's running iOS 5.1 (or later). You can customize your iCloud settings from the Settings app.

Your free iCloud account comes with a predetermined amount of online storage space. Tap the Storage & Backup tab near the bottom of the iCloud screen to manage your existing online storage space or purchase additional online storage space. From the Storage & Backup screen within Settings, you can also turn on or off the Back Up to iCloud feature. This determines whether your iPad automatically and wirelessly backs up your tablet using iCloud.

ADJUSTING THE SETTINGS FOR MAIL, CONTACTS, AND CALENDARS

If you use your iPad for work, three apps you will probably rely heavily on are Mail, Contacts, and Calendars. From the Settings app, you can customize a handful of options pertaining to each of these apps, and you can set up your existing work and personal email accounts to work with your tablet.

> **NOTE** For information about how to use the Settings app to customize app-related options, see Chapter 2, "Working with Email," Chapter 4, and Chapter 5, "Working with the Contacts App."

SETTING UP THE TWITTER APP

The Twitter online social networking service is fully integrated into iOS 5.1 and your iPad, and is accessible from within several different iPad core applications, as well as the actual official Twitter app.

The Twitter features built into the iPad's operating system work with your existing Twitter account; however, you need to download the free, official Twitter app. You can also set up a free Twitter account if you don't already have one. Customize the settings as desired so you can send tweets from a variety of different iPad core apps, including Photos or Safari.

CUSTOMIZING YOUR WEB SURFING EXPERIENCE WITH SAFARI

Safari is the web browsing app built in to the iPad. It's similar to the Safari web browser available on all Mac computers. The Safari app has a handful of settings you can customize using the Settings, such as which search engine to use, whether to show the Bookmarks bar, or whether you want to block pop-up ads. These options, as well as the others found in the Safari settings, are explained in Chapter 3, "Surfing the Web."

CUSTOMIZING THE MESSAGES APP

iMessage is an online-based text messaging service operated by Apple. This service works very much like the text messaging capabilities of your cell phone, but with this service, you can freely send and receive an unlimited number of messages. The service is compatible with all Macs, as well as with iOS-enabled devices, including the iPad, iPad 2, new iPad, iPhone 3Gs, iPhone 4, iPhone 4s, and iPod touch.

From your iPad, the iMessage service must be accessed using the Messages app, which comes preinstalled on the tablet. Tap the Messages option within Settings to set up an iMessage account using your Apple ID and to manage your account. You learn more about the Messages app and iMessage service from Chapter 12, "Conducting Video Conferences and Virtual Meetings."

PERSONALIZING MUSIC SETTINGS

One of the apps built in to your iPad is the Music app, which transforms your tablet into a full-featured digital music player, and enables you to experience the music and audio files you have stored on your tablet. This includes music, podcasts, and audiobooks acquired from iTunes.

Using the Settings app, you can customize a handful of options relating to the Music app. From the left column of the main Settings app screen, tap the Music setting. Then, on the right side of the screen, adjust the Sound Check, EQ, Volume Limit, and Lyrics & Podcast Info options.

PERSONALIZING VIDEO SETTINGS

Use the Videos app that comes on your iPad to watch TV show episodes and movies you've purchased or rented from the iTunes Store. From the Settings app, you can adjust how the Videos app functions by turning on or off various settings.

From the Settings app, tap the Videos setting in the left column. When the Video options appear on the right side of the screen, you can adjust four main options, starting with the Start Playing feature. The default option for this feature is to resume playing a video where you last left off. However, you can change this option so videos always start at the beginning. You can also turn on or off closed captioning, for example.

You learn more about the Videos app in Chapter 15, "Downloading Versus Streaming Online Content."

MAKING APP-SPECIFIC ADJUSTMENTS

You can also customize settings for the preinstalled apps, such as the Photos, FaceTime, Notes, and App Store apps. These are all displayed toward the bottom of the main Settings screen's left column.

To make adjustments that are specific to any of the apps listed, tap the app name (displayed in the left column of the Settings screen), and then adjust the app-specific settings on the right side of the screen. The customizations you can make are specific to each app.

As you begin installing optional apps on your iPad, apps that have customizable options are also adjustable from within the Settings app. When this is the case, those apps are listed within the left column of the main Settings app screen. For example, the Pages, Numbers, and Keynote apps are each listed within the Settings app after you install them.

USING THE NEW iPAD'S DICTATION FEATURE

One feature that is exclusively available to new iPad users is the Dictation mode. When activated, almost anytime the iPad's virtual keyboard becomes active, an extra key with a microphone on it is visible (see Figure 1.15).

Dictation Key

FIGURE 1.15

The new iPad offers the Dictation feature, which enables you to speak directly to your tablet.

Instead of manually typing information into the iPad when using a compatible app, you can tap on the Dictate key once, which causes a larger microphone icon to be displayed (see Figure 1.16). At the same time, the iPad generates a quick tone. At this point, you can begin speaking, in a normal voice, to your iPad.

In Dictation mode, anything you say is recorded by your tablet. Then, when you tap the Dictate key again on the virtual keyboard, your iPad translates whatever you said into text and inserts that text into the app you're using.

This feature works with many different apps on your iPad and can be a huge time saver, as it is a viable alternative to touch-typing or manual data entry. As you're speaking to your iPad when the Dictation mode is active, speak as clearly as possible using a normal volume and speed.

Microphone Icon

FIGURE 1.16

After tapping on the Dictation feature, a larger microphone-shaped icon displays, indicating that your iPad is recording what you're saying, so start speaking.

As you're speaking, you can include punctuation in your text, by speaking that as well. For example, you can say, "comma," "period," "colon," "open quotes," "close quotes," "exclamation point," and so on.

For example, as you're using the Pages or Notes app, you could say, "This is a test of the iPad's dictation mode period I really love this feature exclamation point." Your iPad translates this as, "This is a test of the iPad's dictation mode. I really love this feature!" and enters the text into your Pages or Notes document (as shown in Figure 1.17).

> **NOTE** Using the Dictation feature of the new iPad requires Internet access. If your tablet is connected to the Web using a 3G or 4G connection, using this feature utilizes some of your monthly wireless data allocation.
>
> However, the Dictation feature translates speech to text faster using a Wi-Fi connection.

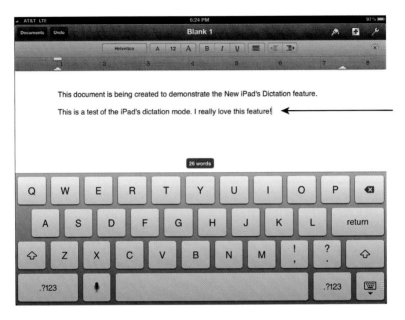

FIGURE 1.17

When the Dictation mode is engaged, what you say is translated into text and inserted into whatever compatible app you're currently using.

Use the new iPad's Dictation mode to enter text into a text editor or word processor, compose tweets or Facebook page status updates, or insert text into virtually any compatible app without having to type. The Dictation feature works with an optional headset, which can be used to reduce background noise if you're using your iPad in a busy area.

NOW, LET'S PUT YOUR iPAD TO WORK

Now that you understand the basics of how to set up and interact with your iPad, let's start putting it to work by focusing on the job-related tasks for which you can use many of the tablet's preinstalled applications, starting in Chapter 2 with surfing the Web using the Safari web browser app.

2

WORKING WITH EMAIL

As long as your iPad has access to the Internet via a Wi-Fi, 3G, or 4G connection, it has the capability to securely access virtually any type of email account. In fact, using the tablet's preinstalled Mail app, you have the ability to manage multiple email accounts simultaneously without having to open and close accounts to switch between them.

> **NOTE** Any model iPad can access an optional 4G Personal Hotspot device via Wi-Fi, or any other wireless device that offers a 4G tethering feature.

Your iPad is also capable of viewing certain types of attachments that accompany emails, including PDF files, photos, and Microsoft Office documents and files. Plus, if you have access to an AirPrint-compatible printer, you can print incoming or outgoing emails from within the Mail app.

Using your iPad, you can easily send and receive email messages, and manage personal and work-related email accounts at the same time, yet keep the content of the various accounts totally separate.

Before you can manage one or more email accounts from your iPad, it's necessary to access the Settings app to configure your tablet to work with your email account(s).

SETTING UP YOUR iPAD TO WORK WITH EXISTING EMAIL ACCOUNTS

The email account setup process described here works with virtually all email accounts. If you have an email account through your employer that doesn't initially work using the setup procedure outlined in this chapter, contact your company's IT department or Apple's technical support for assistance.

> **NOTE** The process for setting up an existing email account to use with your iPad and the Mail app needs to be done only once per account.

Follow these steps to set up your iPad to work with your existing email account:

1. From the Home screen, tap the Settings app icon.

2. On the left side of the main Settings app screen, tap the Mail, Contacts, Calendars option.

3. When the Mail, Contacts, Calendars options display on the right side of the screen (see Figure 2.1), tap the Add Account option that's displayed near the top of the screen, below the Accounts heading. If you've already set up iCloud on your iPad when you initially set up the tablet, your iCloud-related email account is already listed under the Accounts heading, just above the Add Account option.

4. From the Add Account screen, select the type of email account you have: iCloud, Microsoft Exchange, Gmail, Yahoo! Mail, AOL Mail, MobileMe, or Other. Tap the appropriate option (see Figure 2.2). If you have a POP3- or IMAP-compatible email account, tap the Other option and follow the onscreen prompts.

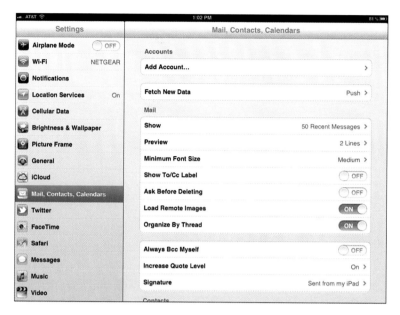

FIGURE 2.1

Tap the Mail, Contacts, Calendars option from within Settings, and then tap the Add Account option.

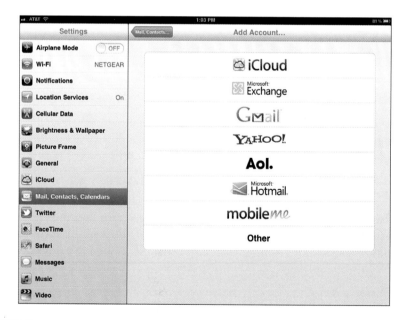

FIGURE 2.2

Select the type of email account you are setting up by tapping the appropriate icon.

If you have an existing Yahoo! Mail account, for example, tap the Yahoo! icon. When the Yahoo! screen appears (shown in Figure 2.3), use the iPad's virtual keyboard to enter the Account Name, Email Address, Password, and a Description for the account.

FIGURE 2.3

Using the iPad's virtual keyboard, enter the details pertaining to your existing email account.

5. Tap the Next button that's located in the upper-right corner of the window.

6. Your iPad connects to the email account's server and confirms the account details you entered.

7. After the account has been verified, a new window with multiple options, such as Mail, Contacts, Calendars, and Notes, is displayed. (The options listed vary based on the type of email account you're setting up.) Each option has a virtual On/Off switch associated with it. These options relate to what account-related data will sync with your iPad.

8. Tap the Save button that's located in the upper-right corner of this window.

9. Details about the email account you just set up are added to your iPad and accessible from the Mail app.

10. If you have another existing email account to set up, from the Mail, Contacts, Calendars screen within the Settings app, again tap the Add Account option, and repeat the preceding steps.

As you're setting up your email account and responding to onscreen prompts within the Settings app, the Name field should include your full name. This is what is later displayed within the From field of all email messages you send. The Address is your email address, and you should enter it in the *yourname@mailservice.com* format.

The Password is the password you currently use to access your existing email account. For the Description, you can enter any text that helps you differentiate the email account from others, such as "AOL Mail Account," "Yahoo! Email," or "Work Email."

> **TIP** If you're trying to set up a POP3, IMAP, or Microsoft Exchange account, for example, and you're prompted for information you don't have, such as your Incoming Mail Server Host Name, Incoming Mail Server Port Number, Outgoing Mail Server, or Outgoing Server Authentication Type, contact your Internet service provider or the company that provides your email account.

Depending on the type of email account you're setting up for use with your iPad, the information you are prompted for varies slightly.

> **TIP** When you purchase an iPad, it comes with free technical support from AppleCare for 90 days. This includes the ability to make an in-person appointment with an Apple Genius at any Apple Store to get help setting up your email accounts on your tablet. To schedule a free appointment, visit www.apple.com/retail/geniusbar. Or call Apple's toll-free technical support phone number and have someone talk you through the email setup process. Call (800) APL-CARE.

CUSTOMIZING YOUR EMAIL ACCOUNT SETTINGS

From the Settings app, as you look at the Mail, Contacts, Calendars screen, you see a variety of customizable options that pertain to your email accounts. Tap each of these customizable options, one at a time, to personalize the settings based on your preferences and needs.

FETCHING NEW DATA

Set up your iPad to automatically access the Internet and retrieve new email messages by tapping the Fetch New Data option and adjusting its settings. You can also make sure the Push option, listed at the top of the Fetch New Data screen (see Figure 2.4), is turned on. This allows the iPad to automatically retrieve new emails from the server on an ongoing basis.

If you turn off the Push option, set the Fetch option to check for new emails every 15 minutes, every 30 minutes, hourly, or manually. Two reasons why you might consider turning off the Push feature and use Fetch to periodically check for emails (or do this manually) is to reduce your 3G or 4G wireless data usage, and to extend your tablet's battery life between charges. (Constantly checking for new emails and downloading those emails depletes the iPad's battery life faster.)

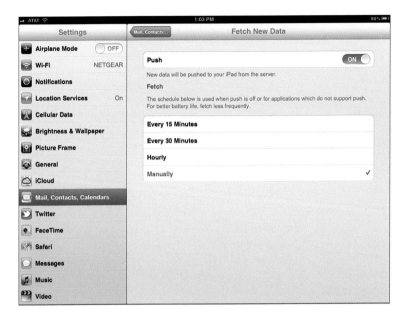

FIGURE 2.4

Turn on the Push option to allow your iPad to automatically check for new emails and retrieve them from the server.

CAUTION When you signed up for a 3G or 4G wireless data plan, you were given a pre-determined wireless data allocation per month. Having your iPad constantly check for new incoming emails (using the Push feature) quickly uses this allocation. This is not a concern, however, if you're using a Wi-Fi Internet connection.

Keep in mind, downloading and reading emails with large attachments, such as photos, Microsoft Office, or PDF files, depletes your monthly wireless data allocation much faster, as does having your iPad check for new emails often.

CUSTOMIZING MAIL OPTIONS

Under the Mail heading of the Mail, Contacts, Calendars screen are a handful of additional customizable features pertaining to how your iPad handles your email accounts. These options include the following:

- **Show:** This feature determines how many messages within a particular email account the Mail app downloads from the server and displays at once. Your options include 50, 100, 200, 500, or 1,000 Recent Messages.

Preview: As you look at your Inbox using the Mail app, you can determine how much of each email message's body text is visible from the Inbox summary screen, in addition to the From, Date/Time, and Subject lines.

Minimum Font Size: Regardless of the font size used by the sender, your iPad can automatically adjust the font size so messages are more easily readable on the tablet's display. The default option is Medium, which is acceptable to most iPad users.

Show To/Cc Label: To save space on your screen as you're reading emails, you can turn off the To and CC label within each email message by tapping the virtual switch associated with this option.

Ask Before Deleting: This option serves as a safety net to ensure you don't accidently delete an important email message. When this feature is turned on, you are asked to confirm your message deletion request before an email message is actually deleted. Keep in mind that, by default, you cannot delete email messages stored on your email account's server. When you delete a message, it is only deleted from your iPad.

Load Remote Images: When an email message has a photo or graphic embedded with it, this option determines whether that photo or graphic is automatically downloaded and displayed in conjunction with the email message. You can opt to have your iPad refrain from automatically loading graphics in conjunction with email messages. This reduces the amount of data transferred to your tablet, and it can help to protect against spammers who use image tracking to verify valid email addresses. You always have the option to tap an icon within the email message to download the graphic content of that message, including photos.

Organize By Thread: This feature enables you to review messages in reverse chronological order if a single message turns into a back-and-forth email conversation, where multiple parties keep hitting Reply to respond to messages with the same topic. When turned on, this makes keeping track of email conversations much easier, especially if you're managing several email accounts on your iPad. If turned off, messages in your Inbox are displayed in reverse chronological order, as they're received, and are not grouped together by subject.

Always Bcc Myself: To ensure you keep a copy of every outgoing email you send, turn on this feature. A copy of every outgoing email is sent to your Inbox if this feature is turned on.

Signature: For every outgoing email that you compose, you can automatically add an email signature. The default signature is "Sent from my iPad." By tapping this option, you can compose one or more customized signatures.

A signature might include your name, mailing address, email address, phone number(s), and so on.

After you make whatever adjustments you want to the Mail app-related options from within the Settings app, exit the Settings app by pressing the Home button on your iPad to return to the Home screen. You're now ready to begin using the Mail app to access and manage your email account(s).

MANAGING YOUR EMAIL ACCOUNTS WITH THE MAIL APP

The Mail app that is preinstalled on your iPad is loaded with features to make managing multiple email accounts a straightforward process.

> **NOTE** If you need to manage multiple email accounts with your iPad, it's important to understand that although the Mail app enables you to view email messages in all of your accounts simultaneously (when the All Inboxes option is selected), the app actually keeps messages from your different accounts separate.

As you view your incoming email messages, by default, the app groups emails together by message thread, enabling you to follow an email-based conversation that extends through multiple messages and replies. When turned on, this feature displays emails within the same thread in reverse chronological order, with the newest message first.

> **NOTE** To send and receive emails using the Mail app, your tablet must be connected to the Internet via a Wi-Fi, 3G, or 4G connection.

After you've initially set up your existing email accounts to work with the Mail app, you can use this app to manage your email accounts from anywhere. Launch the Mail app from the Home screen.

To alert you of incoming messages, without having the Mail app running, access the Settings app to have the iPad display a badge on the Mail app icon that's displayed on the Home screen as new emails arrive.

> **NOTE** A badge is a small number that appears in the upper-right corner of the Mail app's icon on the Home screen. In this case, it indicates how many new emails your iPad has received. Refer to the bottom of Figure 2.5 to see what a badge looks.

Plus, you can set the Notification Center to list incoming emails. If the Notification Center window displays an incoming message alert (shown in Figure 2.5), tap it to automatically open the Mail app and display that new message. You learn more about the Notification Center in Chapter 4, "Using the Calendar, Reminders, and Notification Center Apps."

FIGURE 2.5

This is what the Notification Center window looks like when incoming email message alerts are displayed.

Upon launching the Mail app, you can access the Inbox for one or more of your existing email accounts, compose new emails, or manage your email accounts. Just like the Inbox on your main computer's email software, the Inbox of the Mail app (see Figure 2.6) displays your incoming emails.

FIGURE 2.6

The Mail app's inbox screen. In this example, just one email account is set up to work with the app.

WORKING WITH THE INBOX

On the left side of the Mail app's Inbox screen is a list of the individual emails within your Inbox. A blue dot to the left of a message indicates the message has not yet been read.

> TIP   As shown in Figure 2.7, a blue dot displayed within your Inbox, next to a message on the left side of the screen, indicates that a message is new and unread. A flag icon indicates the message is urgent. A circular, left-pointing arrow icon indicates you have already sent a reply to that message. A straight, right-pointing arrow indicates you have forwarded the message to one or more recipients.

FIGURE 2.7

Small graphic icons displayed to the left of each email message listing within your Inbox indicate different things.

Based on the customizations that you made from within the Settings app that pertain to the Mail app, the Sender, Subject, Date/Time, and up to five lines of the message's body text are displayed for each incoming message.

The email message that's highlighted in blue on the left side of the screen is the one that's currently being displayed, in its entirety, on the right side of the screen. Tap any email item on the left side of the screen to view the entire message on the right side of the screen.

At the bottom of the Inbox message listing (on the left side of the screen) is a circular arrow icon. Tap this icon to refresh your Inbox and manually check for new incoming emails. The Updated message, accompanied by the date and time, indicates the last time your Inbox was refreshed.

At the top of the Inbox message listing are two buttons labeled Mailboxes and Edit. Between these two icons is the Inbox heading, along with a number that's displayed in parentheses. This number indicates how many new, unread messages are currently stored in your inbox.

Just below the Inbox heading is a Search field. Tap this Search field to enter a search phrase and quickly find a particular email message. You can search the content of the Mail app using any keyword, a sender's name, or email subject, for example.

ORGANIZING MAILBOX ACTIONS WITH THE MAILBOXES BUTTON

When looking at your Inbox, the Mailboxes button is displayed in the upper-left corner of the screen. If you're managing just one email account with the Mail app, when you tap on this icon, you can immediately access your Drafts folder, Sent Message folder, Trash folder, Bulk Mail folder, or other folders associated with your email account.

However, if you're managing multiple email accounts using the Mail app, when you tap the Mailboxes button, you see a listing of each mail account's Inbox, as well as each email account, displayed on the left side of the screen.

Tabs for each email account's Inbox are displayed to the upper left. At the top of this listing is an All Inboxes tab. Tap this icon to view a listing of all your incoming emails, from all your accounts, on a single screen. (These messages are displayed together but are actually kept separate by the Mail app.)

> **TIP**   When you're managing multiple accounts, you can tap the Mailboxes tab to switch between individual email account Inboxes. Under the Accounts heading, you can also access the Inbox, Drafts, Sent, Trash, Bulk Mail, or other folders for each account separately.

Depending on the email account, you might be able to add new folders for storing email messages on your iPad. As you're looking at the current list of folders associated with one email account, tap the Edit button that's displayed at the top of the screen next to the Mailboxes heading. Now, at the bottom of the screen, in the lower-right corner of the left mailbox folder column, you see a new button labeled New Mailbox (shown in Figure 2.8).

FIGURE 2.8

For most types of email accounts, you can create an unlimited number of mailbox folders (each with a custom name) for organizing email messages.

Tap the New Mailbox button to manually enter the name of a new folder, and decide under which email account (Mailbox Location) the folder will be displayed.

SELECTING MESSAGES FOR USE WITH AN EDIT BUTTON

Located on top of the Inbox message listing (to the right of the Inbox heading) is an Edit button. When you tap this button, you can quickly select multiple messages from your Inbox to delete or move to another folder (see Figure 2.9).

After you tap the Edit button, an empty circle displays to the left of each email message summary. To move or delete one or more messages from this Inbox listing, tap the empty circle for that message. A red-and-white check mark fills the empty circle when you do this, and the Delete and Move buttons are displayed at the bottom of the screen.

After you've selected one or more messages, tap the Delete button to quickly delete the messages from your Inbox (which sends them to the Trash folder), or tap the blue-and-white Move button, and then select which folder you want to move those email messages to.

FIGURE 2.9

After tapping the Edit button you can quickly delete or move multiple email messages currently stored in your Inbox.

DELETING INDIVIDUAL INCOMING MESSAGES

As you're looking at the listing of messages in your Inbox, with most types of email accounts, you can delete individual messages, one at a time, in several ways. Swipe your finger from left to right over a message listing on the left side of the screen. A red-and-white Delete button displays on the right side of that email message listing. Tap this Delete button to delete the message.

Another way to delete a single message from your Inbox (or any folder) is to tap the message listing that's displayed on the left side of the screen, which highlights the message in blue. At the same time, the entire message is displayed on the right side of the screen. To then delete the message, tap the Trash Can icon displayed near the upper-right corner of the screen.

VIEWING YOUR EMAIL

When a single email message is highlighted on the left side of the Inbox screen, that message is displayed, in its entirety, on the right side of the screen. At the top of the message, you see the From, To, Cc, Bcc, Subject, and Date/Time lines.

In the upper-right corner of the email message is a blue Hide command. If you tap this, some of the message header information is no longer displayed. This enables you to display more of that email's message on the tablet's screen. To make this information reappear, tap the Details command that appears in the upper-right corner of the message.

Located to the right of the Date and Time the email was received is a blue Mark command. When you tap this Mark tab, two new command icons appear, labeled Flag and Mark As Unread.

TIP If you Flag a message, a small orange flag appears next to its listing on the left side of the screen (as shown in Figure 2.10), which indicates the message is urgent. If you tap the Mark As Unread option, that message remains in your Inbox with a blue dot next to it, indicating that it's a new message that has not yet been read.

FIGURE 2.10
As you're reading any incoming email message on your iPad, you can flag it to indicate to your-self that the message is urgent.

ACCESSING INCOMING EMAIL ATTACHMENTS

The Mail app enables you to access certain types of attachment files that accom-pany an incoming email message. You can view and access the following files: photos (in the .JPEG, .GIF, .PNG, and .TIFF format), audio files (in the .MP3, .AAC, .WAV, and .AIFF format), PDF files, as well as Pages, Keynote, Numbers, Microsoft Word, Microsoft Excel, and Microsoft PowerPoint files.

If an incoming email message contains an attachment that is not compatible or accessible from your iPad, you see that an attachment is present but you aren't able to open or access it. In this case, you must access this content from your pri-mary computer.

To open a compatible attached file within an incoming email message, tap and hold down the attachment icon for one to three seconds. If the attachment is compatible with an app that's installed on your iPad, you are given the option to transfer the file to that app and directly open or access the file using that app. Or, you can open a compatible attachment in the Mail app's own viewer.

TRANSFERRING MESSAGES TO OTHER FOLDERS

As you're viewing an email message on the right side of the screen, you can move it from your Inbox to another folder in one of two ways. First, you can tap the Edit button, or you can tap the file folder-shaped icon that's displayed in the upper-right corner of the screen. When you tap this icon, the various folders available for that email account are displayed on the left side of the screen. Tap the folder to which you want to move the message. The folders available vary for different types of email accounts.

FORWARDING, REPLYING, AND PRINTING

From within the Mail app, you can reply to the message, forward any incoming message to someone else, or print the email by tapping the left-pointing arrow icon that's displayed in the upper-right corner of the main Inbox screen (next to the Trash Can icon). A menu is then displayed in the upper-right corner of the screen (see Figure 2.11).

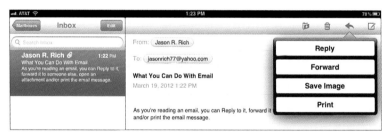

FIGURE 2.11

As you're reading any email message, tap the left-pointing arrow icon to Reply To, Forward, Save/Open Attachments, or Print that message.

To reply to the message you're reading, tap the Reply button. A blank email message template appears on the screen. See the "Composing Messages" section later in this chapter for details on how to write and send an email message from the Mail app.

To forward the email you're reading to another recipient, tap the Forward button. If there's an attachment associated with this email, you are asked if you want to include the attachments from the original email. You see two icons, labeled Include and Don't Include. Choose the appropriate response.

> **NOTE** When you opt to forward an email, a new message template displays. However, within the body of the email message are the contents of the message you're forwarding.

Start the message forwarding process by filling in the To field. You can also modify the Subject field (or leave the message's original Subject) and then add to the body of the email message with your own text. The newly added text displays above the forwarded message's content.

> **TIP** To forward an email to multiple recipients, enter each person's email address in the To field of the outgoing message, but separate each address with a comma. You can also tap the plus icon (+) that appears to the right of the To field to add more recipients.

> **TIP** If you're sending an email to a contact that's stored within your Contact app's database, instead of manually typing the personal's email address, you can begin typing the person's name. The Mail app offers suggestions based on the information stored within the Contacts app.

When you're ready to forward the message to one or more recipients, tap the blue-and-white Send button that appears in the upper-right corner of the email message window. Or tap the Cancel button (located in the upper-left corner of the message window) to abort the message forwarding process.

If you have a wireless printer set up to work with your iPad, you can print incoming or outgoing emails directly from your tablet using the Print command. To learn more about wireless printing from your iPad, see Chapter 8, "Wireless Printing and Scanning via Your iPad."

COMPOSING MESSAGES

From within the Mail app, you can easily compose an email from scratch and send it to one or more recipients. To compose a new email, tap the Compose icon that's displayed near the upper-right corner of the main Inbox screen. The Compose icon looks like a square with a pencil on it.

When you tap the Compose icon, a blank email message template (shown in Figure 2.12) displays. Using the virtual keyboard, fill in the To, Cc, Bcc, and Subject fields. At the very least, you must fill in the To field with a valid email address for at least one recipient. The other fields are optional.

The Microphone (Dictate) Key

FIGURE 2.12

After tapping the Compose icon you can create an email from scratch and send it from your iPad.

You can send the same email to multiple recipients by either adding multiple email addresses to the To field, or by adding additional email addresses to the Cc or Bcc fields.

> **TIP** If you're managing just one email address from your iPad, the From field automatically fills with your email address and is not displayed. However, if you're managing multiple email addresses from the tablet, tap the From field to select the email address from which you want to send the message.

Tap the Subject field and use the virtual keyboard to enter the Subject for your message. As you do this, the Subject displays in the title bar of the Compose window.

To begin creating the main body of the outgoing email message, tap in the main body area of the message template and use the virtual keyboard (or the external keyboard you're using with your iPad) to compose your message.

If you have a new iPad, instead of manually typing an email message, you can use the Dictate feature. To do this, tap the microphone key on your new iPad's virtual keyboard. When then icon enlarges and you hear a tone, begin speaking (dictating) the body of your email message. When you're done, tap the Dictate button again.

Whatever you said is translated by your iPad from speech to text and promptly inserted into the body of your outgoing email message. To learn more about this feature, see the section called, "Using the New iPad's Dictation Feature," at the end of Chapter 1.

CAUTION If you have the Auto-Correction or Spell Check feature turned on (both of which are adjustable from the Settings app) as you type, the iPad automatically corrects anything that it perceives as a typo or misspelled word.

Be very careful when using these features because they are notorious for plugging the wrong word into a sentence. Especially if you're creating important business documents and emails, make sure you proofread whatever you type on your iPad carefully before sending it. Typically, these features are helpful, but they do have quirks that can lead to embarrassing and unprofessional mistakes.

The Signature you set up in the Settings app is displayed automatically at the bottom of the newly composed message. You can return to the Settings app to turn off the Signature feature, or you can change the signature that appears.

When your email is fully written and ready to be sent, tap the blue-and-white Send button in the upper-right corner of the Compose window. Within a few seconds, the message is sent from your iPad, assuming the tablet is connected to the Internet. A copy of the message goes to your Sent or Outbox folder.

SAVING UNSENT DRAFTS OF AN EMAIL MESSAGE

If you want to save a draft of an email (within your Draft folder, for example), without sending it, as you're composing the email message tap the Cancel button that appears in the upper-left corner of the Compose message window. The Delete Draft and Save Draft buttons display. To save the unsent draft, tap Save Draft. This draft is permanently saved in your Drafts folder until you either send it or delete it.

SENDING AN EMAIL WITH AN ATTACHMENT

To send an email message that contains an attachment, such as a Pages document or a photo, those attachments must be sent from within a specific app, not from the Mail app.

For example, you can send a Pages, Word, or PDF document from within the Pages app, a Numbers or Excel (spreadsheet) file from within the Numbers app, or a photo from within the Photos app. Other apps also enable you to attach app-specific files to outgoing emails that are composed and sent from within that app. To do this, tap the Share icon that's displayed within the app and choose the Email option.

> **NOTE** Currently, attachments cannot be added to outgoing messages composed using the Mail app.

ADDITIONAL MAIL APP FEATURES

As you begin using the Mail app to manage one or more email accounts on your iPad, you'll probably discover that this app offers much of the same functionality as the email program you use on your primary computer or on the Web.

In addition to utilizing a built-in spell checker, for example, Mail is compatible with the Select, Copy, Cut, and Paste features built in to the iOS operating system. This enables you to move text and email message content between messages or into other apps with ease.

Plus, the Mail app automatically links with the Contacts app to pull email addresses from your Contacts database. So instead of entering someone's email address into the To field of a message you're composing, you can begin typing the recipient's name, and the app automatically pulls email addresses from your Contacts database and gives you a list of potential recipients.

USING THE WEB OR OTHER APPS TO ACCESS EMAIL

In addition to using the Mail app to access your email, for some types of email accounts, you can also use the Safari web browser to access your email account directly from the server.

By visiting the App Store, you can also find third-party iPad apps that can replace the Mail app and help you better manage one or more email accounts. To find these apps, launch the App Store app, and within the Search field, enter the keyword "email."

If you're a Microsoft Outlook user, for example, you'll discover the Outlook Web Email app ($4.99) or Outlook Mail Pro app ($9.99). For sending emails to groups of people, you can use the MailShot Pro app ($3.99). For people who use Google Gmail, the free Gmail app enables you to better manage this type of email account from your iPad.

IN THIS CHAPTER

- Discover how to use the Safari web browser
- Syncing your Safari bookmarks with your computer and other iOS devices
- Accessing Twitter, Facebook, Google+, LinkedIn, and other online social networking services

3

SURFING THE WEB

Back in the sixteenth century, long before people even dreamed of iPads and the Internet, Sir Francis Bacon stated, "Knowledge is power." In today's cut-throat business world, this statement is truer than ever.

People who possess knowledge, and who consistently stay up to date and in the know, have a distinct advantage over the masses who don't keep their skill set, knowledge, toolset, and education current.

The Safari web browser that comes preinstalled on your iPad offers the ability to access the Internet from virtually anywhere there's a Wi-Fi, 3G, or 4G signal. As a result, your tablet can place a vast amount of information at your fingertips exactly when you need it. Like never before, the iPad is a tool that can keep you in the know and can provide the knowledge you need to be a powerful force in the business world.

> TIP   Your iPad enables you to visit virtually any website and navigate around the World Wide Web with ease using now-familiar finger motions on the tablet's touch-screen.
>
> As you visit web pages using Safari, you can utilize hyperlinks or activate command icons with the tap of the finger, scroll up or down on a web page with a finger swipe, perform a reverse pinch or double-tap to zoom in on specific areas of a web page, or flick your finger to scroll left or right.

If you're already familiar with how to surf the Web on your primary computer using a web browser, such as Microsoft Internet Explorer, Firefox, Google Chrome, or the Mac version of Safari, you should have little trouble surfing the Web on your iPad. The iPad's version of Safari was custom-designed specifically for your tablet to give you the most authentic and robust web surfing experience possible from a mobile device.

CUSTOMIZING SAFARI SETTINGS

The Safari app offers a handful of user-customizable settings adjustable from the Settings app on your iPad. Several of these settings relate to security and privacy.

To access and personalize the settings for Safari, tap the Settings app icon that's displayed on your tablet's Home screen, and then tap the Safari option listed on the left side of the screen under the Settings heading. On the right side of the screen, a handful of Safari-specific options are displayed.

At the top of the Settings screen (on the right), when the Safari option is selected (on the left), you see a General heading with four options below it: Search Engine, AutoFill, Open New Tabs in Background, and Always Show Bookmarks Bar.

As you're actually surfing the Web and looking at the main Safari screen (see Figure 3.1), note the Search field in the upper-right corner of the screen, just below the battery icon. From the Settings app, you can determine whether your default search engine should be Google, Yahoo!, or Bing. This determines which search engine Safari utilizes when you perform a keyword search as you surf the Web.

The AutoFill option has two main uses when it's activated. First, as you're surfing the Web, whenever you're asked to enter your personal information—such as your name, address, phone number, or email address—Safari automatically inserts the information into the appropriate fields on the website.

To use AutoFill, make sure the virtual switch that's associated with the Use Contact Info option is turned on. You also need to tap the My Info option and select your own contact entry from your Contacts database.

Bookmark Bar   Toolbar   Address Field   Search Field   The Open Tab

FIGURE 3.1

The main Safari browser screen looks similar to the web browser screen of a computer.

Farther down on the AutoFill screen is the Names and Passwords option. This is the second main use for AutoFill. When it's turned on, this feature remembers your usernames and passwords for the websites you visit and automatically enters them whenever you revisit websites that require you to otherwise manually enter a user-name or password.

> **CAUTION** If you're concerned about security and other people accessing personal information about you from the Web when they use your iPad, make sure you keep the Names and Passwords option turned OFF. This prevents other users from accessing your account(s) or signing in to websites as you.

The Clear All option at the bottom of the AutoFill screen resets all the names and passwords data from websites you've visited and deletes this information from your tablet.

The next option found under the General heading is the Open New Tabs in Background feature. Safari enables you to open multiple web pages at once using tabs and then instantly switch between them with a tap of the finger.

With the Open New Tabs feature turned on, when a new web page is opened automatically (and a new tab is created), that page does not take precedence over the web page you're currently viewing. You need to tap on the new page's tab to access it.

Also under the General heading is the Always Show Bookmarks Bar option. This option is accompanied by a virtual On/Off switch on the right. As you're surfing the Web using Safari, under the Title Bar command icons at the top of the screen, you can opt to display your personalized Bookmarks bar.

When the Always Show Bookmarks Bar option is turned on, the Bookmarks bar is displayed at all times, giving you one-tap access to your favorite websites. You can assign which websites appear along your Bookmarks bar, or you can sync this information with the browser you use on your primary computer.

When the Always Show Bookmarks Bar option is turned off, one line of onscreen real estate is conserved. The Bookmarks bar, however, is displayed automatically whenever you use the Search field within Safari to perform a search, or when you tap on the address bar.

Under the Privacy heading of the Safari screen within Settings, you can customize a handful of security-related options. For example, you can turn on or off the Private Browsing option, which keeps Safari from storing cookies or other data pertaining to the websites you visit. By default, this option is turned off.

You can also opt to keep Safari from saving cookies related to the websites you visit, or delete cookies that have already been stored by Safari by tapping on the Remove Website Data option that's found under the Privacy heading.

The Accept Cookies option enables Safari to store certain information relating to specific websites you visit so that those sites remember you on subsequent visits. By selecting the From Visited option, only information that relates to websites you have chosen to visit is saved.

TIP   Safari automatically keeps a detailed listing of every website you visit. When you tap the Clear History button, this listing is reset and deleted.

Under the Security heading of the Safari screen with Settings, you can turn on or off the Fraud Warning option. By default, this option is turned on and should remain on for your protection. This option helps prevent you from accidentally surfing to imposter or fraudulent websites, for example.

NOTE Don't mess with the default settings for the next two options, JavaScript and Block Pop-ups, unless you know what you're doing or are instructed by a specialist to change these settings. The JavaScript option enables you to visit and access websites that utilize JavaScript programming. The Block Pop-ups option prevents those annoying pop-up windows (which are usually ads) from cluttering your screen as you're surfing the Web.

Unless you have a programming background or you're told to do so by an AppleCare technical support specialist, refrain from changing any settings found under the Developer or Databases submenus, if and when these options are displayed on the Safari screen within Settings. Simply leave the default settings as is.

To exit the Settings app and automatically save your changes, press the Home button on your iPad. This returns you to the Home screen. From here, you can launch Safari and begin surfing the Web.

WHERE'S THE FLASH?

The one main drawback to surfing the Web using Safari on your iPad is the web browser's inability to display Adobe Flash-based graphics and animations. This limitation is not due to lack of technological capability of your tablet, however. It's the result of ongoing disagreements between Apple and Adobe in regard to offering Flash compatibility through the iOS operating system.

Unfortunately, websites that rely heavily on Flash are not accessible using Safari. However, the optional Photon Flash Web Browser app does support Flash as you surf the Web from your iPad. You can also use a remote desktop app, such as Splashtop, to control your primary computer from your iPad's screen, which enables you to run your computer's web browser to surf the Web to access Flash-based websites.

NOTE You learn more about the Photon Flash Web Browser and Splashtop apps in Chapter 13, "Discovering 'Must Have' Business Apps."

YOU'RE READY TO BEGIN SURFING

To access the Web using your iPad, make sure it's connected to the Internet, and then tap the Safari app icon that's displayed on the tablet's Home screen. The main Safari web browser screen appears.

USING SAFARI'S TOOLBAR FEATURES

Located along the top of the Safari screen is the toolbar, which includes a handful of command icons that you use to navigate around the Web. Although the icons might look different than what you're used to when surfing the Web using the browser installed on your primary computer, their features and functions are similar.

TIP   As you surf the Web using Safari, you can hold your tablet in portrait or landscape mode. Landscape mode makes the portion of the websites you're viewing appear larger on the screen, but portrait mode enables you to see more of the web page vertically.

Located in the upper-left corner of the Safari screen are the Back and Forward arrow-shaped icons used for jumping to a previous web page you've visited.

The icon of the open book on the toolbar (shown in Figure 3.2) enables you to access your Reading List, History, Bookmarks bar, and the bookmarks you've added to your bookmarks list. Later in this chapter, you learn how to sync your bookmarks between Safari on your iPad with the bookmarks stored on your primary computer's web browser software.

FIGURE 3.2

Tap the icon of the open book to access your Reading List (which is explained shortly), as well as your History, Bookmarks Bar listing, and saved bookmarks.

When you're visiting any website, you can tap the rectangular icon with a right-pointing arrow sticking out of it (the Share icon) that's located to the immediate left of the address field to access a submenu with the following five options (see Figure 3.3): Add Bookmark, Add to Reading List, Add to Home Screen, Mail Link to This Page, and Print.

FIGURE 3.3
This submenu offers several useful web surfing options.

NOTE If you have Twitter set up on your iPad (from within the Settings app), a sixth option, labeled Tweet, is displayed within the Share menu, enabling you to send a tweet to your followers, containing your 140-character message and a link to the website you're viewing.

The Share menu offered in other apps, such as Photos, YouTube, and Maps, also displays a Tweet option if you have Twitter turned on and you're signed in to your Twitter account from within the Settings app.

The Add Bookmark command adds the website URL for the page you're currently viewing to your Bookmarks menu or Bookmarks bar. When you tap the Add Bookmark command, the Add Bookmark window displays.

Using the virtual keyboard, enter the title for this web page, or use the default title, and then choose whether you want to store the bookmark within your Bookmarks menu or display it on your Bookmarks bar.

The Bookmarks menu is a pull-down menu that lists your favorite bookmarks. It is a listing you can create and maintain as you're surfing the Web. You can access it by tapping on the open-book icon at the top of the Safari screen.

TIP Be sure to tap the blue-and-white Save button in the upper-right corner of the Add Bookmark window to save your changes before returning to the main Safari screen.

The Add to Reading List option immediately stores the webpage you're viewing in the iPad's memory and enables you to access it later (even if you're offline). When you add a website to your reading list, you can access it by tapping the open-book icon and then tapping the Reading List option. This feature is particularly useful if you find an interesting article or blog entry that you don't have time to read at the moment, but you know you want to refer to later.

Instead of adding a bookmark to the Bookmark menu or the Bookmarks bar, both of which are only visible when Safari is running and you're surfing the Web, you can create a bookmark icon for a specific web page on your Home screen using the Add to Home Screen command.

When you tap a Home screen bookmark icon, the Safari browser launches and automatically loads the bookmarked web page. This enables you to access your favorite websites directly from the iPad's Home screen. Home screen bookmark icons look similar to app icons on your Home screen. However, instead of launch-ing an app when you tap one, Safari launches and opens the specific web page the icon is associated with.

When you tap the Add to Home Screen command, an Add to Home window dis-plays. Using the virtual keyboard, enter the title of the bookmark in the displayed field and then tap the blue-and-white Add button displayed in the upper-right cor-ner of the window. After doing this, when you access your Home screen, the new Home screen bookmark icon appears.

After you add a Home screen bookmark icon, you can treat it like any Home screen app icon, which means you can tap it to launch the website, move it around on the Home screen, or place it into a folder.

TIP   When you tap the Mail Link to This Page command, an email message screen displays. Fill in the To field to specify who should receive the email. A link to the website you're currently viewing is automatically placed in the body of the email. You can add additional text to the body of the email before tapping the Send button.

If you have a printer linked to your iPad that's compatible with the AirPrint fea-ture, you can print web pages you're viewing using the Safari app. Tap the Print command icon to do this. See Chapter 8, "Wireless Printing and Scanning via Your iPad," for more information about using your tablet with a printer.

EDITING YOUR BOOKMARKS

As you're viewing your Bookmarks menu, tap the Edit button displayed in the upper-right corner of the window to edit your bookmarks listing.

After you tap on the Edit command, the Bookmarks menu displays additional icons to the right and left of each bookmark title (see Figure 3.4). On the left side of each user-added bookmark listing is a red-and-white circular icon with a minus sign in it. Tap this icon to delete the bookmark from your Bookmarks menu.

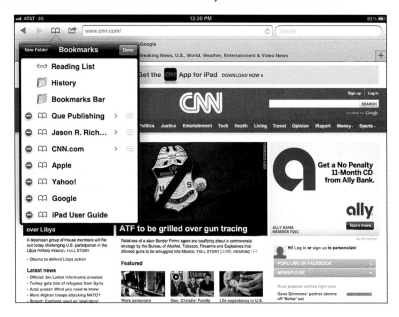

FIGURE 3.4

You can edit the bookmarks listed in your Bookmark menu or Bookmarks bar by tapping the Edit button in the upper-right corner of the Bookmark menu window.

Use the open-book icon or the > symbol (displayed to the right of each bookmark title) to edit the bookmark's title, URL, or where the bookmark is listed.

Located to the extreme right of each user-added bookmark title is an icon with three horizontal lines. Place your finger on one of these icons to drag a bookmark listing up or down on the Bookmarks list, and change the order of the list.

In addition to having all of your bookmarks displayed in one long list within the Bookmarks menu, you can tap the New Folder button in the upper-left corner of this Bookmarks menu window to create separate folders that you can use to better organize your bookmarks by sorting them into custom categories. When you create a new bookmark folder, you must also assign a custom name to it.

When you're done editing the Bookmark menu, be sure to tap the blue-and-white Done button in the upper-right corner of the window to save your changes and return to the regular Bookmark menu.

ACCESSING AND MANAGING YOUR READING LIST

To access and manage your reading list, tap the open-book icon, and then tap on the Reading List option. A new Reading List window appears. Under the Reading List heading are two tabs: All and Unread.

To open a reading list entry, tap its listing, or swipe your finger from left to right across the entry to delete an entry from your reading list. When the red-and-white Delete icon appears, tap it.

To exit out of the Reading List window, either tap on the Bookmarks icon that's displayed in the upper-left corner, or tap anywhere on the tablet's screen that's outside the window.

Your Reading List can be comprised of websites or specific web pages you want to refer to later, in order to read a specific article, new item or blog entry, for example. At any time, if you're reading an article on a website, another way to add it to your reading list is to tap the open-book icon, select the Reading List option, and then tap the plus (+) icon in the upper-right corner of the Reading List window.

SAFARI'S ADDRESS FIELD

Located at the top of the main Safari screen is the address bar. When you tap it, the iPad's virtual keyboard appears and you can manually enter the website address (URL) for any website you want to access, as shown in Figure 3.5. As you begin typing, a list of suggestions, based on past websites you've visited, is displayed.

If a website is already displayed within the address bar, tap the X icon displayed at the right end of the address bar to delete the address bar's contents.

TIP   In Safari, the virtual keyboard includes several specialized keys associated with entering URL addresses, including a colon (:), backslash (/), underscore (_), dash (-), and .com. These keys are located along the bottom row of the virtual keyboard.

These keys enable you to more quickly enter the URL for the website you want to visit. When you're done entering the URL, tap the Go key on the virtual keyboard to surf to that site.

Also, if you hold down the .com key on the virtual keyboard, a pop-up menu enables you to choose .net, .org, .com, .us, or .edu, which are common website extensions.

The Address Bar

The
Go Key

FIGURE 3.5

Enter the URL for any website into the address bar, and then tap the Go key on the virtual keyboard to visit any website.

USING THE SEARCH FIELD

Located in the upper-right corner of the screen is Safari's Search field. Here, you can enter any keyword or search phrase to perform a web search using Google, Yahoo!, or Bing, depending on which default search engine you previously selected from the Settings app.

USING TABS

Tabs enable you to load multiple web pages within Safari simultaneously and then instantly switch between them. The tab bar is displayed below the Bookmarks bar, near the top of the Safari screen.

When you first load Safari, only one tab is open. However, at any time, you can tap the plus (+) icon that's displayed to the extreme right of the tab bar to open a new browser window and create a new tab.

You can have multiple tabs displayed at the top of the Safari screen. When multiple tabs are open, tap any of them to switch to the website to which the tab corresponds.

The website that's actually displayed on the iPad's screen is the active tab. To the left of the active tab's title is an X icon. Tap this X to delete the tab and close the web page associated with it. To keep the web page open but view a different web page, tap on another displayed tab or open a new tab and manually surf to another website.

The ability to quickly switch between web pages that are open (which is referred to as *tabbed browsing*), makes surfing the Web on the iPad fast and convenient.

USING SAFARI'S READER FEATURE

Sometimes, web pages are cluttered with ads, graphics, menus, and other content that makes reading a text-based article confusing. The Reader option that's built in to Safari enables the web browser to automatically strip away this clutter, allowing you to read the text-based article more easily and with no onscreen distractions.

When this option is available, a small Reader icon appears to the right of the web-site's URL in the Address field of Safari (as shown in Figure 3.6). Tap this icon, and the text-based article displays in a new, clutter-free window.

www.nydailynews.com/news/money/holidays-great-time-town-   Reader ⟳

FIGURE 3.6

When the Reader icon appears in the Address Bar of Safari, you can tap it to read the text-based content on that site on a clutter-free screen.

As you're reading a text-based article in Reader, in the upper-left corner of the screen is an aA icon. Tap it to increase or decrease the size of the onscreen text.

UNDERSTANDING THE WEB PAGE VIEWING AREA

Getting back to surfing the Web, displayed below the title bar and the Bookmarks bar (if you have this option turned on) is the main website viewing area of Safari. As you view website content, you can scroll around on the page using upward, downward, left, or right finger swipes.

To instantly jump back to the top of a web page, tap anywhere on the status bar at the top of the iPad's screen (above the title bar). The status bar displays the Internet connection's signal bars, the current time, and the battery life indicator.

To zoom in or out of a particular area of a web page, either double-tap on the area that you want to zoom in on or perform a reverse-pinch finger motion. To zoom out, double-tap on the screen again or perform a pinch finger motion.

If you see a hyperlink or a command button displayed within a web page, tap it to follow the link or activate the button. To see where the link takes you before actually surfing there, hold your finger on the link or button for two to three seconds. The link's URL address is displayed along with a menu containing three commands:

- **Open:** This opens the web page that the link directs you to.
- **Open in New Page:** This opens the web page that the link directs you to but does so within a new Safari browser window.
- **Copy:** This copies the website URL to your iPad's virtual clipboard so you can paste this information elsewhere.

> TIP   As you're viewing almost any graphic or photo that's displayed within a website, you can hold your finger on the image to save it on your iPad, where it becomes accessible from the Photos app.

If for some reason a web page doesn't fully load or you want to refresh the information displayed on a web page you're currently viewing, tap the circular arrow icon that's displayed to the extreme right of the address bar. However, if you want to stop a web page as it is loading, tap the X icon to the extreme right of the address bar during the web page loading process.

Any time you need to enter text or numerical data in a field on a website you're viewing, tap the empty field, which causes the iPad's virtual keyboard to display. To move to another field that requires data entry, either tap your finger on the next field or tap the Next or Previous icon that appears on the screen above the virtual keyboard.

SYNCING BOOKMARKS WITH YOUR PRIMARY COMPUTER

To ensure your web surfing experience is similar to when you're exploring the Web using the web browser on your primary computer, you have the option to sync your bookmarks between your computer and your iPad.

There are two methods for syncing your Safari bookmarks. One happens automatically using the iCloud service, and the other is done through an iTunes sync procedure when your tablet is connected to your primary computer via a USB cable. This sync process works with Safari for the Mac, Microsoft Internet Explorer on a PC, as well as a variety of other popular web browser applications.

If you use the iCloud online service, you can automatically sync your bookmarks wirelessly between your tablet and primary computer (as well as your iPhone). To set this up, after you have an iCloud account, access the Settings app from your tablet's Home screen, and tap the iCloud option that's displayed on the left column. When the iCloud screen appears on the right side of the Settings screen, turn on the Bookmarks option.

ACCESSING SOCIAL NETWORKS ON YOUR iPAD

Whether you use Facebook, Twitter, Google+, or LinkedIn to promote your business, a product, or service to help position yourself as an expert in your field, to meet new people, or simply to stay in touch with your friends and family, you can fully utilize these online social networking sites using specialized apps available from the App Store.

The ability to share information on social networks from virtually anywhere using your iPad brings a new level of interactivity to these services.

WORKING WITH FACEBOOK

The official Facebook for iPad app (free) is available from the App Store. It offers almost all of the functionality of Facebook on your tablet's screen, including the ability to access your Wall, update your Status, send/receive messages, manage your photo albums, upload and share photos shot using your iPad, and chat in real-time with your Friends.

TWEETING FROM YOUR iPAD

There is an official Twitter app, designed specifically for the iPad (free), as well as dozens of third-party apps that work with Twitter.

The official Twitter app, as well as Twitter functionality, has been fully integrated into iOS 5.1, so you can tweet from a variety of different apps as long as the official Twitter app is loaded on your tablet.

To initially set up Twitter on your iPad, access the Settings app and tap the Twitter option displayed on the left side of the screen. On the right side of the screen, you have the option to install the official Twitter app by tapping the Install Now icon.

After installation, launch the Twitter app on your iPad. You can then sign in using one or multiple Twitter accounts, or create a new account (which is also something you can do from the Twitter screen within Settings, by tapping the Create New Account option).

You can use the official Twitter app to create and send tweets, access your Twitter timeline, and see what the people you're following are tweeting about. In addition, various other core apps—including Photos, Safari, Camera, Contacts, YouTube, and Maps—are fully integrated with Twitter and allow you to send tweets with an app-related attachment.

> **TIP** For Twitter integration to work with the core apps built in to your iPad (as opposed to just the official Twitter app), you need to sign in to your Twitter account from within Settings just once.

Figure 3.7 shows the Twitter option in Photos, which is displayed when you view a photo and tap the Share icon. When the Share menu appears, the last option is to tweet the photo from directly within the Photos app.

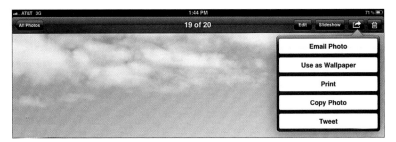

FIGURE 3.7
You can send tweets from within the Photos app as you're viewing a photo. Tap the Share icon, and then choose the Tweet option.

Tap the Tweet option, and within Photos, a Tweet window appears (shown in Figure 3.8), enabling you to compose an outgoing tweet that automatically attaches the photo. If you tap the Add Location option in the lower-left corner of this window, your exact location is automatically added to the outgoing tweet as well.

FIGURE 3.8
When you choose to send a tweet from within an app, a special tweet window appears enabling you to compose and send the 140-character message and (if applicable) automatically attach a photo, URL, or your exact location.

TAPPING IN TO LINKEDIN TO NETWORK WITH BUSINESS PROFESSIONALS

More than 65 million business professionals, working in thousands of different fields and industries, are active participants on the LinkedIn online social networking service (www.linkedin.com).

To access LinkedIn from your iPad, download the free LinkedIn app, called IN. It's available from the App Store. IN is designed for the iPhone, but works flawlessly on the iPad.

MANAGING YOUR GOOGLE+ ACCOUNT FROM YOUR iPAD

Also available from the App Store is the free Google+ app. It enables you to manage most aspects of your Google+ account directly from your tablet. However, the official Google+ app was designed as an iPhone-specific app that works on an iPad, but doesn't fully utilize the tablet's large screen.

In addition to visiting websites, using your iPad to manage multiple email accounts, and accessing the Internet to manage your Facebook page or Twitter account, for example, you also can stream audio and/or video content directly from the Web. To learn more about how to stream content, see Chapter 15, "Downloading Versus Streaming Online Content."

TIP   When using any app, including Safari, you can unlock the virtual keyboard from its fixed location at the bottom of the screen and move it up on the screen. To do this, place and hold your finger on the right edge of the Hide Keyboard icon (located in the lower-right corner of the virtual keyboard) and drag it upward. Or, when a pop-up window with the Undock and Split options appear, tap the Undock option. The virtual keyboard jumps to the middle of the screen. Now, place your finger again on the right edge of the Hide Keyboard key, and drag it up or down to move the virtual keyboard around. To return the keyboard to its default position at the bottom of the screen and lock it there, hold your finger on the edge of the Hide Keyboard key and select the Dock command that appears in the pop-up window. This is a new feature added to iOS 5.1.

4

USING THE CALENDAR, REMINDERS, AND NOTIFICATION CENTER APPS

Appointments, meetings, phone calls, web-based virtual meetings, commuting to and from work, business travel, errands, responding to emails, personal obligations, and vacations are just some of the ways people spend their time.

Those people who are typically the most productive and efficient on the job, and who live with the least amount of day-to-day stress, have often discovered the secrets of effectively managing their time, which enables them to prioritize tasks and their responsibilities, delegate when possible, and keep themselves organized.

You can use your iPad as a time-management and to-do list management tool for keeping track of and successfully juggling your day-to-day schedule, deadlines, and responsibilities.

CALENDAR APP BASICS

The Calendar app comes preinstalled on your tablet. With multiple viewing options for keeping track of the scheduling information, Calendar is a highly customizable scheduling tool that enables you to easily sync your scheduling data with your primary computer's scheduling software (such as Microsoft Outlook on a PC, or iCal or Calendar on a Mac), as well as with your iPhone or smartphone. Like many other apps, Calendar works seamlessly with Notification Center and Apple's iCloud service.

Using Calendar, you can share some or all of your schedule information with colleagues, and maintain several separate, color-coded calendars of your own to keep personal and work-related responsibilities and projects listed separately while still being able to view them on the same calendar.

> **TIP** The Calendar app is designed to work seamlessly with Apple's iCloud service, Microsoft Exchange, and other software and online-based calendar/scheduling programs (including Google Calendar and Yahoo! Calendar, for example). This file compatibility enables you to easily synchronize your scheduling data between your iPad and other devices.

CONTROLLING THE VIEW

When you launch the Calendar app, choose which viewing perspective you'd like to use to display your schedule data in. Your five options, selectable by tapping the tabs displayed at the top-center of the screen, include the following.

DAY VIEW

This view (shown in Figure 4.1) displays your appointments and scheduled events individually on the right side of the screen, based on the time each item is scheduled for.

WEEK VIEW

This view uses a grid format (shown in Figure 4.2) to display the days of the week along the top of the screen and time intervals along the left side. With it you have an overview of all appointments and events scheduled within a particular week (Sunday through Saturday).

FIGURE 4.1
The Calendar app's Day view.

FIGURE 4.2
The Calendar app's Week view.

MONTH VIEW

This month-at-a-time view (shown in Figure 4.3) enables you to see a month's worth of appointments and events at a time. You can tap any single day to immediately switch to the Day view in order to review a detailed summary of appointments or events slated for that day.

FIGURE 4.3
The Calendar app's Month view.

YEAR VIEW

This view (shown in Figure 4.4) enables you to look at 12 mini calendars and see an overview of your schedule. For example, you can block out vacation days, travel days, and so on, and get a comprehensive view of your overall annual schedule.

LIST VIEW

See a complete summary listing of all appointments and events stored within the Calendar app (shown in Figure 4.5). You can tap an individual listing to see its complete details. When you're using this view, a listing of all upcoming appointments is displayed on the left, and the current day's appointments and related notes are displayed on the right side of the screen.

FIGURE 4.4

The Calendar app's Year view.

FIGURE 4.5

The Calendar app's List view.

Regardless of which view you select, at any time you can view the current day's schedule by tapping the Today button located in the lower-left corner of the screen. On the calendar itself, the current date is always highlighted in blue.

NOTE   The Calendar app works in either landscape or portrait mode, so which you choose is a matter of personal preference. Regardless of which direction you hold your tablet, the onscreen information pertaining to your schedule is the same.

ENTERING A NEW APPOINTMENT

No matter which calendar view you're using, to enter a new appointment, tap the plus-sign icon that's displayed in the lower-right corner of the screen. This displays an Add Event window (shown in Figure 4.6). When using the Calendar app, appointments, meetings, and other items you enter are referred to as *events*.

FIGURE 4.6

From the Add Event window, you can add a new appointment to the Calendar app and associate an audible alarm with that event.

The first field in the Add Event window is labeled Title. Using the iPad's virtual keyboard, enter a heading for the appointment or event, such as "Lunch with Bob," "Sales Meeting," or "Call Natalie."

Next, if there's a location associated with the meeting or appointment, tap the Location field that's located below the Title field, and then use the virtual keyboard to enter the address or location of the appointment. Entering information into the Location field is optional. You can be as detailed as you want when entering information into this field.

To set the time and date for the new appointment to begin and end, use the Starts and Ends fields. A new Start & End window (see Figure 4.7) displays, temporarily replacing the Add Event window.

FIGURE 4.7

From the Start & End window, select the start and end times and the dates for each new appointment you manually enter into the Calendar app.

When viewing the Start & End window, tap the Starts option so that it becomes highlighted in blue, and then use the scrolling Date, Hour, Minute, and AM/PM dials to select the exact start time for your appointment.

After entering the start time, tap the Ends option, and again use the scrolling Date, Hour, Minute, and AM/PM dials to select the exact end time for your appointment. Or, if the appointment lasts the entire day, tap the All-Day virtual switch, moving it from the Off position to On.

You can also adjust the Time Zone option if the meeting will be taking place in a different time zone than the one you're currently in. So, if you're based in Los Angeles but the meeting or appointment will take place at 2:00pm EST because it will be held in New York, you can enter the correct time for the location of the meeting and the iPad adjusts accordingly when you travel.

After you enter the start time and end time for the appointment, you must tap the blue-and-white Done button to save this information and return to the Add Event window.

> **TIP** If the appointment you're entering repeats every day, every week, every two weeks, every month, or every year, tap the Repeat option and choose the appropriate option. The default for this option is Never, meaning it is a nonrepeating, one-time only appointment.

ASSOCIATING ONE OR TWO ALARMS WITH EACH EVENT

To set an audible alarm for the appointment, tap the Alert option displayed below the Repeat option within the Add Event window. The Event Alert window temporarily replaces the Add Event window. In the Event Alert window, tap to specify when you want the audible alarm to sound to remind you of the appointment. Your options are None (which is the default), At Time of Event, 5 Minutes Before, 15 Minutes Before, 30 Minutes Before, One Hour Before, Two Hours Before, One Day Before, or Two Days Before. When you tap your selection, a check mark that corresponds with that selection displays on the left side of the window.

Again, tap the blue-and-white Done button that's displayed in the upper-right corner of the Event Alert window to save the information and return to the Add Event screen.

Upon adding an alert, a Second Alert option now displays in the Add Event window. If you want to add a secondary alarm to this appointment, tap the Second Alert option and when the Event Alert window reappears, tap when you want the second alarm to sound. Again, don't forget to tap the Done button.

ADDITIONAL WAYS TO CUSTOMIZE EACH EVENT LISTING

When you return to the Add Event window, if you're maintaining several separate calendars within the Calendar app, you can choose which calendar you want to list the appointment or event by tapping on the Calendar option and then selecting the appropriate calendar.

As you scroll down within the Calendar window, you see an optional URL and Notes field. Using the virtual keyboard, you can manually enter a website URL that corresponds to the event or meeting. Or, tap the Notes field and manually type notes pertaining to the appointment (or paste data from other apps within this field). On the new iPad, you can also use the Dictation feature as another way to input Notes or other Calendar data.

CAUTION It is essential that you tap the blue-and-white Done button to save the new appointment information. Otherwise, the information you entered will not be saved to your calendar and will be lost.

TIP The Calendar app works with several other iPad apps, including Contacts and Notification Center. For example, within Contacts, you can enter someone's birthday within their record, and that information can automatically be displayed within the Calendar app. To display birthday listings within Calendar, tap the Calendars button, which is displayed in the upper-left corner of the screen, and then tap the Birthdays option to add a check mark to that selection. All recurring birthdays stored within your Contacts app now appear within Calendar.

The alternative to manually entering appointment information into the Calendar app is to enter your scheduling information within a scheduling program on your primary computer, such as Microsoft Outlook (PC), iCal or Calendar (for Mac), or Microsoft Entourage (Mac), and then sync this data with your iPad using the iTunes sync process, iTunes Wireless Sync process, or via iCloud.

You can also sync scheduling data with your iPhone, as well as several different online or network-based scheduling applications. Chapter 9, "Syncing Your iPad via iTunes or iCloud," focuses more on how to sync data between your iPad and other devices or computers.

NOTE If you've updated your Mac to run the OS X Mountain Lion operating system, you'll discover that the iCal app is now called Calendar, and it looks even more like the iOS version of Calendar that's currently running on your iPad.

VIEWING INDIVIDUAL APPOINTMENT DETAILS

From the Day, Week, Month, or List view within the Calendar app, tap any individual event (appointment, meeting, and so on) to view all the details related to that item. When you tap a single event, a new window opens. In the upper-right corner of the window is an Edit icon. Tap it to modify any aspect of the event listing, such as the title, location, start time, end time, alert, or notes.

To delete an event entry entirely, tap the red-and-white Delete Event icon that's displayed at the very bottom of the Edit window. Or, when you're done making changes to an event entry, tap on the blue-and-white Done button that's displayed in the upper-right corner of the window to save your updated event information.

SUBSCRIBING TO CALENDARS

From within Calendar, it is possible to subscribe to read-only Google, Yahoo!, or iCal or Calendar calendars saved in the .ics format. To subscribe to a calendar, which enables you to read calendar entries created on other devices or services but not edit or create new events within those calendars, follow these steps:

1. From the iPad's Home screen, access the Settings app.

2. From the left side of the Settings screen, select the Mail, Contacts, Calendars option.

3. Under the Accounts heading on the right side of the Settings screen, tap the Add Account option.

4. From the bottom of the list of account types, tap the Other option.

5. When the Other screen appears on the right side of the display, tap the Add Subscribed Calendar option.

6. Within the Subscription window that appears, enter the address for the calendar you want to subscribe to within the field labeled Server. Enter this information using the following format: *myserver.com*/cal.ics.

7. Tap the Next icon that's located in the upper-right corner of the screen to validate the subscription, and then tap the Save button. Your tablet must be connected to the Internet to do this.

If you use iCal or Calendar on a Mac, for example, you can publish (and share) a Calendar via a web server, and make it available to be subscribed to on your iPad. From iCal or Calendar on your Mac, select the calendar you want to publish from the listing on the left side of the iCal or Calendar screen (on your Mac). After it's highlighted, click the Calendar pull-down menu and select the Publish option. Add check marks next to your desired options, and then click the Publish icon. The URL for the calendar displays. Enter this URL into the Calendar app on your iPad using the steps outlined earlier in this section.

The Apple website also publishes dozens of read-only calendars that you can subscribe to on your iPad. These read-only calendars list major holidays, game schedules for your favorite sports teams, moon phases, new song releases on iTunes, new DVD releases, and more. For a listing of these calendars, visit www.apple.com/downloads/macosx/calendars.

TIP If your primary work schedule is handled on a computer or network that is compatible with the industry-standard CalDAV or .ics file format, you can easily sync this data with the Calendar app on your iPad. To subscribe to a CalDAV or .ics calendar, launch the Settings app on your iPad, and then choose the Mail, Contacts, Calendars option. Tap the Add Account option, and then choose Other from the bottom of the list.

When the Other screen appears, select the Add CalDAV Account option. A CalDAV window displays, and you are prompted to enter the server address (cal.*example.com*), your username, password, and a description for the calendar. This is information you can obtain from your company's network system administrator or IT department.

After entering all the requested information in the CalDAV window on your iPad, tap the Next button to verify the account. Tap the Save button when this process is completed. The appointments and events included in the calendar you just subscribed to now appear in their own color-coded calendar when you launch the Calendar app on your iPad.

FINDING AN APPOINTMENT

In addition to viewing the Day, Week, Month, or List view within Calendar to find individual appointments, you can use the Search field in the upper-right corner of the Calendar app. Tap the Search field and then use the virtual keyboard to enter any keyword or phrase associated with the appointment you're looking for.

Or, from the iPad's Home screen, swipe your finger from left to right to access the tablet's main Spotlight Search screen. In the Search field that appears, enter a keyword, search phrase, or date associated with an appointment. When a list of relevant items is displayed, tap the appointment you want to view. This launches the Calendar app and displays that specific appointment.

VIEWING CALENDARS

One of the more useful features of the Calendar app is that you can view and manage multiple, color-coded calendars at once on the same screen, or you can easily switch between calendars.

To decide which calendar information you want to view, tap the Calendars icon. When the Show Calendars window displays, select which calendar or calendars you want to view on your iPad's screen. You can view one or more calendars at a time, or you can select to view data from all of your calendars on one screen simultaneously. Each calendar is color-coded, so you can tell entries apart when looking at multiple calendars on the screen at once.

INVITING PEOPLE TO MEETINGS OR EVENTS

The Calendar app is compatible with Microsoft Exchange. Thus, if you have the appropriate feature turned on, and your company uses a CalDAV supported scheduling app on its network, you can invite other people on that network to your events and respond to other people's event invites.

To respond to a meeting, appointment, or event invitation, your iPad must have access to the Internet. When you receive an invitation, the event is displayed in your calendar with a dotted line surrounding it. Tap it to see options enabling you to see who the invitation is from and who is attending the event. You can also set your iPad to alert you of the meeting and add comments of your own that pertain to the meeting invite.

As the invitee, you can then accept or decline the invitation, or tap the Maybe option. The person who invited you to the meeting or event receives your response.

CUSTOMIZING THE CALENDAR APP

As you begin using the Calendar app, you'll discover there are many ways to customize it beyond choosing between the Day, Week, Month, or List calendar view or subscribing to read-only calendars. For example, from within the Calendar app you can set audible alerts to remind you of appointments, meetings, and events. To customize the audio alert you hear, launch the Settings app and select the General option from the left side of the screen. Next, tap the Sounds option displayed on the right side of the screen.

Make sure the Calendar Alerts option, displayed within the Sounds screen, is turned on. If this option is turned off, a text-based message displays on the iPad's screen as an event reminder instead of an audible alarm sounding.

> TIP   If you have the ability to receive meeting or event invites from others, from the Settings app, tap the Mail, Contacts, Calendars option. Then scroll down to the Calendars heading and make sure the New Invitations Alerts option is turned on. This enables you to hear an audible alarm when you receive a new invitation.

Also from Settings, listed under the Calendars heading on the right side of the display, you can determine how far back in your schedule you want to sync appointment data between your primary computer and iPad. Your options include Events 2 Weeks Back, Events 1 Month Back, Events 3 Months Back, Events 6 Months Back, or All Events.

When the Time Zone Support option is turned on and you've selected the major city that you're in or near, all alarms are activated based on that city's time zone. However, when you travel, turn off this option. With Time Zone Support turned off, the iPad determines the current date and time based on the location and time zone you're in (when it's connected to the Internet) and adjusts all your alarms to go off at the appropriate time for that time zone.

To access the Time Zone Support feature, launch the Settings app, and select the Mail, Contacts, Calendars option. On the right side of the screen, scroll down to the options listed under Calendars and then tap the Time Zone Support option. When the Time Zone Support screen appears, you see a virtual On/Off switch. When it's turned on, below the switch is a Time Zone option. Tap it and then choose your home city (or a city within the time zone you're in).

SYNCING SCHEDULING DATA WITH YOUR PRIMARY COMPUTER OR SMARTPHONE

Depending on whether you want to sync your Calendar app with a standalone PC or Mac, or wirelessly access scheduling data on a network, the process for setting up the connection and syncing scheduling data is slightly different.

SYNCING CALENDAR DATA WITH A PC OR MAC USING iTUNES SYNC

The process for syncing data between the Calendar app and your primary computer using the iTunes sync process involves connecting the two devices using the white USB cable that came with your iPad. You also need the free iTunes software to be running on your primary computer. Customize the Sync Calendars option within iTunes on your computer, which is found under the Info tab when your iPad is connected to your PC or Mac and iTunes is running.

For more information about the iTunes Sync process, and how to use it to exchange different types of data between your tablet and computer and maintain a complete backup of your iPad, be sure to read Chapter 9, "Syncing Your iPad via iTunes or iCloud."

SYNCING CALENDAR DATA WIRELESSLY USING iCLOUD

It's also possible to sync your Calendar data with other iOS mobile devices, as well your primary computer, using Apple's iCloud online service. After you have created an iCloud account, set up your iPad for automatic Calendar syncing. To do this, launch the Settings app and select the iCloud option that's displayed on the left side of the screen. On the right side of the screen, when the iCloud menu screen appears, make sure the Calendars option is turned on.

You also need to turn on Calendar syncing via iCloud on your primary computer, iPhone, and/or other iOS mobile devices that are linked to the same iCloud account.

TIP When your Calendar data is syncing in real-time with iCloud, you can access that information anytime from any computer or mobile device that connects to the Internet. Simply visit www.icloud.com/#calendar, and sign in using your Apple ID and password. You'll find a free, online-based application that looks almost identical to the Calendar app on your iPad. Your personal scheduling data will be displayed.

SYNCING CALENDAR DATA WIRELESSLY WITH SCHEDULING SOFTWARE ON A MICROSOFT EXCHANGE-COMPATIBLE NETWORK

To set up the Calendar app to sync data with Microsoft Exchange-compatible scheduling software used in a corporate environment, launch the Settings app on your tablet and choose the Mail, Contacts, Calendars option.

Tap the Add Account option, and then select Microsoft Exchange from the menu displayed on the right side of the screen. Enter your account information when prompted. This information is typically supplied by your company's system administrator or IT department.

As you're setting up the Microsoft Exchange connection with your iPad, be sure to add a check mark next to the Calendar option so you can sync this data.

TIP Many company networks and virtual private networks (VPNs) utilize scheduling software that is CalDAV-compatible. To synchronize your scheduling information between your tablet and a CalDAV-compatible calendar/scheduling software package on a corporate network, contact your company's IT department or system administrator to obtain the necessary account settings and passwords to make this connection.

On your iPad, set up this connection from the Settings app. If your company's system administrator or IT department is not able to help you sync your tablet with the company's network, make an appointment with an Apple Genius at any Apple Store, or call AppleCare's toll-free phone number (800-APL-CARE) and have a technical support person walk you through the setup process.

SYNCING CALENDAR DATA WIRELESSLY WITH GOOGLE CALENDAR OR YAHOO! CALENDAR

If you maintain your scheduling information using an online-based scheduling application, such as Google Calendar or Yahoo! Calendar, you can use your iPad (when it's connected to the Internet) to wirelessly sync scheduling data.

To set this up, launch the Settings app on your iPad, select the Mail, Contacts, Calendars option, and then tap the Add Account option.

Choose the Google, Yahoo!, or AOL option based on where you maintain an online-based calendar. When prompted, enter your name, the existing email address and password used for that service, and a brief description for the account.

Finally, tap the services you want to link with your iPad, such as Calendars, Contacts, and so on. The available options vary based on the service you use.

USING THE REMINDERS APP

On the surface, Reminders is a straightforward to-do list manager. However, after you start using this innovative but easy-to-use app, you'll discover it offers a plethora of interesting and useful features.

Reminders works seamlessly with Notification Center and iCloud, and easily syncs with the Reminders app on your Mac if you're running OS X Mountain Lion, or iCal if you're running OS X Lion. The Reminders app also can sync with Microsoft Outlook running on your primary computer. Plus, you can create as many separate to-do lists as you need to properly manage your personal and professional life, or various projects you're responsible for.

> **NOTE** Using iCloud, Reminders can automatically sync with your primary computer, iPhone, or other iOS devices. Be sure to turn on the iCloud functionality for Reminders from within the Settings app to initiate real-time, automatic syncing. OS X Mountain Lion for the Mac now includes the Reminders app, which makes syncing to-do lists easy via iCloud.

To make it easier for you to juggle tasks and keep track of deadlines and ongoing responsibilities, you can give every item on your to-do list a unique alarm, which can be associated with specific times, dates, or both.

> **TIP** You can set a reminder alarm to warn you of an upcoming deadline and then have a second alarm alert you when that deadline has arrived.

When you launch Reminders for the first time, on the left side of the screen you see the control center for this app. On the right side of the screen (shown in Figure 4.8) is a simulated sheet of lined paper, with the heading Reminders at the top.

FIGURE 4.8
This is what the Reminders screen looks like when you launch the app for the first time.

To begin creating a single to-do list under this Reminders heading, tap the top empty line of the simulated sheet of paper, or tap the plus-sign button that's displayed near the upper-right corner of the screen. The iPad's virtual keyboard displays. Enter the first item to be added to your to-do list and tap the Return key on the keyboard.

Upon tapping on the Return key, an empty checkbox displays in the margin to the left of the to-do list item you just entered (as shown in Figure 4.9). You can mark the completion of this task later by tapping this checkbox to add a check mark to it. The item then moves to the master Completed list, which is accessible from the left side of the screen under the Completed heading.

TIP If you're a new iPad user, you can also enter to-do items and related information into the Reminders app using the Dictation feature. To learn more about this new iPad-specific feature, see "Using the New iPad's Dictation Feature," at the end of Chapter 1, "Activating and Customizing Your iPad."

FIGURE 4.9

As soon as you create an item for a to-do list and tap the Return key on the keyboard, a checkbox displays to the left of it.

As soon as you're done entering the to-do list item, you can tap it to make the app's Details window appear. Set a Remind Me alarm by tapping the Remind Me option. Or, you can tap the Show More option to set a due date and priority for the to-do item.

If you're managing multiple to-do lists, you can also assign the to-do item to a specific list. When you scroll down the Details window, you see a Delete option. Tap it to delete the item from your list.

> **NOTE** Alarms can be associated with each item in each of your to-do lists. You also have the option of creating a to-do list item without associating any type of alert or alarm with it.
>
> When any alarm goes off with a to-do list item, a notification automatically displays in your iPad's Notification Center window, assuming you have this feature turned on.
>
> To ensure Reminders works with the Notification Center, launch the Settings app and tap the Notifications option. When the Notifications screen appears on the right side of the screen, tap the Reminders option and make sure the Notification Center option is turned on.

When it comes to managing your to-do list and accomplishing tasks listed within it, as you complete each listing, tap the checkbox associated with that item. This causes a check mark to appear within the checkbox, and the to-do list item is moved to the Completed section (displayed on the left side of the screen).

At any time, you can view your list of completed items by tapping the Completed heading on the left side of the screen.

MANAGING MULTIPLE TO-DO LISTS SIMULTANEOUSLY

The Edit button is in the upper-left corner of the Reminders screen. Tap this button to create a new list, delete an existing list, or change the order in which your lists are displayed on the left side of the screen.

As soon as you tap one of the Create New List options, the iPad's virtual keyboard displays, and you can enter a name or title for the new list (see Figure 4.10).

FIGURE 4.10

In Edit mode, you can create a new list, delete entire lists, or change the order of lists.

Also while in Edit mode, you can delete a list by tapping the red-and-white circle icon with a minus sign displayed in it that is associated with the list you want to delete. Or, to change the order of your lists, place your finger on the icon that looks like three horizontal lines and drag it upward or downward. To exit Edit mode, tap the Done button in the upper-left corner of the screen.

When the List button that is displayed near the top-left corner of the screen is selected, the left side of the Reminders screen lists the various list names, enabling you to view any of them with a single tap. However, when you tap the Date button that's displayed to the immediate right of the List button, the left side of the Reminders screen is replaced with month-by-month calendars. You can tap a specific date to view upcoming deadlines or due dates associated with specific to-do list items.

> **TIP** To quickly find items within any of your to-do lists, tap the Search Reminders field displayed in the upper-left portion of the screen, and then use the virtual keyboard to enter any text that is associated with what you're looking for.

After you get into the habit of entering all of your to-do list items, upcoming dead-lines, or various other tidbits of information into the Reminders app, you quickly discover it can be used to manage many different types of information in your per-sonal and professional life.

KEEPING INFORMED WITH THE NOTIFICATION CENTER

Whenever an alarm from the Calendar app goes off, you can be alerted by the Notification Center. Likewise, you can be alerted if you receive a new incoming email, a missed call in FaceTime, a new message via iMessage, or other types of notifications generated by other apps.

The Notification Center (shown in Figure 4.11) is fully customizable. By default, whenever a new alert or alarm goes off, if something happens in an app that requires your attention, Notification Center displays a message within a window that appears at the very top of the display.

FIGURE 4.11

The Notification Center window shown here displays only Calendar-related events. It can simul-taneously show alerts, alarms, and notifications from multiple apps, however.

TIP   To access the Notification Center anytime, you can use your finger to swipe down from the top of the iPad. Notification Center serves as a central window where all of your alerts can be displayed in one convenient and easy-to-access location.

The Notification Center is always running in the background and works regardless of what apps are currently being used. To customize the Notification Center and determine what alerts, alarms, and messages are displayed, as well as what audible alerts and alarms you hear, launch the Settings app and select the Notifications option on the left side of the screen.

When the Notifications window appears on the right side of the screen (shown in Figure 4.12), you see all Notification Center-compatible apps listed under the In Notification Center heading. Keep in mind that as you add new apps to your iPad, many of these will also be compatible with Notification Center.

FIGURE 4.12

For each app that is compatible with Notification Center, you can customize how you will receive alerts and alarms.

Tap one app listing at a time that's displayed under the In Notification Center heading, starting with Calendar. When you do this, the Notification Center customization options for that app display on the right side of the Settings screen (as shown in Figure 4.13).

From the first option, you can determine whether Notification Center pays attention to alerts and alarms created using the Calendar app. To use this app with Notification Center, turn this virtual switch to the on position.

Next, determine how many items (individual alerts, alarms, and so on) display for that app at any given time within Notification Center. Your options include 1, 5, or 10 recent items.

By turning on the View in Lock Screen option, you can determine whether the alerts and alarms associated with Calendar appear on the iPad's Lock Screen when the tablet is in Sleep Mode. You can also adjust the Alert Style and decide whether the visible alert window displays as a banner at the top of the screen or as an alert in the middle of the screen.

The Notification Center Virtual Switch

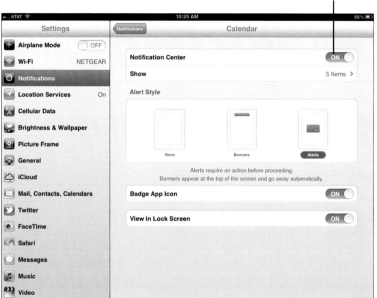

FIGURE 4.13

The Notification Center customization screen for the Calendar app, which can be found within Settings.

A banner display appears and then automatically disappears after a few seconds. However, an alert remains on the screen until you tap the appropriate icon in the alert window to make it disappear. Depending on the app, you can also turn on or off Badge App Icons, which display on the Home screen as part of that app's icon.

When you're viewing the Notification Center window, you can tap any item, alert, or alarm listed in it, and the appropriate app automatically launches. For example, if you tap an alert for an upcoming appointment within Calendar, when you tap that listing within Notification Center, the Calendar app launches, and details for that specific appointment appear on the screen. Likewise, if you tap an incoming new email message alert, the Mail app opens and the new email message is displayed.

When a new incoming alert or alarm is set off, the Notification Center window automatically appears at the top of the screen. You can stop whatever you're doing and address that alert or alarm, or you can continue doing whatever you were doing on your iPad uninterrupted, and then address that alert or alarm at your convenience.

> **TIP** While your iPad is in Sleep Mode, the Notification Center continues to function. From Settings, you can optionally set the Notification Center to display new alerts, alarms, and related content on your tablet's Lock screen. Thus, when you wake up your iPad, you immediately see all new alerts, alarms, and messages. From the Lock screen, you can swipe any of the Notification Center listings to unlock the iPad and access the appropriate app and content.

After it's set up and customized based on the apps you most rely on, the Notification Center is a powerful tool for helping you stay up to date on all your responsibilities and obligations. As you'd expect, the Notification Center also works with the Reminders app (for maintaining interactive to-do lists), Twitter, Messages, Mail, and FaceTime, so you can more easily stay connected with your friends, family, co-workers, customers, and clients.

CHOOSING THE RIGHT SCHEDULING APP

When you visit the App Store, with a little bit of research, you can find optional scheduling, time-management, project-management, and other related apps, each of which offers a different collection of features and functions.

To help you select the app that's best suited to your unique needs and work habits, first carefully determine those needs. The following are some considerations:

- Does the iPad app you select for scheduling, time management, project management, and so on need to be compatible with a software package you're currently using on your PC, Mac, or a company network? Or does the data need to be compatible with an online-based application used within your company or organization?

- Does the iPad app enable you to sync or back up data with your primary computer using a wireless, cloud-based file-sharing service (such as iCloud or Dropbox) or a direct connection method (via iTunes Sync and a USB cable)?

- Does the iPad app work seamlessly with other apps already installed on your iPad, such as the Contacts or Maps?

- What current time-management or scheduling challenges or problems will implementing an app help you solve?

- Do the app's features, functions, and user interface fit nicely with your existing work habits?

- Can you easily share data between the app and your employer, co-workers, and clients as needed?

TIP If you want the functionality of Contacts, Calendar, and Reminders in one app that's designed for relationship management, be sure to read Chapter 7, "Using VIPorbit for Contact and Schedule Management." VIPorbit is a powerful, third-party app that can meet the needs of many types of business professionals and streamline how you use the iPad to manage a variety of contact relationship management (CRM) tasks.

Simply by choosing the right app for the time-management or scheduling tasks you need to handle, you're more apt to be able to use your iPad as a tool to help you become more productive and better organized.

IN THIS CHAPTER

- Getting started using the Contacts app
- Syncing data with other contact management software
- Using Contacts data with other apps

5

WORKING WITH THE CONTACTS APP

The art of networking is all about meeting new people, staying in contact with them, making referrals and connections for others, and tapping the knowledge, experience, or expertise of the people you know to help you achieve your own career or work-related goals.

If you become good at networking, regardless of which field or industry you work in, over time you establish a contact list comprised of hundreds, or even thousands, of individuals.

In addition to the contacts you establish and maintain within your network, your personal contacts database might also include people you work with, customers, clients, family members, people from your community who you interact with (doctors, hair stylist, barber, dry cleaners, and so on), and friends.

The easiest way to keep your contacts database organized is to utilize some type of contact management application on your primary computer. On a Mac, you might use the popular Address Book or Contacts software, or Microsoft Entourage. Or, on a PC, Microsoft Outlook is a popular tool. There are also many web-, network-, and online (cloud)-based contact management applications available that are used by businesses of all sizes.

> **NOTE** If you've updated your Mac to run the OS X Mountain Lion operating system, you'll notice that the Address Book app is now called Contacts, and it looks even more like the iOS version of the Contacts app currently running on your iPad.

CUSTOMIZING THE CONTACTS APP

Chances are that the contacts database that you rely on at your office can be synced with your tablet and made available to you using the Contacts app. As you're about to discover, Contacts is a customizable contact management database that works with several other apps that also came preinstalled on your iPad, including Mail, Calendar, Safari, FaceTime, and Maps.

Of course, Contacts can also be used as a standalone app on your iPad, enabling you to enter new contact entries as you meet new people and need to keep track of details about them.

The information you maintain within your Contacts database is highly customizable, which means you can keep track of only the information you want or need. For example, within each contact entry, you can store a vast amount of information about a person, including the following:

- First and last name
- Name prefix (Mr., Mrs., Dr., and so on)
- Name suffix (Jr., Sr., Ph.D., Esq., and so on)
- Job title
- Company
- Multiple phone numbers (work, home, cell, and so on)
- Multiple email addresses
- Multiple mailing addresses (work, home, and so on)
- Multiple web page addresses
- Facebook, Twitter, Skype, Instant Message, or other online social networking site usernames

You can also customize your contacts database to include additional information, such as each contact's photo, the person's nickname, associated spouse's and assistant's names, birthdays, as well as detailed notes about the contact.

Using the Contacts app, your entire contacts database is instantly searchable using data from any field within the database, so even if you have a database containing thousands of entries, you can find the person or company you're looking for in a matter of seconds.

> **NOTE** For each entry within Contacts, you can enter as much or as little detail about each person as you want. However, the more information you include, the better. Several other apps on your iPad automatically tap into your Contacts database to obtain relevant information as it's needed.

ALLOWING THE CONTACTS APP TO WORK SEAMLESSLY WITH OTHER APPS

After your contacts database has been populated with entries, other apps can utilize that information in a handful of ways. Here are some examples:

- When you compose a new email message from within Mail, in the To field you can begin typing someone's full name or email address. If that person's contact information is already stored within Contacts, the relevant email address automatically displays within the email's To field.

- If you're planning a trip to visit a contact, using the Maps app, you can pull up someone's address from your Contacts database in order to obtain driving directions to the person's home or work location.

- If you include each person's birthday in your Contacts database, that information can automatically be displayed within the Calendar app to remind you in advance to send a card.

- As you're creating each contact entry, you can include a photo of that person by either activating the Camera app from within the Contacts app to snap a photo, or use a photo that's already stored in the Photos app and link it with a contact.

- From within FaceTime, you can create a Favorites list of people you video conference with often. You can compile this list from entries in your Contacts database, but access it from within FaceTime.

- From within the Messages app, it's possible to access your Contacts database when filling out the To field as you compose new text messages to be sent via iMessage. As soon as you tap the To field, an All Contacts window appears enabling you to select contacts from your Contacts database (or you can manually enter the recipient's info).

- If you're active on Facebook, for example, you have the option of adding each contact's Facebook profile page URL within the contact entry. When you use the official Facebook app, however, you can download each entry's Facebook profile picture and insert it into your Contacts database.

GETTING STARTED USING THE CONTACTS APP

When you first launch this app, its contents are empty. However, you can create and build your contacts database in two ways. The first way is to sync the Contacts app with your primary contact management application on your computer, network, or on an online (cloud-based) service, such as iCloud. You can also manually enter contact information directly into the app.

Ultimately, as you begin using this app and come to rely on it, you can enter new contact information or edit entries on either your tablet or within your primary contact management application, and keep all the information synchronized, regardless of where the entry was created or modified. (The easiest way to do this is with iCloud, if you want to sync data with your primary computer, iPhone, or other iOS devices that are linked to your iCloud account.)

From the iPad's Home screen, tap the Contacts app to launch it. On the left side of the screen are alphabetic tabs. Near the top of the screen is the All Contacts heading, and below it is a Search field (as shown in Figure 5.1).

After you have populated your contacts database, the entries are all listed alphabetically on the left side of the screen below the Search field. Quickly find a particular entry by entering any keyword associated with an entry, such as a first or last name, city, state, job title, or company name, into the Contact app's Search field. You can also use the Spotlight Search feature of your iPad, which is accessible from the Home screen, by swiping your finger from left to right or by pressing the Home button once from the Home screen.

The Search Field

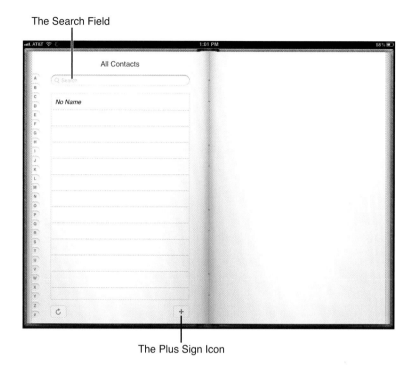

The Plus Sign Icon

FIGURE 5.1

This is the main Contacts screen when the contacts database is empty. Tap the plus-sign icon to create a new entry.

You can also tap a letter tab on the left side of the Contacts screen to see all entries "filed" under that letter by either a contact's last name, first name, or company name, depending on how you set up the Contacts app from within the Settings app's Mail, Contacts, Calendars option.

To see the complete listing for a particular entry, tap its listing on the left side of the screen. That entry's complete contents are displayed on the right side of the screen (as shown in the sample entry in Figure 5.2).

The Selected Entry

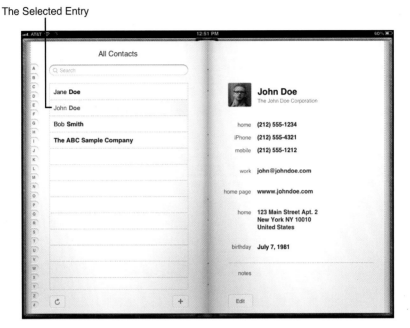

FIGURE 5.2

When you select a contact entry from the left side of the screen, all information pertaining to that particular contact displays on the right side of the screen. The entry highlighted in blue is the selected entry.

CREATING NEW CONTACT ENTRIES

To create a new contact entry, tap the plus icon that's displayed near the bottom center of the Contacts screen. When you do this, the main Contacts screen is replaced by an Info screen and the iPad's virtual keyboard displays.

Within the Info window are a handful of empty fields related to a single contact entry, starting with the First Name field. By default, the fields available in this app include First Name, Last Name, Company, Photo, [Mobile] Phone Number, Email Address, Ringtone, Home Page (Website) URL, Address, and Notes (see Figure 5.3).

Some of these fields, including Phone, Email, and Mailing Address, enable you to enter multiple listings, one at a time. So you can include someone's home phone, work phone, and mobile phone numbers within the entry. Likewise, you can include multiple email addresses, as well as home and work addresses for an individual.

FIGURE 5.3

From the Info window, you can enter details about a new contact and create a new entry in the Contacts app.

Begin by filling in one field at a time. To jump to the next field, tap it. For example, after using the virtual keyboard to fill in the First Name field, tap the Last Name field to fill it in, and then move on to the Company field, if applicable, by tapping it.

For each type of field, the iPad's virtual keyboard modifies itself accordingly, giving you access to specialized keys. You can change the label associated with certain fields (which are displayed in blue), by tapping the field label itself. This reveals a Label menu, offering selectable options for that field.

For example, Figure 5.4 shows the Label options for the Phone Number field, which include Mobile, iPhone, Home, Work, Main, Home Fax, Work Fax, Pager, and Other. At the bottom of this Label window, you can tap the Add Custom Label option to create your own label if none of the listed options apply. Tap the label title of your choice. A check mark appears next to it, and you are returned to the Info window.

NOTE As you're creating each contact entry, you can fill in any fields you want. You can always go back and edit a contact entry to include additional information later.

FIGURE 5.4

For any field that has a blue label, you can tap that label (not within the empty field) to change the label. Upon doing this, a Label window displays. Tap on your new label selection.

When you enter a contact's phone numbers, it's important to differentiate between a mobile phone number and an iPhone phone number. If you know someone has an iPhone, use the iPhone label because the FaceTime and Messages apps use what's in this field to identify someone's FaceTime or Messages User ID (which, if they're an iPhone user, is usually their iPhone's phone number).

As you scroll down in the Info window and fill in each field, at the bottom of the window you discover an Add Field option. Tap this to reveal a menu containing additional fields you can add to each contact entry, such as Middle Name, Job Title, Nickname, Instant Message username, Twitter username, Facebook Profile, or Birthday.

There's also a field to add Related People, such as the names of your contact's mother, father, parent, brother, sister, child, friend, spouse, partner, assistant, manager, or other. You can even add your own titles for the Related People field.

A green-and-white plus icon next to a field (on the left) means that you can have multiple entries for that field, such as several phone numbers, email addresses, or mailing addresses.

If there's a field displayed that you don't want to utilize or display, tap the red-and-white minus sign icon to delete the field from the Info window.

> **TIP** When entering a phone number, you can simply enter the 10 digits of that number. There is no need to include parentheses around the area code or a dash between the exchange and main number. This formatting is done for you by the app. The Contacts app can also accommodate international phone numbers, along with related country codes or dialing prefixes.

ADDING A PHOTO TO A CONTACT ENTRY

To the immediate left of the First Name field is a square box that says Add Photo. When you tap this field, a submenu with two options, Take Photo and Choose Photo, is displayed. If you tap Take Photo, the iPad's Camera app launches from within the Contacts app so that you can snap a photo to be linked to the contact entry you're creating.

If you tap on the Choose Photo option, the Photos app on your iPad launches so that you can choose any digital image that's currently stored on your tablet. When you tap the photo, a Choose a Photo window displays on the Contacts screen, enabling you to move and scale the image with your finger, as shown in Figure 5.5.

FIGURE 5.5

Select a photo stored within the Photos app and link it to someone's contact entry. After choosing the photo, you must move and scale the image.

After cropping or adjusting the photo selected, tap the Use button in the upper-right corner of the Choose Photo window to link the photo with that contact's entry.

If you also use an iPhone or use FaceTime on your iPad, from the Ringtone option in the Info window you can select the ringtone you hear each time the contact calls you. Your iPad has 25 preinstalled ringtones (Marimba is the default); however, from iTunes, you can download thousands of additional ringtones, many of which are clips from popular songs.

NOTE Each time you add a new mailing address to a contact's entry from within the Info screen, the Address field expands to include a Street, City, State, ZIP, and Country field (as shown in Figure 5.6).

FIGURE 5.6

Using the virtual keyboard, you can add multiple addresses, one at a time, for each contact in your Contacts database. This enables you to include a home address and a work address, for example.

In the Notes field, you can enter as much information pertaining to that contact as you want. Or, you can paste content from another app into this field using the iOS's Select, Copy, and Paste commands and the multitasking capabilities of your iPad to quickly switch between apps. Press the Home button twice to access multitasking mode in order to quickly switch between apps.

TIP Contacts is fully compatible with the new iPad's Dictation feature. Instead of manually typing information into any of the contact entry fields, including the Notes field, tap the Dictation key on the tablet's keyboard, and then say the information you want to include within each field. For more information about using the new iPad's Dictation feature, refer to the "Using the New iPad's Dictation Feature" section at the end of Chapter 1, "Activating and Customizing Your iPad."

After you have filled in all of the fields for a particular entry, tap the Done button, which is in the upper-right corner of the Info window. Your new entry displays within your contacts database.

EDITING OR DELETING AN ENTRY

As you're looking at the main Contacts screen, you can edit an entry by selecting it from the left side of the screen. Tap its listing to view the complete entry on the right side of the screen. Now, tap the Edit button displayed near the bottom of the screen to edit the selected entry.

When the Info window appears, tap any field to modify it using the virtual keyboard. You can delete any fields by tapping the red-and-white minus icon.

You can also add new fields within an entry by tapping any of the green-and-white plus icons and then choosing the type of field you want to add.

> **TIP** When you're done editing a contact entry, be sure to tap the Done button to save your revisions. If you have the iCloud sync function activated, your revisions are automatically reflected on your primary computer and other iOS devices within seconds.

You can also delete an entire entry from your Contacts database. As you're editing a contact entry and looking at the Info window for that entry, scroll down to the bottom of it and tap the Delete Contact button. Keep in mind that if you have your Contacts database set up to use the iCloud sync feature, the entry is also immediately deleted from all of the computers and devices that are linked to your iCloud account.

> **TIP** Whenever you're viewing a contact entry, tapping a listed email address causes the iPad's Mail app to launch, which enables you to compose an email message to that recipient. The To field of the outgoing email is filled in with the email address you tapped from within Contacts.
>
> Likewise, from within any Contacts entry, tap a website URL that's listed and the iPad launches the Safari web browser with the appropriate webpage automatically loaded.
>
> This technique also works with the Twitter field (if you have the Twitter app installed). Or, if you tap a street address, it automatically launches the Maps app, which displays that address. (From that point you can tap the Directions icon that's displayed near the upper-left corner of the screen to obtain directions to that contact's location.)

When you're in edit mode to modify content within a contact's entry, scroll down to the very bottom of the window (below the red-and-white Delete contact icon) to find a small icon with a silhouette of a head with a plus sign next to it. Tap this icon to link this contact with one or more other contacts in your database.

SHARING CONTACT ENTRIES

From the main Contacts screen, tap a contact from the left side of the screen that you want to share details about. When the contact's entry is displayed on the right side of the screen, scroll to the bottom of the entry until you see the Share Contact button displayed (see Figure 5.7) and tap it.

The Share Contact Icon

FIGURE 5.7

From within Contacts you can share someone's contact entry with other people by tapping the Share Contact button displayed at the bottom of each contact entry.

An outgoing email message form displays on your iPad's screen. Fill in the To field with the person or people you want to share the contact info with. The default subject of the email is Contact; however, you can tap this field and modify it using the virtual keyboard.

The contact entry you selected (stored in .vcf format, which is an industry standard format used by many contact management applications) is already embedded within the email message. When you've filled in all the necessary fields in the outgoing email form and added additional text to the body of the message, tap the blue-and-white Send icon that's located in the upper-right corner of the Contact window to send the email message to the intended recipient(s). After doing this, you are returned to the Contacts app.

Within a minute or two, the recipient should receive your email. When she clicks on the email's attachment (the contact entry you sent) she can automatically import that data into her contact management application as a new entry, such as within Address Book on her Mac or Contacts on her iPad or iPhone.

If someone sends you an email with a Contacts entry attached, it is displayed within the body of the email as an attachment. After tapping the email's attachment icon, tap the Create New Contact or Add to Existing Contact option to incorporate this information into your Contacts database.

SYNCING CONTACT DATA WITH OTHER CONTACT MANAGEMENT SOFTWARE

If you maintain your primary contacts database using Address Book or Contacts on your Mac, for example, you can sync the Contacts app via an iTunes Sync, or you can sync the contacts wirelessly using iCloud (which is a more convenient and fully automated method).

You can also synchronize your contacts database on your iPad with Microsoft Outlook on a PC, Microsoft Entourage on a Mac, any Microsoft Exchange-compatible contact management software that is running on your company's network, or a variety of other online (cloud)-based contact management tools. To synchronize contacts data wirelessly, you must first do some initial setup (just once) using the Settings app on your iPad.

SYNCING CONTACTS DATA FROM YOUR iPAD WITH iCLOUD

After setting up a free iCloud account, access the Settings app on your iPad. On the left side of the screen, tap the iCloud option and enter your Apple ID and password to turn on the main iCloud functionality. Next, scroll down the iCloud menu screen and make sure the virtual switch associated with the Contacts option (shown in Figure 5.8) is turned on.

NOTE From the Settings app, tap on the Mail, Contacts, Calendars option to personalize settings related to the Contacts app. Scroll down on this screen to the Contacts heading.

The Contacts Option

FIGURE 5.8

For the iCloud sync feature to work with Contacts, it must be turned on from within the Settings app.

Turning on the Contacts option enables your iPad to automatically sync your Contacts data with your iCloud account (as long as your tablet is connected to the Web). Also make sure you turn on iCloud functionality—as well as the Contacts sync feature—for your primary computer, iPhone, and other iOS devices that are linked to the same iCloud account.

TIP   After your Contacts data is automatically syncing with iCloud, you can access your contacts database from any computer or web-enabled mobile device by pointing its web browser to www.icloud.com/#contacts. Sign in using your iCloud username and password (which is typically your Apple ID and password) to access a free, online-based app that is almost identical to the Contacts app. It contains all of your up-to-date contact entries.

SYNCING WITH MICROSOFT EXCHANGE-COMPATIBLE APPLICATIONS

From the iPad's Home screen, tap Settings, and then choose the Mail, Contacts, Calendars option. Tap the Add Account option displayed under the Accounts heading on the right side of the screen. Choose to set up a Microsoft Exchange account. When prompted, enter your email address, domain, username, password, and an account description. This is information that should be supplied by your network administrator or IT department. Next, turn on the contacts option and save your new settings.

Contacts is compatible with any contact management software that uses the industry-standard CardDAV and LDAP format. Thus, if you have a Microsoft Exchange account and activate the contacts sync feature, you can wirelessly keep your primary contacts database perfectly synchronized with your Contacts database as long as your iPad has access to the Web.

SYNCING WITH CARDDAV- OR LDAP-COMPATIBLE APPLICATIONS

To set up the wireless sync process between a CardDAV-compatible application and Contacts, access the Settings app on your iPad and select the Mail, Contacts, Calendars option. From under the Add Account heading, tap the Other option. Next, choose either the Add LDAP account or Add CardDAV account option, depending on the application you are syncing with.

You are prompted for a server address, username, password, and an account description. Obtain this information from your network administrator or company's IT department.

HOW DOES SYNCING YOUR CONTACTS INFO HELP YOU?

After the iPad is set up to sync your Contacts app with another contact management application, whenever you make a change, deletion, or addition to your contacts database (either from your iPad, your primary computer, or your smartphone that's also synced with the database), those modifications are automatically reflected on all of the devices that you access your contacts database from.

If you have questions about how to configure your iPad to sync correctly with your primary contact management application, make an appointment with an Apple Genius at any Apple Store or call AppleCare's toll-free phone number at (800) APL-CARE, and have a technical support specialist talk you through the setup and initial data sync process.

NOTE In addition to or instead of using the Contacts app to manage your contacts, the App Store has a selection of optional third-party apps that offer slightly different, or sometimes enhanced, functionality when compared to Contacts. When visiting the App Store, enter the search phrase "Contact Management" or "Contacts" into the Search field. There you can also find utility apps, such as Remove Duplicate Contacts ($0.99), which can help you streamline your contacts database and avoid duplicates.

IN THIS CHAPTER

- Access the App Store from your iPad
- Discover why some apps are free and some are not
- Find and download the best apps for you
- Keep your apps up-to-date with the latest versions

6

FINDING AND INSTALLING APPS FROM THE APP STORE

Yes, the iPad is a sleek piece of hardware with lots of capabilities, but it's ultimately the iOS 5.1 (or later) operating system and the collection of apps on your tablet that make it capable of doing so much. From the App Store, you can find, download, and install optional apps for your iPad that greatly expand its capabilities.

However, with more than 200,000 iPad-specific apps currently available, plus more than 500,000 iPhone apps that work on the iPad, the task of finding the right app(s) to meet your personal needs can be daunting.

For every task the iPad can perform using an app, there are most likely a handful of app choices, from different developers, that offer very similar functionality.

When you start browsing through the apps offered, you'll discover the pricing for them varies greatly. Plus, a growing number of apps allow for or require in-app purchases or a paid subscription to fully utilize them.

NOTE After you purchase an app from the App Store, all future updates to that app are free. You simply need to download and install the updates as they become available.

APPLE'S APP STORE: ONE-STOP SHOPPING FOR iPAD APPS

If you want to add apps to your iPad, the only way to do this is to acquire them from Apple's App Store. There are two ways to access the App Store to find, purchase, download, and install apps onto your tablet.

First, you can use the App Store app, which comes preinstalled on your iPad. To use it, your tablet must have access to the Internet.

NOTE Some apps that have a large file associated with them cannot be downloaded and installed using the App Store app if you're connected to the Internet via a 3G or 4G connection. Either a Wi-Fi connection is necessary, or you'll need to download certain apps using iTunes on your primary computer, and then transfer those apps to your tablet using the iTunes sync process. The majority of apps, however, which are less than 50MB in size, can be downloaded and installed directly onto your iPad using a 3G, 4G, or Wi-Fi connection via the App Store app.

The second option for finding, purchasing, downloading, and installing apps is to access the App Store through the iTunes software on your primary computer, and then transfer the acquired apps to your tablet using the iTunes sync process or iCloud.

Regardless of how you visit the App Store, you need to set up an Apple ID account and have a major credit card or debit card linked to the account to make purchases.

TIP If you don't have a major credit card or debit card that you want to link with your Apple ID account so you can purchase apps from the App Store, you can purchase prepaid iTunes gift cards from Apple or most places that sell prepaid gift cards, such as convenience stores, supermarkets, and pharmacies.

iTunes gift cards can be used to make app purchases. iTunes gift cards (which are different from Apple gift cards, which are redeemable at Apple Stores or Apple.com) are available in $15.00, $25.00, and $50.00 denominations.

UNDERSTANDING THE APP STORE

From your iPad's Home screen, tap the blue-and-white App Store icon. Your tablet must have access to the Internet via a 3G, 4G, or Wi-Fi connection.

When you access the App Store via the App Store app (shown in Figure 6.1), you'll discover a handful of command icons and tabs displayed at the top and bottom of the screen that are used to navigate your way around the online-based store.

— Search Field

— Command Icons

FIGURE 6.1

The main App Store screen.

If you already know the name of the app you want to find, tap the Search field, which is located in the upper-right corner of the App Store app's screen. Using the virtual keyboard, enter the name of the app. Tap the Search key on the virtual keyboard to begin the search. You can also perform a search based on a keyword or phrase, such as word processing, to-do lists, time management, or photo editing. The search results can then be filtered even more by category, customer rating, or release date, for example.

Within a few seconds, matching results are displayed on the App Store screen. When you access the App Store from your iPad (using the App Store app), iPad-specific and hybrid apps are always listed first. Scroll down on the search results screen to also see iPhone apps, which also work on your iPad.

TIP   Within each App listing is a price icon. If you notice a plus-sign icon displayed in the upper-left corner of the price icon, this indicates that the app you're
looking at is designed for both the iPad and iPhone, and adapts accordingly, based
on the device it's being used on.

In general, when choosing apps for your iPad, look for iPad-specific apps first, and
then look for hybrid apps that are designed for both iPad and iPhone. Apps that
are iPhone-specific also run fine on an iPad, but the app's graphics and user interface are formatted for the iPhone's smaller screen.

At the bottom of the main App Store screen are six command icons: Featured,
Genius, Top Charts, Categories, Purchased, and Updates. If you don't know the
exact name of an app you're looking for, these icons help you browse the App
Store and discover iPad apps that might be of interest to you.

DISCOVERED FEATURED APPS

Tap the Featured icon to see a listing of what Apple considers to be new or noteworthy apps. These are divided into two categories: New and Noteworthy and Staff
Favorites.

Under the New and Noteworthy heading of the Featured screen, you see six app
listings. Use a horizontal swipe motion with your finger to scroll between the four
New and Noteworthy sections. You can also tap the See All command that's displayed next to the New and Noteworthy heading to see all of the relevant listings
presented on one screen.

SORT APP LISTINGS BY RELEASE DATE OR POPULARITY

As you're looking at the Featured page of the App Store, you see three tabs displayed at the top center of the screen: New, What's Hot, and Release Date. Each of
these tabs reveals a different collection of Apple-recommended apps.

If you scroll down to the bottom of the Featured screen (with the New or What's
Hot tab selected), you see a subsection labeled Quick Links. It offers six options for
finding apps related to a particular area of interest.

The Quick Link options change periodically, but might include Apple Apps, App
Starter Kit, Games Starter Kit, Essentials, Previous Apps of the Week, and Previous
Games of the Week. Tap any of these options to see a collection of apps you might
be interested in.

From the Featured screen, tap the Release Date tab at the top of the screen to see
the most recently released apps available from the App Store, starting with the
newest and working backward by date.

GENIUS: ANALYSIS AND SUGGESTIONS

The App Store keeps track of all apps you purchase. When you tap the Genius icon at the bottom of the App Store screen, the App Store analyzes your past app purchases and offers suggestions for other apps you might be interested in.

TOP CHARTS: SEE WHAT OTHER iPAD USERS ARE BUYING

Tap the Top Charts icon at the bottom of the App Store app's screen to access listings of the most popular free and paid iPad apps. This is a general listing of all currently popular apps, so it constantly changes.

If you're primarily interested in apps that fall into a specific category, such as Business, Productivity or Travel, tap the Categories icon that's displayed in the upper-left corner of this screen (shown in Figure 6.2). A listing of 22 different app categories are displayed. Choose a category by tapping it.

FIGURE 6.2

Choose the category you're most interested in seeing the bestselling apps from.

When you tap a specific category, such as Business, the Top Chart listings displayed on the left side of the screen features the Top Paid iPad Business Apps, and the chart displayed on the right side of the screen features the Top Free iPad Business apps. At the bottom of the screen is a listing of Top Grossing iPad apps in that category.

CATEGORIES: FIND APPS BY TOPIC OR GENRE

Although tapping the Top Charts icon reveals a listing of the top-selling apps within a specific category, you can tap the Categories icon at the bottom of the App Store app's screen to access all of the apps that fall into any one of the App Store's 22 main categories.

Upon tapping the Categories icon, a listing of all app categories displays (shown in Figure 6.3). The app icon shown for each category is the current number-one most popular paid app within that category. Tap the category that most interests you in order to browse through listings of all apps within that category.

FIGURE 6.3

Browse all apps within that App Store that fit into a specific category by first selecting a category that's of interest.

By default, the apps are displayed in order based on release date (with the most recently released apps displayed first). However, you can change the sort order by tapping the Sort By icon that's displayed near the upper-right corner of the screen. Your options include Name (for an alphabetical listing), Most Popular (starting with the best-selling apps), or Release Date.

As you're looking at the app listings, you can learn more about a particular app by tapping on its graphic icon or title. Or, you can purchase, download and install the app by tapping its price icon. (For free apps, when you tap the Free icon, the app automatically downloads and installs after you enter your Apple ID password).

MANAGING YOUR APP STORE ACCOUNT OR iTUNES GIFT CARDS

When you scroll to the very bottom of the main Featured, Genius, or Top Charts sections of the App Store (as well as several other subsection pages within the App Store), you see three icons: Account [Your Apple ID Username], Redeem, and Support.

Tap the Account icon to manage your Apple ID account and update your credit card information, if necessary. Tap the Redeem icon to redeem a prepaid iTunes Gift Card. If you experience problems using the App Store, or have questions, tap the Support icon.

ACCESSING YOUR PURCHASED APPS

When you tap the Purchased command icon that's displayed at the bottom of the App Store screen, a complete listing of all apps you've purchased to date using your Apple ID is displayed. This listing includes apps not currently stored on your iPad. Any of the listed apps, which are now stored online within your iCloud account, can be downloaded and installed onto your tablet, including your previous iPhone or iPod touch app purchases. To do this, simply tap the iCloud icon displayed in conjunction with an app's listing.

> **TIP** If you also own and use an iPhone or iPod touch that's linked to the same iCloud account, anytime you purchase an iPad/iPhone hybrid app, you can install it on any or all of your iOS devices without having to purchase the same app multiple times.

UNDERSTANDING THE APP LISTINGS

Each app listing contains the app's name, what category the app falls into (such as Business, Reference, News, Lifestyle, or Games), the app's original release date, the average star rating the app has received from your fellow iPad users, the total number of ratings the app has received, and a graphic icon that features the app's logo.

Figure 6.4 shows a sample app listing. Also displayed within each app listing is the app's price icon. If the app is free, the word FREE is displayed. If the app listing is for a paid app, the price of the app is displayed.

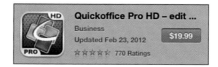

FIGURE 6.4

A sample app listing contains important information about the app, including its price.

CAUTION Some free apps are, in fact, free. However, they might ultimately require you to pay for a content subscription or make in-app purchases to fully utilize the app. How app pricing works is explained later in this chapter. When looking at an app's Description screen, if in-app purchases are possible (or required), this will be mentioned on the left side of the screen under the heading Top In-App Purchases.

To purchase an app (or download and install a free app), tap its price icon. The price icon changes from gray-and-white to green-and-white. If it's a free app, this new icon is labeled Install App. If it's a paid app, the green-and-white icon says Buy App. Tap the icon to confirm your purchase decision.

An Apple ID Password window displays on the screen. Your Apple ID username is already displayed, but you need to manually enter your Apple ID password. Type your Apple ID password and then tap the OK icon. The app automatically downloads and installs itself on your iPad. This process can take between 15 seconds and several minutes. When the app is installed, the app icon for the new app appears on your tablet's Home screen.

NOTE It is necessary to enter your Apple ID Password whenever you attempt to download and install any app, even if it's a free app.

LEARNING ABOUT AN APP BEFORE MAKING A PURCHASE

Before committing to a purchase, as you're looking at an app's listing from within the App Store, you can tap its title or graphic icon to reveal a detailed Description page for the app.

An app's Description page (like the one shown in Figure 6.5) displays the app's title and logo near the top of the screen, along with a detailed description of the app under the Description heading.

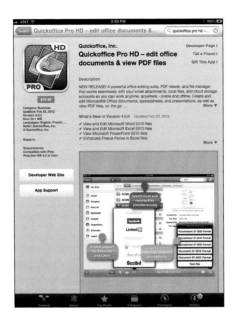

FIGURE 6.5

From an app's Description screen, you can learn all about a specific app. This information can help you decide whether it's of interest to you or relevant to your needs.

Below the Description is information about what new features have been added to the app in the most recent version. As you scroll down this screen, you see one or more actual screen shots from the app.

Displayed under the app's screen shots are the Customer Ratings for that app. You can sort these ratings by tapping the Current Version or All Versions tabs displayed on the right side of the screen.

The Customer Ratings are based on a five-star system. Anyone who purchases or downloads an app has the option to rate it. A top-rating is five stars. From the Ratings Summary chart (shown in Figure 6.6), you can see how many people have rated an app, discover the app's average rating, and then see a breakdown of how many one-star, two-star, three-star, four-star, and five-star ratings the app has received.

Obviously, an app with a large number of five-star ratings is probably excellent, and an app that consistently earns three-stars or less is probably not so great or is loaded with bugs.

Keep scrolling down to read full reviews that your fellow iPad users have written about that app. These reviews often describe the best features of the app and/or its worst problems.

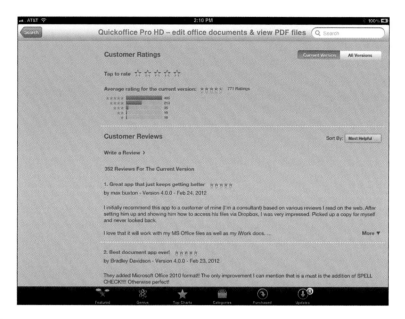

FIGURE 6.6

Every app description contains an average rating and a rating summary chart. Use it to quickly see what other iPad users think about the app you're currently looking at.

At the bottom of the app's Description page is a section labeled Customers Also Bought. These are listings for other apps, usually similar in functionality to the app you're looking at, which other customers have also purchased and downloaded.

Back near the top of an app's Description page is the app's price icon. You'll find it just below the app's logo, on the left side of the screen. Specific information pertaining to that app, including its category, the date it was last updated, the current version of the app, the file size of the app, what language the app is in, and the seller or publisher of the app is also displayed in this area.

Scroll back down to see additional notes related to the app's content (also on the left side of the screen), including whether the app requires in-app purchases or a paid subscription to fully utilize it.

The system requirements for the app are also displayed along the left margin of every app's Description page (when you're using the App Store app). This helps you identify if it's an iPad-specific app, for example, and what iOS operating system version it works with.

After reviewing an app's Description page, if you want to be reminded of the app's existence (without downloading it), or you want to tell a friend about the app, tap the Tell a Friend icon that's displayed in the upper-right corner of the Description page, and then complete the email form that appears.

> **TIP** Using the Gift This App option in the upper-right corner of an app's description page, you can purchase an app and send it to another iPad or iPhone user electronically.

To exit an app's Description page and continue browsing the App Store, tap the left-pointing arrow that's labeled App Store. It's displayed in the upper-left corner of the screen.

VISITING THE APP STORE FROM iTUNES ON YOUR COMPUTER

The second method of finding, purchasing, downloading, installing, and updating apps is to use the latest version of the iTunes software running on your primary computer in order to access the iTunes Store.

Click the iTunes Store option displayed on the left side of the screen, under the Store heading. Your computer must be connected to the Internet to access the iTunes Store.

When the main iTunes Store launches within iTunes, click the App Store tab at the top of the screen. You see a screen that's similar to the Featured page of the App Store when you access it from your iPad using the App Store app.

HOW APP PRICING WORKS

Originally, when the App Store opened, there were two types of apps: free apps and paid apps. The free apps were often demo versions of paid apps (with limited functionality), or fully functional apps that displayed ads within the app. Most paid apps were—and continue to be—priced between $.99 and $9.99 (although some are priced higher).

As the App Store has evolved, additional payment options and fee structures for apps have been introduced, giving app developers new ways to generate revenue, and giving iPad users different methods of paying for apps and content.

Here's a summary of the different types of apps from a pricing standpoint:

FREE APPS

Free apps cost nothing to download and install on your tablet. Some programmers and developers release free apps out of pure kindness and to share their creations with the iPad-using public. These are fully functional apps.

There are also free apps that serve as demo versions of paid apps. These are scaled down versions of apps, or they have some type of limitation in terms of how long they can be used for (usually 30 days). In some cases, basic features or functions of the app are locked in the free version, but are later made available if you upgrade to the paid or premium version of the app.

A third category of free apps are fully functional apps that display ads as part of their content. In exchange for using the app, you have to view ads, which offer the option to click on offers from within the app to learn more about the product or service being advertised.

A fourth category of free apps serve as a shell for premium (paid) content that must be loaded into the app to make it fully functional.

The final type of free app is fully functional, but it enables the user to make in-app purchases to add features or functionality to the app or to unlock premium content. The core app, without the extra content, is free.

PAID APPS

After you purchase an app, you own it and can use it as often as you like without incurring additional fees. You simply pay a fee for the app upfront, which is typically between $.99 and $9.99. All future upgrades of the app are free of charge. In some cases, paid apps also offer in-app purchase options to access premium content.

SUBSCRIPTION-BASED APPS

Apps based on subscriptions, such as monthly magazines, are typically free, but you pay a recurring subscription fee for content, which is automatically downloaded into the app. Many digital editions of newspapers, such as *The New York Times* and *The Wall Street Journal,* utilize a subscription app model, as do hundreds of different magazines.

IN-APP PURCHASES

The ability to make in-app purchases is a special function within some free and paid apps. The important thing to note is that, as you're actually using the app, you can purchase additional content or add new features and functionality to the app by making in-app purchases. The ability to make in-app purchases has become very popular, and is being used by app developers in a variety of different ways.

As you view an app's description within the App Store, carefully read the text included within the left margin of the app Description screen to see if in-app purchases are required.

CAUTION The price you pay for an app does not translate directly to the quality or usefulness of that app. There are some free or very inexpensive apps that are extremely useful and packed with features and that can really enhance your iPad experience. However, there are costly apps that are poorly designed, filled with bugs, don't live up to expectations, or don't offer the functionality promised within the app's Description page (which is content provided by the app's developer, not Apple).

The price of each app is set by the developer or programmer that created or is selling the app. Instead of using the price as a determining factor if you're evaluating several apps that appear to offer similar functionality, be sure to read the app's customer reviews carefully and pay attention to the star-based rating the app has received. The user reviews and ratings are a much better indicator of the app's quality and usefulness than the price of the app.

QUICK TIPS FOR FINDING APPS

As you explore the App Store, it's easy to become overwhelmed by the sheer number of apps that are available for your iPad. If you're a new iPad user, spending time browsing the App Store introduces you to the many different types of apps that are available and provides you with insight about how you can utilize your tablet in your personal or professional life.

However, you can save a lot of time searching for apps if you already know the app's exact title, or if you know what type of app you're looking for. In this case, you can enter either the app's exact title or a keyword description of the app within the App Store's Search field to see a list of relevant matches.

If you're looking for vertical market apps with specialized functionality that caters to your industry or profession, enter that industry or profession (or keywords associated with it) within the Search field. For example, enter keywords such as medical imaging, radiology, plumbing, telemarketing, or sales.

As you're evaluating an app before downloading it, use these tips to help you determine if it's worth installing onto your tablet:

- Figure out what type of features or functionality you want to add to your iPad.
- Using the Search field, find apps designed to handle the tasks you have in mind. Chances are that you can easily find a handful of apps created by different developers that are designed to perform the same basic functionality. You can then pick which is the best based on the description, screen shots, and list of features each app offers.

  Compare the various apps by reading their descriptions and viewing the screen shots. Figure out which app will work best for you based on your unique needs.

- Check the customer reviews and ratings for the app. This is a useful tool to quickly determine if the app actually works as described. Keep in mind that an app's description within the App Store is written by the app's developer, and is designed to sell apps. The customer reviews and star-based ratings are created by fellow iPad users who have tried out the app firsthand.

- If an app has only a few ratings or reviews, and they're mixed, you might need to try out the app for yourself to determine if it will be useful to you. However, if an app has many reviews that are overwhelmingly negative (three stars or less), that's a strong indication that app does not perform as described or that it's loaded with bugs.

- If an app offers a free (trial) version, download and test out that version of the app before you purchase the premium version. You can always delete any app that you try out but don't wind up liking or needing.

- Ideally, you want to install apps on your iPad that were designed specifically for the iPad, so if you have a choice, opt for the iPad-specific edition of an app first.

KEEPING YOUR APPS UP TO DATE

Periodically app developers release new versions of their apps. To make sure you have the most current version of all apps installed on your iPad, visit the App Store using the App Store app on your tablet and tap the Updates icon displayed at the bottom of the screen.

A red-and-white circle in the upper-right corner of the Updates icon (as shown within Figure 6.7) indicates that one or more of your apps has an update available. The number in the red circle tells you how many app updates are available. You can download updates directly from your iPad if it's connected to the Internet.

After launching the App Store app, tap the Updates command icon to display a list of apps with updates available and then tap the Update All icon or an individual app icon that's displayed on the Updates screen to automatically download the new version of the app and install it. Doing this replaces the older version of the app.

To check for app updates using the iTunes software on your primary computer, click the Apps option displayed under the Library heading on the left side of the iTunes screen. The app listings for every app you've downloaded for your iPad (and iPhone, if applicable) display, even apps not currently installed on your tablet are included.

When you have the Apps option selected in iTunes on your Mac or PC, in the lower-right corner is an option that says how many app updates are currently available. Click this option. You can then click individual apps you want to update or click the Download All Free Updates option that's displayed in the upper-right corner of the My App Updates screen.

After the app updates have been downloaded to your primary computer, perform an iTunes sync with your iPad to transfer the updated versions of the apps currently installed on your tablet.

Updates Icon

FIGURE 6.7

Keep your apps up to date with the latest versions.

TIP   To ensure you have the latest versions of your most commonly used apps installed on your iPad, check for app updates once every week or two. Each time Apple releases an update to the iOS operating system, it's common for app developers to also release an updated version of their apps.

TIP   To conserve your monthly 3G or 4G wireless data allocation, it's a good strategy to update your apps using a Wi-Fi Internet connection, especially if multiple apps need to be updated at once.

7

USING VIPorbit FOR CONTACT AND SCHEDULE MANAGEMENT

Your iPad that's running iOS 5.1 comes with the Contacts, Calendar, and Reminders apps preinstalled. Although these apps can work together, they are three separate apps designed for different tasks commonly utilized by businesspeople.

Available from the App Store is VIPorbit for iPad ($8.99), a full-featured, mobile contact (or customer) relationship manager (CRM) that's designed for building, managing, and cultivating business relationships. Created by the co-designer of ACT! for the PC, VIPorbit enables you to manage your personalized contacts database, schedule, and to-do lists all from one app that also nicely integrates your data with other iPad apps.

NOTE Initially, VIPorbit for iPad is designed to be a stand-alone CRM (contact relationship manager) app. However, a separate iPhone version is also currently available. In the near future, a Mac version of VIPorbit will be released separately, along with an in-app purchase for the iPad and iPhone versions that allow your data to be synced between all versions of the VIPorbit app and software.

VIPORBIT HAS A MULTITUDE OF USES

The goal behind the VIPorbit app is to help business professionals become more efficient when it comes to managing their contacts and building relationships. The premise of VIPorbit is that in addition to creating a personalized database of your individual contacts (which is what the Contacts app is designed to do), you can categorize your contacts into groups and establish connections between them. Plus, within each contact entry it's possible to include details about the contact that goes well beyond name, company affiliation, address, phone number, and email address.

The contact management aspect of VIPorbit enables you to customize up to six fields within each entry and attach a digital photo or graphic to each entry as well. In addition, you can add unlimited, free-form notes to each entry over time.

MANAGE YOUR CONTACTS OR CUSTOMERS

The VIPorbit app greatly differs from the Contacts app and becomes a valuable business tool because with VIPorbit each time you make contact with someone you've saved in your contact database you can record details about the interaction and automatically save those notes and activities in chronological order.

Because the app has a built in scheduling and to-do list manager, as you're speaking or corresponding with a contact, you can quickly schedule a follow-up meeting and set a related alert or alarm, or set a reminder to initiate a future call or email, plus include detailed notes about what you've already discussed and what you need to discuss during your next communication.

It's this functionality within VIPorbit that enables you to better manage your contacts and build relationships. The app automatically helps you keep track of even the most minute details related to each interaction you have with a contact so nothing falls through the cracks, and you never forget to follow through on tasks or responsibilities related to each contact.

PLAN YOUR SCHEDULE

If you need to schedule a meeting for next week, remember to send the contact a follow-up email in a month, or want to remember an important date related to a contact, you can easily handle it with a few taps on the screen in VIPorbit.

Unlike when you use the Contacts, Calendar, and Reminders apps separately, the VIPorbit app allows you to link activities, meetings, and scheduled events directly to contact entries. The app then reminds you of upcoming to-do items or appointments and automatically keeps track of completed activities.

Because you can link contacts or place them into groups within VIPorbit, a single task, to-do item, or scheduled item can also be linked with multiple contact entries or a group. And, because everyone's work habits are slightly different, the calendar/scheduling module of VIPorbit is customizable, so you can view calendars in multiple formats, or filter a calendar view by activity type or date range.

NOTE Data already stored within the Contacts and Calendar apps (or iCal or Calendar events on your Mac) can easily be imported into VIPorbit, eliminating the need for repetitive data entry.

COMMUNICATE MORE EFFICIENTLY

The VIPorbit app works seamlessly with other apps installed on your iPad, and offers email, text messaging (via Messages), Twitter and Facebook integration, and Skype integration (for Internet-based voice and video conference calls via your iPad). As a result, you can stay in contact with people in your database with ease without having to manually launch multiple apps or cut and paste information between apps.

As you interact with your contacts, VIPorbit automatically maintains a detailed log of all phone conversations, emails, online communication, and in-person meetings, so you can quickly refer to interactions that have transpired and see alerts for upcoming required actions related to each contact.

TIP VIPorbit is not compatible with iCloud or iTunes Sync. So if you want to maintain a full backup of your VIPorbit database (which is highly recommended), you need to utilize the app's proprietary Backup My Stuff feature, which requires an in-app purchase ($4.99). This, however, is not a solution for syncing data between the iPad and iPhone versions of the app. App-specific data syncing functionality is slated to be released later.

VIPorbit is a powerful and highly customizable tool for business executives, sales-people, lawyers, real estate professionals, or anyone who regularly interacts with employees, customers or clients.

Like the original ACT! Contact and Customer Management Software for PCs, which was first released in 1987, VIPorbit is designed to cater to users' personal work habits and make them more organized and productive. Because the app handles a wide range of tasks simultaneously, it does require an initial learning curve as you begin using it.

IMPORTING YOUR EXISTING DATA INTO VIPORBIT

Upon purchasing and downloading the VIPorbit for iPad app from the App Store, you first need to import your existing Contacts and Calendar data. When you launch the app, the main Dashboard screen is displayed (shown in Figure 7.1).

FIGURE 7.1

The main Dashboard screen of VIPorbit. It's from here you can look up contacts data, check your schedule, review your Tasklist (to-do list items and pending deadlines), back up your data, and access the app's other main functions.

To import your existing contacts, tap the Tools icon (the gear) that's displayed in the lower-left corner of the main VIPorbit screen and then tap the Import Contacts option. From the Smart Important Contacts screen (shown in Figure 7.2), choose to import your Apple (Calendar) contacts, Google Contacts, or your existing contacts from Facebook, Twitter, and/or LinkedIn.

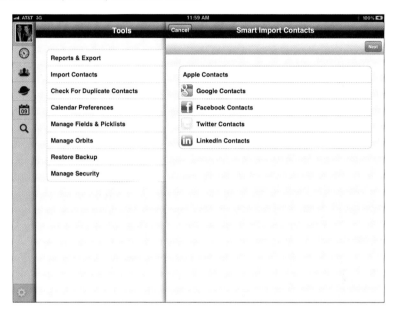

FIGURE 7.2

You can import existing contacts data from the iPad's Contacts app and/or Google Contacts, as well as your existing Facebook, Twitter, and LinkedIn accounts.

Then, from the Tools menu, tap the Calendar Preferences option to turn on automatic importing of iCal (Calendar app) data and/or Google Calendar data. You can also set up a password for accessing the VIPorbit app by tapping the Manage Security option from the Tools menu.

Before starting to manage your contacts using VIPorbit, tap on the Manage Fields & Picklists option from the Tools menu to customize the User Defined Fields for each entry and set up personalized pick list options related to contacts, activities, and logs.

When your pre-existing data has been imported into the VIPorbit app, you can easily add new contacts, scheduling information or do-to items from within the app. Return to the main Dashboard screen by tapping on the Dashboard icon that's displayed near the top-left corner of the screen.

USING VIPORBIT'S DASHBOARD

From the Today You Have box that's displayed near the top-left corner of the Dashboard, you can tap the Calls, Meetings, or ToDos icon to quickly see what tasks you have pending for that day. You can also tap on the Contacts, Orbits, or Today icons to separately view your complete contacts list, Orbits (grouped contacts) list, or schedule. The Tasklist window displayed on the Dashboard lists currently pending activities, to-do items, alerts, and deadlines.

> TIP   To quickly add a contact, tap the Add a New Panel box that's displayed on the Dashboard, and then tap the Add a Contact option. From the Add a Panel menu, you can also add an Orbit, create Saved Search parameters, or add a URL for later reference. When you Add a New Panel (shown in Figure 7.3), a sticky note–like window is created on the Dashboard.

Jason R. Rich Panel

FIGURE 7.3

The Add a New Panel feature enables you to create sticky note–like windows on the Dashboard for quick reference or later referral. It's yet another customizable way to organize information.

The easiest way to navigate around the VIPorbit app is to tap the command icons displayed along the left vertical margin of the main app screens. Tap the photo in the upper-left corner of the app screen to set up your personal contact information and select a photo to use with the app. After you set up your account information, you can quickly send a Twitter, Facebook, and/or LinkedIn status update by tapping your photo icon and then tapping the Social tab that's displayed along the top of the screen.

You can use the Contacts icon to access the app's All Contacts list. From here, use the Search field to quickly find any contact entry by typing a contact's name or any keyword or phrase associated with a contact. You can also view all contact listings in alphabetical order from the All Contacts screen and then tap any single contact listing to view the detailed entry.

Use the Orbits icon to access linked or grouped contacts and all information pertaining to them. You can use the Calendar icon to view the calendar module of the app.

After tapping on the Calendar command icon, switch between a month, week, day or list view by tapping the appropriate command tab. These tabs are located along the left vertical margin of the screen (shown in Figure 7.4).

FIGURE 7.4

Once populated with data, the Calendar module of VIPorbit displays all appointments, calls, meetings and to do list items you have scheduled for the day, week, or month, based on the Calendar view you select.

When viewing any of the Calendar views, tap the plus-sign icon in the top-right corner of the screen to add a new appointment. Alternatively, you can tap the Filter icon to choose a specific calendar or activity type (calls, meetings, to-do items) that you want to highlight and view within the Calendar.

As you use the VIPorbit app over time, it accumulates a vast amount of information pertaining to your contacts, schedule, and to-do list items. To quickly find and view any data stored within the app, tap the Find icon that's located along the left verti-cal margin of the app's screen. The Find command has two modes: Find a Contact or Advanced. Use the Advanced option to locate data beyond someone's name, company, status, city, state, or country.

Like any contact relationship manager, scheduling, or database application, what you get out of VIPorbit depends on how diligent you are entering relevant con-tact-, scheduling-, and to-do list–related data, and how proactive you are when it comes to personalizing the app with custom fields and picklists that cater to your work habits and needs.

NOTE When it comes to selecting the right app, you always have options (beyond what's preinstalled on your iPad). By performing a search within the App Store, you'll find a large selection of third-party apps that can supplement or replace your need to use the Contacts, Calendar, or Reminders app on your iPad. In the App Store you'll find many other apps that offer similar functionality in terms of contact (customer) relationship management tasks.

THE FUTURE OF VIPORBIT

Right now, VIPorbit is a powerful and versatile standalone contact and relationship management app for the iPad that streamlines the functionality of several other apps into a single app. However, when the Mac version is released in late 2012, and data can be synchronized between a Mac, iPad, and iPhone, the usefulness and versatility of VIPorbit will be greatly enhanced.

TIP To discover other apps for the iPad that offer similar functionality when it comes to managing contacts, calendars, and/or to-do list management, visit the App Store, and enter the phrase "Contact Management," "Scheduling," "CRM" (Contacts Relationship Manager), or "To Do Lists" into the Search field.

If you're a PC user who currently utilizes Microsoft Dynamics CRM (http://crm.dynamics.com/en-us/home) for contact relationship management, there are a variety of iPad-specific apps that give you full access to your Microsoft Dynamics database via your tablet, including Resco Mobil CRM for Microsoft Dynamics CRM, Mobile Client for Microsoft Dynamics CRM, Mobile CRM+ for MS Dynamics, and CWR Mobile CRM for iPad. These apps require Internet access to function.

NOTE VIPorbit was designed and created by the co-creator of ACT! for the PC, which is now owned and distributed by Sage (http://offer.act.com). While an iPad version of ACT! is not available, you can access the subscription-based ACT! Connect online service from an iPad that's connected to the Web. ACT! Connect gives ACT! users access to their contact details, notes, history, meetings, and activities via a cloud-based service.

IN THIS CHAPTER

▦ Using iOS 5's AirPrint feature
▦ Other wireless printing options for non-AirPrint printers
▦ Scanning documents into your iPad

8

WIRELESS PRINTING AND SCANNING VIA YOUR iPAD

Unlike laptop or netbook computers, the iPad does not contain a USB port that can be used to directly connect a printer or scanner to your tablet. However, built into iOS 5.1 is the AirPrint feature, as well as Bluetooth, which are two separate technologies that allow printers or scanners, for example, to wirelessly communicate with your tablet.

As a result, any app that integrates the AirPrint feature, or taps into the iPad's Bluetooth capabilities, can be used to access and utilize external peripherals, such as a printer or scanner. When it comes to wireless printing, Apple has teamed up with several printer manufacturers to incorporate AirPrint technology into a growing number of printer models. You learn more about AirPrint functionality shortly.

However, if your home or office printer is not AirPrint compatible, there are options for making your iPad compatible with your existing laser, inkjet, or photo printer. You must

use third-party software, such as Printopia 2, on your Mac that's connected to the same wireless network as your iPad, or you can connect a peripheral, such as the Lantronix xPrintServer, to your home or office wireless network. The xPrintServer enables you to share printers currently being used by PCs or Macs with an iPad or other iOS devices.

In addition to wireless printing functionality that's available from an ever-growing selection of iPad apps, including Contacts, Calendar, Safari, Mail, Photos, Pages, Numbers, Keynote, and PDFpen, several companies have released portable scanners that can be connected to the iPad, enabling you to take paper-based documents and photos and scan them into the tablet to create full-color digital files that can be viewed on the tablet's screen, manipulated using compatible apps, and then shared with others. You learn more about scanning options later in this chapter.

WIRELESS PRINTING FROM YOUR iPAD

Depending on your printer make and model, there are a variety of ways to establish a wireless connection between an iPad and a laser, inkjet, or photo printer. The option you ultimately choose is based on the printer make and model you'll be using.

If your printer is AirPrint compatible, you do not need any additional software, apps, or hardware to establish a wireless connection between the printer and iPad, as long as they're both connected via Wi-Fi to the same wireless network. If your printer is not AirPrint compatible, additional software and/or hardware is necessary to wirelessly print from your tablet.

NOTE   Unlike a desktop, laptop, or netbook computer, your iPad does not have the ability to connect directly to a printer using a USB cable connection. Thus, some type of wireless connection must first be established before you can utilize the Print command that's now built into many iPad apps.

USING THE AIRPRINT FEATURE TO WIRELESSLY PRINT FROM YOUR iPAD

AirPrint is a wireless printing feature that enables you to connect your tablet to a compatible printer without using cables. The printer and iPad, however, need to be connected (wirelessly via Wi-Fi) to the same network.

After the wireless connection is made, you can freely use the Print command that's built into an ever-growing selection of apps. So, if you're creating or editing a document using Pages, for example, and you're ready to print the document, fol-low these steps:

1. Tap the wrench icon in the upper-right corner of the Pages screen.

2. Tap the Share and Print option (shown in Figure 8.1).

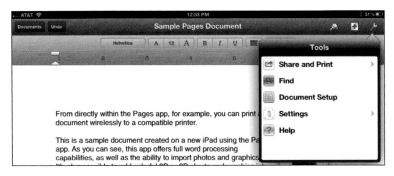

FIGURE 8.1

To wirelessly print a document from within any of the iWork apps (Pages, Numbers, or Keynote), tap the wrench icon and choose the Share and Print option.

3. Select the Printer option from within the Share and Print window.

4. Choose which printer you want to utilize (shown in Figure 8.2).

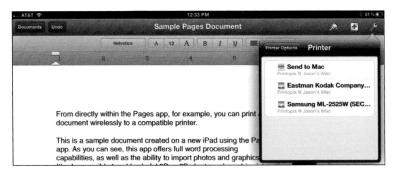

FIGURE 8.2

After tapping the Print option, choose which compatible printer you want to print to.

5. Determine the number of copies of the document you want to print.

6. Tap the Print command icon within the Printer Options window.

The Print command has been incorporated into many popular apps, including Safari (shown in Figure 8.3). After you set up the AirPrint feature once to establish the wireless connection between your tablet and an AirPrint-compatible printer, printing from your tablet is easy.

The Print Command

FIGURE 8.3

From within many apps, including Safari, to print a file, image, or document, first tap the Share icon and then select the Print option.

TIP As you're using many apps, such as Safari or Photos, for example, you'll discover the Print command by tapping on the app's Share icon.

Within the past two years or so, Brother, Canon, Epson, HP, and Lexmark have released AirPrint-compatible laser, inkjet, and/or photo printers. Thus, there are currently approximately 100 printer models that are AirPrint compatible, starting in price at less than $100.00.

NOTE The AirPrint feature only works between an AirPrint-compatible printer and the iPad when the two devices are connected wirelessly (via Wi-Fi) to the same wireless network. A printer that is connected to a wireless network using Bluetooth or a USB cable connection does not support the AirPrint feature.

To see an up-to-date list of compatible AirPrint printers, visit http://support.apple.com/kb/HT4356. Click or tap the Brother, Canon, Epson, HP, or Lexmark heading to view a listing of compatible printer models from each manufacturer.

PRINTING FROM AN iPAD TO A NON-AIRPRINT– COMPATIBLE PRINTER

If your printer is not AirPrint-compatible, there are three options for establishing a wireless connection between your tablet and printer. These options include

1. Using the Printopia 2 software on your Mac (or similar software). The Mac can be connected to the printer using a Wi-Fi, Bluetooth, USB, or Ethernet connection, but the Mac needs to be connected to your network via a Wi-Fi connection.

2. Connect the Lantronix xPrintServer device to your home or office network's wireless router via an Ethernet cable. Up to 10 printers that are on a network (connected to other PCs or Macs within the network) instantly become AirPrint compatible and accessible from your iPad regardless of the printer make and model.

3. Download and install a third-party app on your iPad that enables you to connect wirelessly to your home or office's wireless network in order to print from your tablet to printers that are connected to that network.

USING THE PRINTOPIA 2 SOFTWARE VIA A MAC

Printopia 2 ($19.95, http://ecamm.com) is an easy-to-use program that enables an iPad to wirelessly access any printer that's already connected to a Mac, as long as the Mac is also connected via Wi-Fi to a home or office network.

When Printopia 2 is installed on the Mac, the printers that are connected to that Mac are displayed on your iPad whenever you access the Print command from an AirPrint-compatible app. This works even if the printer itself is not AirPrint compatible (as shown in Figure 8.4).

> **NOTE** AirPrint Activator 2 for the Mac is offered as freeware and offers functionality similar to the Printopia 2 software. To download this software, visit http://netputing.com/airprintactivator/airprint-activator-v2-0/.

FIGURE 8.4

The Samsung laser printer that's shown here is not AirPrint compatible, but it can be used with an iPad as if it were AirPrint compatible when the Printopia 2 software is running on a Mac.

USING XPRINTSERVER TO ACCESS PRINTERS ON A NETWORK

Regardless of whether you utilize Windows-based PCs or Macs, if you have a home or office wireless network, when you connect the xPrintServer device ($149.95) to your wireless router, up to 10 different printers that are also on that network (no matter how they're connected to the network) instantly become AirPrint compatible, enabling you to access them from your iPad as long as the iPad can connect wirelessly (via Wi-Fi) to the same network.

Developed by Lantronix (www.lantronix.com), the xPrintServer is a small device (measuring 4.5" × 2.37" × .87") that connects directly to any network's wireless router using a standard Ethernet cable connection (an RJ45 connector). When the device is connected to a network, it seeks out all printers on that network and instantly makes them AirPrint compatible. Within seconds, each printer becomes accessible from an iPad that's running any AirPrint-compatible app (or an app with a Print command). Absolutely no configuration, special printer drivers, or optional software is required.

The xPrintServer works with laser, inkjet, or photo printers from HP, Toshiba, Lexmark, Canon, Brother, Xerox and Epson. In some cases, the printer must connect to the network via Wi-Fi or an Ethernet cable (as opposed to a USB connection) to work properly from an iPad using the AirPrint feature.

> **NOTE** The xPrintServer device is available online, directly from the Lantronix website (800-422-7055, www.lantronix.com).

USING A THIRD-PARTY PRINTING APP ON YOUR iPAD

There are a variety of third-party apps available from the App Store that enable the tablet to connect wirelessly to specific printer makes and models that are connected to the same wireless home or office network as the iPad. In some cases these apps first send the document, image, or file to a PC or Mac that's also connected to the network, and then prints the desired content from that computer.

If you're interested in creating prints from digital images stored on your iPad (within the Photos app), there are also apps available from the App Store, such as Kodak Gallery (free), that enable you to order prints, photo books, or photo gifts directly from the Kodak Gallery service via the Web and have them shipped directly to you.

> **TIP** To determine whether there's a specialized iPad app available that can facilitate wireless printing using your existing printer, visit the App Store. In the Search field, enter the manufacturer of your printer, such as Epson, Canon, or Kodak.

SCANNING DOCUMENTS ON THE GO INTO YOUR iPAD

Depending on the type of work you do, you might find it extremely useful to be able to scan paper-based documents directly into your iPad while you're on the go. This might include letters and documents, research materials, receipts, reports, photos, or other paper-based printed content.

Using one of several portable scanners currently available from Brookstone and Doxie, for example, you can scan any document or image into your iPad to save it, and then you can store, view, edit, annotate, print, and share it using a variety of third-party apps.

The iConvert Scanner for iPad ($149.00, www.brookstone.com) is an extremely lightweight and portable, 300 dots-per-inch resolution scanner that enables you to scan any full-color or black-and-white document or photo that's between 2" and 8.5" wide.

The scanned documents are then saved in a JPEG format, which is compatible with a variety of iPad apps. The iConvert Scanner (shown in Figure 8.5) comes with a free iConvert Scan scanning app that gets downloaded from the App Store. This app is used to scan and save the JPEG files. Then, you can use other apps to view, organize, store, edit, annotate, and share the digitally scanned files.

FIGURE 8.5

The iConvert Scanner for iPad is available from Brookstone stores, as well as from www.brookstone.com.

Unlike other scanners that are compatible with the iPad, the iConvert Scanner connects to the tablet via the tablet's built-in Dock port. This port is located on the bottom of the tablet. Thus, to use the scanner, simply set the iPad on top of the scanner and launch the iConvert Scan app.

The scanner itself measures 12.1" × 4.4" × 2.8", and it weighs 1.44 pounds. The iConvert Scanner is not battery powered, so you need to plug it in to an AC power source to operate it.

Another portable scanning option is the Doxie Go + Wi-Fi portable scanner from Apparent Corporation ($239.00, www.getdoxie.com). This is a compact, battery-powered scanner that you can use anywhere.

After you scan paper-based documents (up to 8.5" wide) into the scanner, the scanner connects to any wireless network via Wi-Fi, and transfers the scanned documents to the online (cloud-based) service of your choice, such as iCloud, Dropbox, Flickr, or Evernote. The files can also be sent directly to your own FTP site.

After being uploaded, you can access the scanned files using an iPad that's connected to the Internet so that you can view, save (in a choice of formats), edit, and share them using your tablet.

Unlike the iConvert Scanner from Brookstone, the Doxie Go + Wi-Fi can create searchable PDF files from scanned documents, so you can use optional third-party apps, such as PDFpen or Evernote, to edit or annotate the scans. Or, if the scanned file is a graphic or photo, you can save it in the JPEG format and use it with the iPad's Photos app (or any third-party photo-editing and sharing app).

The Doxie Go + Wi-Fi Scanner measures 10.5" × 1.7" by 2.2", weighs 14.2 ounces, and can easily be transported within a briefcase or computer bag, making it perfect for a mobile executive.

The Doxie Go + Wi-Fi scanner has a 600 dots-per-inch resolution and can scan an 8.5" × 11" page in eight seconds (in 300 dpi resolution). The scanner's internal memory holds up to 600 pages or 2,400 photos. You can connect an optional USB flash drive or SD card to the scanner to provide more internal storage until you can sync files with an iPad or computer.

Using either of these scanning solutions with an iPad, it's easy to manage, access, and store documents, files, and photos from virtually anywhere. When combined with wireless printing capabilities and the functionality of various apps for viewing, editing, and sharing documents, photos, and files, the iPad gains capabilities that were once exclusive to desktop or notebook computers.

> TIP   Use a portable scanner with your iPad to create a more paper-free work environment for yourself while maintaining full access to your important documents, files, and photos on the go.
>
> A scanner that utilizes OCR technology (Optical Character Recognition), such as the Doxie Go + Wi-Fi, can convert text-based information from a scanned document into data that can be manipulated or edited using a spreadsheet app, expense manager, word processor, or annotation app on your iPad.
>
> Also, in addition to scanning photos, these scanners can be used to import and store digital versions of drawings or other graphics on your tablet, which you can then view, edit, and share using various third-party apps related to photography.

UNDERSTANDING FILE FORMATS CREATED BY SCANNERS

A scanner that utilizes OCR technology can take a text-based paper document and transform it into an editable digital file accessible from your iPad. You can edit it using Pages, Evernote, Notes, or another word processing app. An applicable word processing or text editing iPad app is required to view, edit, print, or share the scanned text-based document.

If the scanner can transform the scanned document into a PDF file, using a third-party app, such as PDFpen (available from the App Store), you can annotate and edit any PDF file, as well as view, print, and share it from within the app.

The scanned documents or files created by a scanner that can only create JPG files are treated like digital photos by your iPad. You can view, print, or share them using the Photos app or another photography-related app that's available from the App Store. Some photography apps, such as Skitch for iPad, enable you to annotate digital images.

> **NOTE** Without using a portable scanner connected to your tablet, you can still create a scanned document using your desktop or notebook computer that's connected to any type of scanner. Then you need to transfer the file to your iPad to view, store, edit, print, or share it.

IN THIS CHAPTER

- Sync your iPad with your computer using iTunes Sync
- Sync your iPad with your computer using iTunes Wireless Sync
- Take advantage of iCloud for backing up and syncing files and data on your iPad

SYNCING YOUR iPAD VIA iTUNES OR iCLOUD

Thanks to the iOS 5.1 operating system, your iPad is designed to work seamlessly with Apple's online-based iCloud service, enabling you to maintain a backup of your tablet wirelessly, plus sync app-specific files and data with both iCloud and your Mac(s) and other iOS devices that are linked to the same iCloud account.

Apps such as Contacts, Calendar, Music, iBooks, Safari, Photos, Reminders, Notes, iTunes, Videos, Pages, Numbers, Keynote, and iPhoto, for example, all have iCloud functionality built in, so data, files, and documents utilized by these apps can automatically back up and sync to the iCloud service.

NOTE For iCloud functionality to work, you must set up a free iCloud account, turn on the iCloud feature from within Settings on your iPad, and also activate iCloud with each app it's compatible with. After doing this once, however, your tablet syncs data and backs itself up to iCloud.

When used with iCloud, your iPad no longer needs to be connected to your primary computer (a PC or Mac), via a USB cable, in order to transfer documents, sync data, or back up files. However, this continues to be a viable option. The benefit to using iCloud for data syncing and file backups is that you can access important information from anywhere your iPad has an Internet connection because the files are stored "in the cloud." When you use iTunes Sync, the backup or synced files are stored on your primary computer, and you must connect the tablet to that computer. This is not necessarily conducive if you're away from your primary computer or traveling, for example.

With iCloud turned on, you can back up your tablet directly to the iCloud service via the Internet. Meanwhile, the iTunes Sync process stores backup files and synced data on your primary computer. A third option for backing up and syncing data is to use iTunes Wireless Sync, which enables your iPad to wirelessly back up and sync data with your primary computer as long as both devices are connected to the same wireless network.

When it comes to syncing or backing up data related to your iPad, using the iTunes Sync process is considered "old school." Let's explore how the iTunes Sync process, which is a viable option for many iPad users, works.

NOTE If your business has a need to keep multiple iPad tablets uniformly synced so they all contain the same information, configuration, and apps, Apple offers easy solutions to do this. To learn more, visit www.apple.com/support/ipad/enterprise.

MAKING THE iTUNES SYNC CONNECTION

Whether you use a PC or Mac, you need to download and install the most current version of iTunes onto your computer to take full advantage of the iTunes sync process. To do this, visit www.apple.com/itunes, or while iTunes is running on your computer, click the iTunes pull-down menu at the top of the screen and select the Check for Updates option.

NOTE   You use the iTunes software for your PC or Mac for a variety of purposes. You can initiate the iTunes Sync process between your computer and iPad,
or you can use iTunes on your computer to access the iTunes Store and make
content purchases. You also use the software to manage and enjoy your iTunes
content on your primary computer.

On your iPad, however, you use the iTunes app specifically to acquire music,
movies, TV show episodes, audiobooks, podcasts, and iTunes U content. To listen
to audio content on your iPad, you use the Music app. To watch video content
obtained from iTunes, you use the Videos app.

Next, connect the white USB cable that came with your iPad to a USB port on your
computer (or to a USB hub that's connected to your computer) as well as to the
30-pin dock connector port that's located on the bottom of your tablet.

If your computer is turned on when the two devices are connected, the iTunes
software automatically launches on your computer and establishes an iTunes sync
connection.

On your primary computer, iTunes is designed to handle a range of tasks, from
managing your digital music library to enabling you to purchase (or, in some
cases, rent) a vast selection of content, including apps, eBooks, digital newspapers,
digital editions of magazines, music, TV show episodes, movies, audiobooks, and
podcasts.

Ultimately, from your primary computer, you can use the iTunes Sync process to
handle the following iPad functions:

- Initially set up your iPad after purchase.
- Create and maintain a backup of your iPad's data, apps, personalized set-
  tings, and content. You can also restore your iPad from a backup using
  iTunes.
- Transfer or sync digital music.
- Transfer or sync apps.
- Transfer or sync address book, contacts, Safari bookmarks, notes, and email
  accounts. (If you're using the online Calendar apps offered by Google or
  Yahoo!, for example, these too can be synced using iTunes.)
- Transfer or sync TV show episodes and movies.
- Transfer or sync digital photos.
- Transfer or sync your iBooks eBook library, as well as digital editions of news-
  papers and magazines.

- Transfer or sync podcasts and other digital content.
- Transfer or sync certain app-specific files and data, such as documents, spreadsheets, and presentations for use with the Pages, Numbers, or Keynote apps.
- Update the iOS operating system of your iPad (when Apple releases updates that you need to download and install).

> **NOTE** These tasks can also be accomplished wirelessly by using Apple's iCloud service, which eliminates the need to connect your tablet directly to your primary computer via a USB cable. An Internet connection is required, however.

After you make the iTunes Sync connection between your primary computer (a Mac or PC) and tablet, you can customize the iTunes software's settings to automatically transfer or sync only the data, apps, and content you want or need. Thus, you should set up the iTunes software and customize the sync process to best meet your needs.

CUSTOMIZING THE iTUNES SYNC PROCESS

After making the iTunes sync connection between your primary computer and iPad, under the Devices heading on the left side of the iTunes screen, you see your tablet listed. Click this listing to select and highlight your tablet.

Near the top of the main iTunes screen, when the two devices are connected, you see a handful of options, including Summary, Info, Apps, Music, Movies, TV Shows, Books, and Photos. Based on content stored within iTunes, options for Ringtones and Audiobooks might also be listed. The default is the Summary screen, which is displayed in the main area of the iTunes screen on your Mac or PC.

Each command option reveals a separate screen containing additional (relevant) menus for customizing the iTunes sync process. From these screens, you can control the flow of data, content, and information between your iPad and your primary computer. You must adjust the settings within the iTunes software on your computer to customize the sync process; you cannot customize the sync process from your tablet.

UNDERSTANDING THE iTUNES SUMMARY SCREEN

The Summary screen within iTunes on your computer (shown in Figure 9.1) is comprised of four sections: iPad, Version, Backup, and Options. Near the top of the Summary screen is the iPad section. Within this box, your iPad's device name (which you created when you first set up the tablet), its memory capacity, what version number of the iOS operating system is installed on the tablet, and its serial number are displayed.

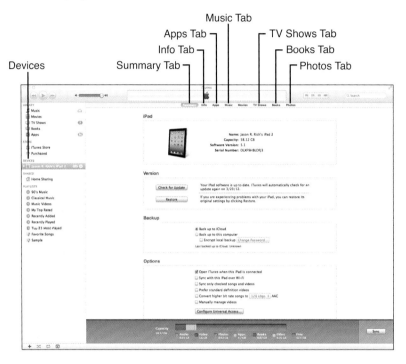

FIGURE 9.1

When your computer and iPad make a connection via the iTunes Sync process, the main iTunes Summary screen looks like this.

Within the Version section of the iTunes Summary screen is an option to check for updates related to the iOS operating system running on your tablet. Click the Check for Update button to determine if an updated version of the operating system is available.

If an iOS update is available, follow the on-screen prompts to download the new version of the operating system from Apple and then install it on your iPad. This process is almost totally automated, but it can take as long as 15 minutes.

Should you have a problem with your iPad that requires you to restore its entire contents from a saved backup, use the Restore option that's displayed within the Version section of the Summary screen. This option also enables you to restore your iPad to its factory settings, which undoes any settings you've adjusted yourself.

From the Backup box of the Summary screen within iTunes, you can determine if your iPad backs itself up wirelessly to the iCloud service or to your primary computer using the iTunes Sync or iTunes Wireless Sync process.

The Options section of the Summary screen includes a handful of other customizable settings. To turn on any of these options, use the mouse to add a check mark within the checkbox that corresponds to the desired option.

The first option displayed in the Options section enables you to set iTunes to automatically launch as soon as you connect the iPad with your computer using the USB cable. The second option, for example, enables you to perform an iTunes Wireless Sync, which works exactly the same as the iTunes Sync process, but it's done wirelessly (without a USB cable connection) when your computer and tablet are connected to the same wireless network.

TIP If you're using your iPad for storing data that you need to keep private, be sure to add a check mark next to the Encrypt Local Backup option that's displayed within the Backup box of the Summary screen.

Activating the Encrypt Local Backup option encrypts the data within the iPad backup files that are stored on your computer, making it much more difficult for an unauthorized person to access this data from your primary computer.

On the iPad itself, you should also activate the Passcode option from the Settings app. This protects the data stored on your tablet and keeps unauthorized people from using your iPad because it is passcode protected.

ADJUSTING SYNC OPTIONS WITH THE iTUNES INFO SCREEN

If you'll be using the iTunes Sync or iTunes Wireless Sync process to back up or sync app-specific data between your primary computer and iPad, tap the Info tab that's displayed near the top of the iTunes screen in order to adjust settings related to syncing data from Contacts, Calendar, Notes, and Mail, as well as your Safari bookmarks.

SYNCING YOUR APPS WITH THE iTUNES APP SCREEN

The iTunes App Screen is used to manage all the apps you've downloaded from the App Store. It enables you to determine which apps should be installed on your iPad. To use the features within this section of iTunes, first add a check mark next to the Sync Apps heading.

On the left side of the iTunes App screen (shown in Figure 9.2) is a complete list of all apps you've downloaded and that are stored (or backed up) on your primary computer. On the right side of the iTunes App Screen is an interactive re-creation of your iPad 's Home screen, which displays all of the apps currently installed on your tablet. Use the mouse to move apps around on your Home screen to change their location.

FIGURE 9.2

When your iPad is connected to your computer and you access the App screen, your iPad's Home screen is re-created on the computer screen, plus you can view a complete list of apps that you own.

From the left side of the screen, add check marks to the apps stored on your primary computer that you want to transfer and install on your iPad. You can also remove check marks that correspond to listed apps to uninstall them from your tablet, but still keep copies of the apps stored on your primary computer.

At the bottom of the app listing, on the left side of the screen, is the Automatically Sync New Apps option. When this option is turned on, anytime you purchase a new app on any device from within the App Store, that new app is automatically transferred to and installed on your tablet when a sync is next initiated.

If you make any changes to the options displayed within the App screen, be sure to click the Apply icon, found in the lower-right corner of the iTunes screen, to save those changes.

TRANSFERRING APP-SPECIFIC DATA OR FILES BETWEEN YOUR COMPUTER AND iPAD

Some apps, such as Pages, Numbers, Keynote, and many others, enable you to use the iTunes sync process to transfer app-specific data between an iPad app and specific software on your primary computer, such as Microsoft Word, Microsoft Excel, and Microsoft PowerPoint.

If you install an app that allows for app-related files to be transferred using the iTunes sync process, those apps are displayed within the File Sharing section, which appears at the bottom of the App screen of iTunes on your computer.

To transfer an app-specific file, from the File Sharing section (shown in Figure 9.3), click the app name listed on the left side of the screen, under the Apps heading. If you click on Pages, for example, on the left side of the screen, a Pages Documents section within iTunes displays. Click the Add button in the lower-right corner of the screen to choose documents stored on your computer's hard drive to be transferred to your iPad during the next sync.

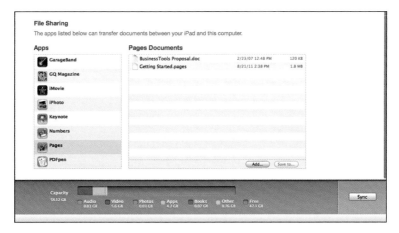

FIGURE 9.3

Under the File Sharing heading, you can set up the iTunes Sync process to synchronize app-specific data between your iPad and computer. This feature works only with compatible apps, such as Pages, Numbers, and Keynote.

SYNCING YOUR MUSIC WITH THE iTUNES MUSIC SCREEN

If you use iTunes on your primary computer to manage your digital music library, and you want to transfer some or all of your music so you can enjoy it on your iPad using the Music app that comes preinstalled on the tablet, click the Music option near the top of the iTunes screen and then place a check mark next to the Sync Music heading.

TIP If you're a paid subscriber to Apple's optional iTunes Match service ($24.99 per year), your tablet is capable of accessing your entire digital music library directly from iCloud. To learn more about this premium service, visit www.apple.com/itunes/itunes-match.

Within the Sync Music section are several customizable options that enable you to determine which music files should be synced with your iPad. For example, you can sync your entire music library, or choose specific songs, playlists, genres, or artists. You can also select entire albums to be synced between the two devices, not just individual songs.

SYNCING YOUR MOVIES WITH THE iTUNES MOVIES SCREEN

If you have purchased and downloaded movies from iTunes and want to transfer those movie files to your iPad to view them using the Videos app, click the Movies option displayed near the top of the iTunes screen and then place a check mark in the checkbox displayed next to the Sync Movies heading. You can choose which movies you want to transfer to your iPad (or vice versa).

However, if you have used iTunes to rent movies, you need to click on the Movies option and use the Rented Movies section to choose which movies you want to transfer from your primary computer to your iPad (or vice versa) by clicking the Move icon that's associated with each rented movie.

On the left side of the screen (shown in Figure 9.4) are the rented movies currently stored on your primary computer. The box on the right side of the Rented Movies screen represents your tablet and the rented movie content stored (or to be stored) on it.

NOTE Unlike movies you have purchased, rented movies can only be stored on one system or device (your primary computer or your iPad) at any given time.

FIGURE 9.4

Movies rented from iTunes can only be stored on one computer or iOS device at a time. So, if you download a rental movie on your primary computer but want to watch it on your iPad, you first need to transfer the file using the Move button.

SYNCING YOUR TV SHOWS WITH THE iTUNES TV SHOWS SCREEN

From the iTunes Store, you can purchase TV show episodes or entire seasons of your favorite TV series. If you've used the iTunes software on your primary computer to acquire and download this content, you can transfer it to your iPad by clicking the TV Shows tab and then adding a check mark in the checkbox next to the Sync TV Shows heading.

> TIP You can purchase movies, TV episodes, and complete TV series seasons from the iTunes app that comes preinstalled on your iPad (if you're using a Wi-Fi Internet connection) and then later transfer those files to your primary computer using the iTunes sync process.
>
> Or, while the files are stored on your tablet, you can use the AirPlay feature with an Apple TV device to stream the TV show or movie content from your iPad to your HD television set or home theater system.

After you add a check mark to the Sync TV Shows heading, determine which TV show episodes or seasons should be transferred between devices during the next sync. For example, you can select all unwatched episodes, or pick one or more TV series, and then select specific episodes of those series.

SYNCING YOUR EBOOKS WITH THE iTUNES BOOKS SCREEN

In addition to finding, purchasing, and downloading eBooks from iTunes on your primary computer (from Apple's iBookstore), you can manage your eBook library from iTunes and decide which eBook titles to keep on your iPad and which to store on your primary computer.

Click the Books tab at the top of the iTunes screen, and then add a check mark next to the Sync Books heading if you want the iTunes sync process to automatically back up your eBook library. With this option selected, you can choose to sync all eBook titles or only selected titles.

If you scroll down when viewing the Books screen within iTunes, you also see a section for syncing audiobooks. If you plan to download audiobooks from iTunes and want to listen to your audiobooks using the Music app on your iPad, add a check mark next to the Sync Audiobooks option.

> **TIP** If you enjoy listening to audiobooks, in addition to buying audiobook content from iTunes to listen to on your iPad using the Music app, you can download the optional Audible app, and then purchase audiobook content from Audible.com (which is owned by Amazon.com).

SYNCING YOUR DIGITAL IMAGES WITH THE iTUNES PHOTOS SCREEN

If you're a Mac user, the iPhoto software that came bundled with your computer is designed to work seamlessly with the Photos app (and optional iPhoto app) on your iPad. Thus, you can quickly and easily transfer digital images between the two devices using the iTunes sync process.

To sync digital images (pictures) between the two devices, click the Photos option displayed near the top center of the iTunes screen and add a check mark to the Sync Photos From heading.

You can then choose to sync photos from a particular application on your primary computer, such as iPhoto, or choose a specific directory on your computer's hard drive (such as Pictures) that contains images that you want to copy over to your iPad.

> **TIP** iCloud's Photo Stream feature is a wireless method of syncing photos between your primary computer, iPad, and other iOS devices. Your iPad requires a Wi-Fi Internet connection to utilize this feature.

From this screen, you can also sync videos you've shot that are stored on your primary computer or videos that you shot using the Camera app of your iPad. As you scroll down the Photos screen within iTunes, you can pick and choose which images you want to sync.

For example, if you use a Mac you can choose specific Albums or Events from iPhoto or choose specific people based on iPhoto's Faces face-recognition feature. The photos you transfer from your primary computer are then accessible from the Photos app (or optional iPhoto app) on your iPad, or from other apps that can access images stored on your tablet (such as Contacts or optional photo-editing apps, such as Photoshop Touch).

Based on your selections, the number of photos to be synced between your primary computer and tablet is displayed in the upper-right corner of the screen. Keep in mind that this is a syncing process, so your images remain intact at their current location, but you can also duplicate, transfer, and save them on the other device.

As always, after you make your selections from the Photos screen, be sure to click the Apply or Sync button in the lower-right corner of the screen to save your changes.

ADDITIONAL iTUNES COMMANDS AND FEATURES

When your iPad is linked with your primary computer via the iTunes sync process, you can see a graphic depiction of your tablet's memory near the very bottom of the iTunes screen. This display (shown in Figure 9.5), shows how much of the iPad's internal storage space is currently being utilized and what type of data is taking up the space.

FIGURE 9.5

Using the iTunes software, you can quickly see how much of your iPad's internal storage is being utilized and by what type(s) of data.

After you adjust the settings to personalize the iTunes sync process, those settings are utilized the next time you initiate the sync process. At any time, however, you can adjust the settings to change what data, files, apps, and content are transferred or synced between your primary computer and tablet.

During the actual sync process, a rotating circle is displayed in the upper-left corner of the iPad's screen (to the immediate right of the 3G/4G and Wi-Fi signal indicators). At the same time, the progress of the sync is displayed at the very top of the iTunes screen on your primary computer.

> **TIP**   Maintaining a backup of your iPad's contents and data is a smart strategy to use on an ongoing basis. Get into the habit of performing a sync at least once every few days, or more often if you make significant changes to data stored on your iPad or need additional apps or content transferred between your tablet from your primary computer.

CHARGING YOUR iPAD'S BATTERY WHILE IT'S CONNECTED TO YOUR COMPUTER

Depending on your primary computer, the USB connection between the PC or Mac and your iPad might be adequate to charge your iPad's battery. If this is the case, the battery icon displayed in the upper-right corner of your tablet's screen shows a lightning bolt within it to indicate that the device is charging.

However, if you see the Not Charging message next to the battery icon, your computer's USB port (or its USB hub) does not provide enough power to the iPad to recharge its battery. If this is the case, you need to connect the two devices to perform an iTunes sync, but you ultimately need to plug your iPad into an electrical outlet (using the USB cable and the power adapter supplied with your tablet) to charge its battery. Or, you can use another charging method.

WORKING WITH iCLOUD

iCloud is a remote file-sharing service that stores your music, photos, apps, calendar data, contacts, documents, and other types of files and makes them available (wirelessly) via the Internet to your various computers and iOS devices.

The majority of services offered by iCloud are free. When you set up your free iCloud account, you're given a unique email address and 5GB of online storage space. You can purchase additional online storage space if you need it. Extra space is provided for free to accommodate all of your iTunes Store, App Store, iBookstore, and Newsstand purchases.

> **NOTE** Think of iCloud as a remote hard drive storage solution in cyberspace that gives you access to all the data and files you transfer to it.

Apple's iCloud service does much more than just store data and files in cyberspace. It can automatically sync your iPad with your primary computer and other iOS devices (such as your iPhone or iPod touch). It even manages and automatically stores all of your iTunes purchases so they're always available on all of your computers and devices that are connected to the Internet.

For example, you can purchase a song on iTunes using your computer, store that song on your computer's hard drive (and automatically on the iCloud service), and then wirelessly and almost instantly access that song purchase (for no additional charge) on your iPad, iPhone, or iPod touch via the Internet.

> **NOTE** If you upgrade your iCloud account to include the iTunes Match feature (for an additional fee of $24.99 per year), you can wirelessly share your entire music collection, including content not purchased from iTunes, between your Macs, Apple TV, and all your iOS devices. This includes music you've ripped from your own CD collection or recorded yourself.

> **TIP** When your iPad syncs Contacts, Calendar, iCloud Mail, or iWork for iPad documents and files with iCloud, you can access this data from any computer or mobile device that's connected to the Internet. Visit www.iCloud.com, log in using your Apple ID and password, and then click the Mail, Contacts, Calendar, or iWork icon that's displayed on the screen.

For sharing digital photos between computers and mobile devices linked to the same iCloud account, use the Photo Stream feature. It enables you to store up to 1,000 digital photos on the iCloud servers.

When using the Photo Stream service through iCloud, a complete master photo library is maintained on your PC or Mac; however, up to 1,000 images remain instantly accessible to all your devices via iCloud.

One of the most convenient features of iCloud is that you can easily transfer (wirelessly) documents, data and work-related files between your primary computer and iPad. Thus, you can take a Microsoft Word, Excel, or PowerPoint file created on your PC or Mac; for example, transfer it into a Pages, Numbers, or Keypoint file format, send it to iCloud, and make it instantly accessible to your iPad that's connected to the Web.

Not only does this feature make it easy to transfer files and documents between your devices, it also insures that each computer and device always has the latest edited version of your file or document.

Your iPad can also use iCloud to back up and access your collection of apps and eBooks. All your app purchases, whether they're currently stored on your iPad or not, are automatically stored in iCloud, and they're accessible to you at any time (assuming your iPad is connected to the Web). iCloud also keeps a backup of all your Newsstand purchases.

> **TIP** To find out how iCloud can be used to sync your Safari bookmarks, see Chapter 3, "Surfing the Web."
>
> Discover how iCloud can sync your Reminders and Calendar data by referring to Chapter 4, "Using the Calendar, Reminders, and Notification Center Apps."
>
> To learn how iCloud can be used for syncing your Contacts data, see Chapter 5, "Working with the Contacts App."

MAINTAINING A BACKUP OF YOUR ENTIRE iPAD VIA iCLOUD

Instead of backing up your iPad by connecting it to your primary computer via a USB cable and using the iTunes sync process, you can create and automatically maintain a daily backup of your tablet wirelessly using iCloud.

To make the backup process quick, only information that has changed on your iPad is sent to the iCloud service and is incorporated into your backup archive. The backup files are stored in cyberspace (on the iCloud servers), not on your primary computer.

After a backup has been stored on iCloud, you can perform a wireless restore if something goes wrong with your tablet causing data to be deleted. When you initially set up your iPad, you are prompted to set up a free iCloud account. You can then customize that account from within the Settings app.

At any time, however, you can turn on the iCloud Backup feature. To do this, launch Settings from your iPad's Home screen. On the left side of the screen, tap the iCloud option.

When the iCloud screen appears on the right side of the screen (shown in Figure 9.6), turn on the iCloud feature and then scroll to the bottom of the screen and tap the Storage & Backup option.

FIGURE 9.6

You can control iCloud features available to your iPad from this iCloud screen, which is accessible from within Settings.

From the Storage & Backup screen within Settings (shown in Figure 9.7), tap the virtual switch associated with the iCloud Backup option to turn it on. Next, tap the Backup Now icon to create a manual backup of your iPad that is stored on iCloud. This can be done at any time (to supplement or replace the automatic daily backup).

When the iCloud Backup feature is turned on, your tablet automatically creates an updated back up once per day, as long as it's plugged into an external power source, has access to a Wi-Fi connection, and is not otherwise being used. While some iCloud features work with a 3G/4G or Wi-Fi Internet connection, the iCloud Backup feature must be used with a Wi-Fi connection.

CAUTION Keep in mind that, to access the iCloud service from your iPad the tablet must have access to a Wi-Fi or 3G/4G Internet connection. If you know you're about to board an airplane that doesn't offer Wi-Fi, or if you're leaving a 3G/4G wireless data coverage area, access and transfer whatever files you need on your tablet from iCloud before the Internet connection is shut down or lost.

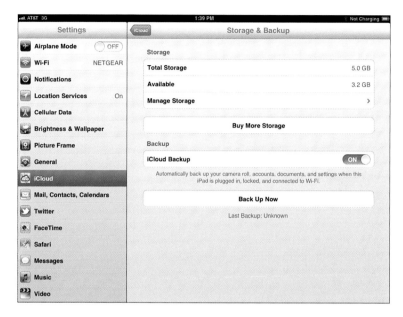

FIGURE 9.7

Access the Storage & Backup screen to turn on or off the iCloud Backup feature, to manually initi-
ate an iCloud Backup, or to return your iPad from iCloud backup files.

10

WORKING WITH PAGES, NUMBERS, AND KEYNOTE

For business users, three of the best designed, most versatile, and feature-packed apps available for the iPad are Pages, Numbers, and Keynote, which together make up Apple's trio of iWork for iPad apps. Each app, however, is sold separately for $9.99. Although each has its own purpose, they all utilize the same basic user interface and menu structure. This design similarity between apps greatly reduces the learning curve for getting the most use out of them.

If you're not familiar with what each app in the iWork for iPad trio is designed for, here's a quick overview:

■ Pages is a full-featured word processor for the iPad. It is Microsoft Word (for PC and Mac) compatible, as well as fully compatible with the Pages software for the Mac.

- Numbers is an extremely powerful spreadsheet management tool that was designed specifically for the iPad. However, its capabilities rival Microsoft Excel running on a desktop computer. In fact, Numbers is compatible with Excel (for PC and Mac), as well as with the Numbers software for the Mac.

- Keynote is a versatile digital slide show presentation tool that enables you to create and showcase presentations on your iPad. After you create a presentation, you can connect your iPad to an HD television or LCD projector, for example, in order to share it with a group. Or, you can take advantage of the new iPad's superior Retina display to convey information graphically (using animated digital slides) to one or two people at a time. Keynote is compatible with both Microsoft PowerPoint (for PC and Mac) and Keynote for the Mac.

In addition to enabling you to import Word, Excel, or PowerPoint documents or files into the appropriate app in order to view, edit, print, or share them, you also have the ability to create documents or files from scratch and export them into Word, Excel, or PowerPoint format, as well as PDF format, before transferring them to your primary computer or another device.

> **NOTE** If you use iWork for Mac (Pages, Numbers, or Keynote), files transfer easily between a Mac and iPad without requiring that you change file formats during the import or export process. Pages, Numbers, and Keynote (sold separately) are available for the Mac from the Mac App Store for $19.99 each.

One of the most useful features of the iWork for iPad apps is that you have several options for easily importing and exporting files between your Mac or PC (or another iOS device) and your tablet. You can email files as attachments to or from the iPad, or you can sync files using the iTunes Sync process. However, the easiest method of transferring files is to use iCloud or another compatible cloud-based file-sharing service.

Unlike most other iPad apps, Pages, Numbers, and Keynote can be seamlessly integrated with iCloud, so your files and documents always remain synchronized (wirelessly) with your primary computer and other devices.

Using this feature, if you make a change to a Pages document on your iPad, for example, within seconds, the revisions are transferred to iCloud and sent to all of the computers and iOS devices that are linked to the same iCloud account. The process happens in the background and is fully automated.

> **TIP** Because Pages, Numbers, and Keynote require significant data entry, consider using these apps with an optional external keyboard. In addition to making touch-typing easier, an external keyboard offers navigational arrow keys that make moving around within a document or file more efficient. All three apps, however, make excellent use of the iPad's virtual keyboard.

Thanks to Pages, Numbers, and Keynote, the capability of your iPad to serve as a powerful business-oriented tool increases exponentially. Using these apps, many businesspeople find they can rely on their iPads for a much broader range of tasks while on the go, and they can often leave their laptop computers or netbooks behind in favor of being able to work directly from the iPad.

> **TIP** If you're using a new iPad, data entry is possible using the tablet's new Dictation feature. Instead of typing, tap the Dictate button on the virtual keyboard, and when prompted, begin speaking.

NEW FEATURES OFFERED BY THE iWORK FOR iPAD APPS

When iOS 5.0 was released for the iPad, the Pages, Numbers, and Keynote apps underwent a major redesign to incorporate a handful of new features, including iCloud integration. In conjunction with the release of the new iPad and iOS 5.1 in March 2012, the trio of apps were again updated by Apple to include some impressive new features.

> **TIP** Make sure you're running the most current version of Pages, Numbers, and Keynote (version 1.6 or later) on your iPad. To check for updates, launch the App Store app, and then tap the Updates button near the bottom-right corner of the screen. If new app updates are available, tap the Update All button (in the upper-right corner of the screen) or tap on the Free icon that appears next to the app listing on the Updates screen.

In addition to a newly designed menu structure which has been streamlined, giving you easier access to various commands and features within the three apps, the iWork for iPad apps now fully support the new iPad's Retina display, and they all allow for the creation and incorporation of colorful 3D bar, line, area, and pie charts into documents and files.

WHAT'S NEW IN PAGES

When you launch Pages, Numbers, and Keynote, the main Library screen showcases thumbnails of the documents or files stored within that app in much the
same way as it was in the previous versions of the apps (shown in Figure 10.1).

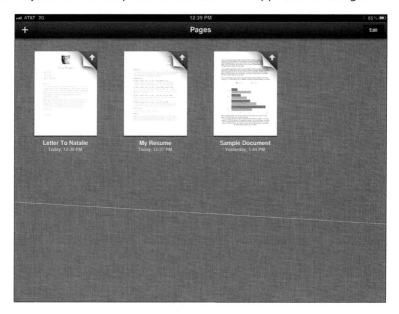

FIGURE 10.1

*The main Library screen of Pages. From here, you can manage, import, or export your document
files. Similar functionality is offered by Numbers and Keynote.*

From the Library screen, you can create a new document or file from scratch;
rename a document; or import a document or file manually by tapping on the
plus-sign icon. Or, you can tap on the Edit icon to select and then share (export),
copy, or delete a document or file from the app you're working with.

> **NOTE** When exporting a Pages, Numbers, or Keynote document or file from
> your iPad, you can keep it in its current format or export it in Word, Excel, or
> PowerPoint format (depending on which app you're using). All three apps also
> allow files to be exported as PDF files.

To open a document or file, tap on its thumbnail while viewing the Library screen.
When in the document-editing mode of Pages (shown in Figure 10.2), at the top
of the screen there are some new command icons. Near the top-left corner of the
screen is the Documents button, which returns you to the app's Library screen.

To the immediate right is the Undo icon. It enables you to undo your most recent actions within the app.

Displayed near the top-center of Pages' editing mode screen is the active document's filename. Near the top-right corner of the screen are three new command icons.

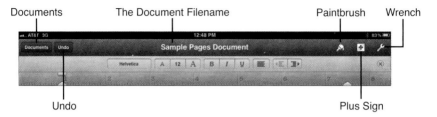

FIGURE 10.2
The main editing mode screen of Pages.

The paintbrush icon is context sensitive and adapts based on what type of content you're working within Pages. For example, if you're working with traditional text, tapping this icon reveals a pop-up window containing menu options for formatting text. Near the top of this window are three command tabs: Style, List, and Layout (shown in Figure 10.3).

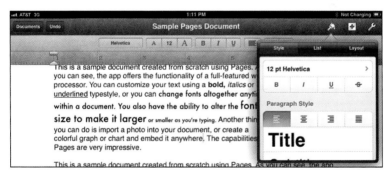

FIGURE 10.3
The Paintbrush command icon reveals a pop-up menu window with three command tabs.

When you tap on the Style tab, you can easily apply a font, type style (bold, italics, underlined, and so on), paragraph style, heading style, add a bulleted or numbered list to a document. You can also create a header and footer.

Upon tapping on the List tab, you can adjust tabs and indents and format a bulleted or numbered list. For example, you can control the size of the bullet or opt to use letters or numbers for creating an outline. Tap the Layout tab to create multiple columns within a document and control line spacing.

THE PLUS-SIGN ICON WITHIN PAGES

When you tap on the new plus-sign icon that's displayed near the top-right corner of the Pages' editing mode screen, a pop-up menu window displays with four command tabs along the top. Each command tab reveals separate submenu options.

Tap the Media tab to import a photo that's stored on your iPad into the document you're working on. Tap the Tables tab to create and format a table within the document. When you tap the Charts tab, two additional command tabs appear to enable you to create colorful 2D or 3D bar, line, area, or pie charts that can be fully customized. As you're looking at this menu, be sure to scroll up and down, as well as left and right, within the menu window in order to reveal all of your chart options.

Tap the Shapes tab to import and customize colorful shapes into your document. You can resize these shapes and place them over or under text, or you can make the text wrap around the shapes.

ACCESSING THE TOOLS MENU WITHIN PAGES

By tapping on the Tools icon, which is the wrench icon that's displayed near the top-right corner of the Pages app's editing screen, the Tools menu is revealed (shown in Figure 10.4).

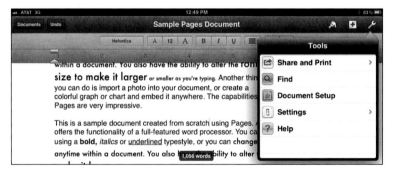

FIGURE 10.4

The Tools icon reveals a handful of submenu options for customizing documents in Pages. Similar functionality is offered when you access this menu in Numbers or Keynote.

The following options are available from the Tools menu:

■ **Share and Print:** Reveals a submenu that enables you to email a document from within Pages, print a document wirelessly to a printer that's set up to work with your iPad, or upload and share the document you're working on via iWork.com, iDisk, or WebDAV (which are cloud-based file-sharing services that the iWork for iPad apps are all compatible with, in addition to iCloud).

- **Find:** Enables you to search for any keyword or phrase within the document you're using. When the Search field appears, tap the gear icon to access the Find, Find and Replace, Match Case, and Whole Words features. Or, if multiple results are found for your search, tap the left- or right-pointing arrow keys to scroll through and display each result within the document.

- **Document Setup:** Enables you to adjust the margins of the document you're working with, including the header and footer. For example, from the Document Setup screen you can add and format page numbers or line breaks.

- **Settings:** Enables you to control the auto Spell Check feature built into Pages, as well as the Word Count feature. You can also turn on or off the Center Guides, Edge Guides, and Spacing Guides that can be displayed within a document. These guides are useful when sizing and placing photos, charts, or graphics into a document.

- **Help:** Accesses the interactive help feature that's built into each iWork for iPad app.

> **TIP** Many of the document formatting commands available under the Style command tab are also available within the main toolbar that's displayed near the top of the main Pages editing screen (just above the ruler). However, to save on-screen real estate, you can remove the toolbar and ruler by tapping the "X" icon that's displayed to the extreme right of the toolbar.

USING THE NEW DOCUMENT NAVIGATOR FEATURE

If you're working with a multipage document, you can easily scan thumbnails of the entire document thanks to the newly designed Document Navigator (shown in Figure 10.5). As you're viewing, creating, or editing a document, hold your finger on the right margin of the document. An oversized magnifying glass icon displays along with a vertical slider. Drag your finger up or down to scan the entire document.

> **TIP** Using the Document Navigator, you can scroll down within a document by dragging your finger. When you release your finger, you can continue viewing or editing the page you scrolled to in the document.

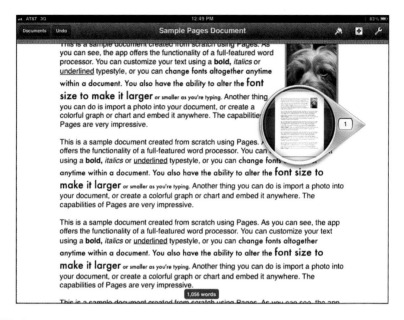

FIGURE 10.5

The Document Navigator feature is exclusive to the new version of Pages. It makes it easier to scroll through a long document to see thumbnails of each page or jump to a specific page within the document you're using.

WORKING IN FULL-SCREEN MODE

As you're proofreading a document, or if you're using an optional external keyboard for typing, position your iPad in portrait mode and take advantage of Pages' full-screen viewing mode to fully utilize the on-screen real estate to view your document (shown in Figure 10.6).

NOTE When typing using the iPad's virtual keyboard, the individual keys appear larger on the screen when the iPad is positioned in landscape mode. The larger keys make it easier to touch-type. However, less of your document can be displayed on the screen at any given time.

In full-screen mode, most of the formatting buttons, the on-screen ruler, and the virtual keyboard disappear, giving you almost the entire screen to see and read your document.

To remove the on-screen keyboard, tap the hide keyboard key on the virtual keyboard. It's the key located at the bottom-right corner of the keyboard.

FIGURE 10.6

When you position your iPad in a portrait position and use the full-screen viewing mode, you can see an entire page on the screen at once.

To remove the formatting bar and on-screen ruler from the screen, tap the circular X icon that's displayed on the right side of the toolbar.

Swipe your finger on the screen to scroll up, down, left, or right while in full-screen mode. Tap and hold your finger anywhere on the screen (within the document) for a second or two to exit out of full-screen mode.

WHAT'S NEW IN NUMBERS

Like Pages, the Numbers app has been updated to now fully utilize the new iPad's Retina display. However, the app continues to function perfectly on the iPad 2 and various iPhone and iPod touch models. Whereas Pages is for word processing, the Numbers app is used for organizing, analyzing, and crunching numbers and for creating powerful spreadsheets and beautifully rendered, full-color charts and tables that showcase numeric data graphically.

The latest version of Numbers offers the ability to create, display, and print customizable, 3D bar, line, area, and pie charts in full-color using spreadsheet data (as shown in Figure 10.7). Plus, when it comes to navigating your way around a complex spreadsheet, the app also now offers a series of highly intuitive sliders, steppers and pop-up menus that makes it easier to work with your numeric data on the tablet's screen.

FIGURE 10.7

Create 3D charts from spreadsheet data that look amazing on the new iPad's Retina display. Charts created in Numbers can be cut and pasted into Pages documents or Keynote presentations.

When it comes to performing complex mathematical calculations, Numbers has it covered. Built into the app is a calculations engine that can handle more than 250 different functions. When the numbers have been crunched, you can decide exactly how you want to view them in either a spreadsheet, table, or graphical form, and you can customize every aspect of the product you choose.

Like all the iWork for iPad apps, Numbers is fully AirPrint compatible. Before printing, however, you can see an on-screen preview of exactly what a spreadsheet, chart, table or graph will look like. Then, you can format the printed page with headers, footers, and page numbers.

If you're already familiar with the Pages app, the Numbers app (and the Keynote app) offer a very similar user interface and menu layout. Upon launching the Numbers app, you see the Library screen. From here, you can create a new spreadsheet from scratch, rename an existing spreadsheet, open a spreadsheet file that's stored on your tablet, or import a spreadsheet from iTunes, iDisk, or WebDAV. (Remember, iCloud file syncing can be automatic.)

By tapping the Edit icon on the Numbers' Library screen, you can select a file and then share (export) it via email, iWork.com, iTunes, iDisk, or WebDAV, copy the file (to make a duplicate of it with a different filename), or delete the file altogether from your iPad.

To open a spreadsheet file, tap on its thumbnail on the app's Library screen. Just like within the Pages app, as you're viewing, creating, or editing a spreadsheet within Numbers, you see a handful of command icons displayed along the top of the screen.

Located near the top-left corner of the screen is the Spreadsheets icon. Tap it to return to the Library screen within Numbers. Next to the Spreadsheets icon is the Undo icon. Tap on it to undo the last actions (or last several actions) you performed within the app.

Displayed near the top-right corner of the Numbers screen are three new command icons (which are similar to what's offered within Pages). These icons include the Formatting icon (which is shaped like a paintbrush), the plus-sign icon, and the Tools menu icon (which is shaped like a wrench).

THE FORMATTING ICON WITHIN NUMBERS

When you tap the Formatting icon, it reveals a pop-up menu window. However, the command tabs and menu options displayed within this window vary based on the type of data you currently have selected within the spreadsheet.

For example, if you have a headline or text highlighted, the command tabs that are displayed at the top of the menu window are Style, Text, and Arrange. Upon tapping on any of these command tabs, various formatting options are revealed. However, if you have a specific cell within a spreadsheet highlighted, the command tabs displayed are Table, Headers, Cells, and Format, and the command options relate to the number-crunching features of the app.

Likewise, if you have a chart or graph selected when you tap the Formatting icon, you see an entirely different selection of submenus, which you can use for creating and editing 2D or 3D charts and graphics.

THE PLUS-SIGN ICON WITHIN NUMBERS

When you want to import a photo or shape into your spreadsheet, or you want to create a table or chart from scratch, tap the plus-sign icon. The pop-up window that appears displays four command tabs at the top: Media, Tables, Charts, and Shapes. Each of these command tabs reveals a separate submenu. Tap the Chart tab (shown in Figure 10.8) to select a chart style and color scheme that you can fully customize.

FIGURE 10.8
The latest version of Numbers for the iPad 2 or new iPad enables you to choose between full-color 2D or 3D graphs.

ACCESSING THE TOOLS MENU WITHIN NUMBERS

The Tools menu includes a Share and Print submenu option, along with Find, Settings, and Help features. The menu layout and what's offered here is very similar to what's offered within Pages.

> **TIP** When you opt to create a document from scratch in Pages, a spreadsheet from scratch in Numbers, or a presentation from scratch in Keynote, the app gives you a selection of templates to choose from. Numbers, for example, offers 16 different templates, including Blank, Checklist, Loan Comparison, Budget, Mortgage Calculator, Expense Report, Invoice, Employee Schedule, and Auto Log. Each template, within each app, is fully customizable.

WHAT'S NEW IN KEYNOTE

When it comes to creating, viewing, and giving presentations on the iPad, one of the most powerful tools at your disposal is the Keynote app. Using Keynote, you can create a digital slide show, complete with animated slides and eye-catching transitions. Or, you can import and utilize presentations created on a PC or Mac using Microsoft PowerPoint.

> **TIP** To give presentations to groups, you might want to check out the Keynote Remote app ($0.99). It enables you to control a Keynote presentation on your Mac, iPad, iPhone, or iPod touch from another iPad, iPhone, or iPod touch in the room as long as both devices are connected to the same Wi-Fi network.

In addition to the revamped user interface offered by the latest version of Keynote, version 1.6 (or later) enables you to create, animate, and display visually impressive 3D bar, line, area, and pie charts within your presentations.

The new version of Keynote also includes a handful of new slide animations and animated slide transition effects. The functionality available from the Library screen of the app (when it's launched) is pretty much the same as in the previous version. You can create a new presentation from scratch; rename an existing presentation; import a presentation from iTunes, iDisk, or WebDAV; email a presentation; export a presentation to iTunes, iDisk, or WebDAV; copy a presentation and save it with a new filename; or delete a presentation from your iPad.

It's from the Library screen that you can also load an existing presentation in order to view or edit it. Tap any presentation thumbnail to load it from the iPad's internal storage into the app.

> **NOTE** Just as with Pages and Numbers, iCloud integration is built into Keynote. After you initially set it up, the integration works automatically, in the background, to make sure all of your presentation files are synchronized between your iPad, other iOS devices, and the Mac(s) that are linked to the same iCloud account.

After you begin creating or editing a Keynote presentation, the now familiar command icons from the other iWork for iPad apps are displayed along the top of the Keynote screen.

Tap the Presentations button to return to the Library screen of the app. Use the Undo button (displayed to the immediate right of the Presentations button) to undo the last action you took using the app. The presentation's filename that you're working with is displayed near the top-center of the screen.

Near the upper-right corner of the Keynote screen are four command icons, including the Formatting, Plus Sign, Tools, and Play icons. As you can see in Figure 10.9, the thumbnails for each slide in your presentation are displayed along the left margin of the screen while you're creating or editing slides.

FIGURE 10.9

You can change the order of slides by using your finger to drag their thumbnails (displayed along the left margin of the screen) up or down.

THE FORMATTING ICON WITHIN KEYNOTE

When you tap the Formatting icon (the paintbrush) within Keynote, you see three command tabs: Style, Text, and Arrange. Each reveals a separate submenu you use for formatting text within slides. For example, from the Style command tab, you can change the appearance of text, including font and background colors, borders, shadows, and other effects.

The Text command tab offers menu options for choosing a font, type size, type-style, and justification, among other things. Tap the Arrange tab to access the Move to Back/Front feature to create layers within a slide. You can also adjust text alignment, adjust spacing, or add multiple columns to a slide.

However, if a graphic or photo is selected within a slide, the paintbrush icon reveals the Style and Arrange tabs, which offer commands used for customizing the appearance of graphics and photos.

THE PLUS-SIGN ICON WITHIN KEYNOTE

Just like in the other iWork for iPad apps, tapping the plus-sign icon enables you to import photos or shapes into a slide, create or modify tables, or create 2D or 3D charts, depending on which command tab you tap.

ACCESSING THE TOOLS MENU WITHIN KEYNOTE

From the Tools menu within Keynote, you can access the Share and Print, Find, Help features (which are similar to the what's found in Pages and Numbers).

The Tools pop-up window also reveals a Transitions and Builds submenu you can use to add animations to individual slides or to establish slide transition effects for the presentation (as shown in Figure 10.10). There's also a Presenter Notes feature that enables you to compose and later view notes to yourself as you're giving the presentation.

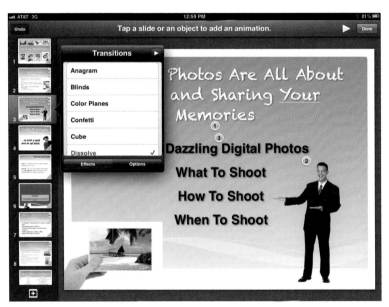

FIGURE 10.10

The latest version of Keynote includes new slide animations and transitions, such as Iris, Shimmer, Wipe, Flame, Perspective, Swing, Object Push, Object Zoom, and Face Through Color. Each looks spectacular when viewed on the new iPad's Retina display, but the features also work with the iPad 2.

The Advanced menu option enables you to automatically number each slide in the presentation, add on-screen guidelines when formatting your slides, incorporate interactive hyperlinks into slides, set up a presentation type, turn on and off the Loop presentation or self-playing features, and turn on or off the Enable Remotes feature (also used when giving a presentation).

THE PLAY ICON WITHIN KEYNOTE

The Play icon (the right-pointing arrow) is used to transition the Keynote app from the slide creation and edit mode to the app's presentation mode. Tap it to display your presentation in full-screen mode. You can use the iPad's AirPlay feature (or optional cables) to showcase the presentation on an HD television, monitor, or LCD projector.

USING THE iWORK FOR iPAD APPS WITH iCLOUD

After you set up a free iCloud account (see Chapter 9, "Syncing Your iPad via iTunes or iCloud"), you can set up Pages, Numbers, and Keynote to automatically sync documents and files with your other Mac and iOS devices via iCloud.

For each of the iWork for iPad apps, the iCloud functionality needs to be set up separately. However, after you've set it up, as long as your iPad has access to the Internet changes you make to a document or file are reflected almost instantly on your Mac and other iOS devices.

Most other apps that are compatible with iCloud have a manual sync feature. Pages, Numbers, and Keynote are among the very few apps that offer automatic iCloud integration and file synchronization that works behind the scenes.

To set up Pages, Numbers, and Keynote on your iPad to work with iCloud, follow these steps:

1. After installing Pages, Numbers, and Keynote onto your iPad, launch the Settings app from the tablet's Home Screen.

2. From the main Settings menu, tap the iCloud option.

3. At the top of the iCloud screen, turn on iCloud functionality and enter your Apple ID and password.

4. Also on the iCloud screen within Settings, tap the Documents & Data option.

5. When the Documents & Data screen is displayed, tap the virtual switch associated with Documents & Data to turn it on (as shown in Figure 10.11). If you want your iPad to automatically sync your iWork for iPad documents and files using a 3G or 4G cellular network (as opposed to Wi-Fi), which utilizes some of your monthly wireless data allocation, turn on the virtual switch that's associated with the Use Cellular option. Otherwise, to only sync files and data when your iPad is connected to the Internet using a Wi-Fi connection, leave the Use Cellular option in the default off position. (This applies only to iPads capable of accessing a 3G or 4G data network.)

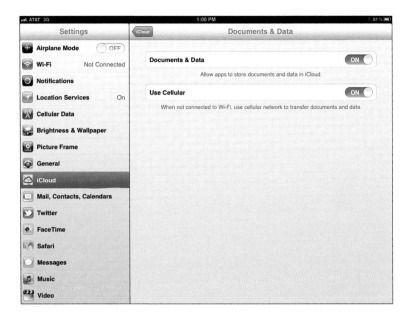

FIGURE 10.11

For iCloud file syncing to work with Pages, Numbers, and Keynote, the iCloud feature needs to be turned on from within Settings.

6. If you have Pages installed on your iPad, on the left side of the Settings screen, scroll down within the Settings menu to the Pages option and tap it.

7. When the Pages screen appears within Settings (shown in Figure 10.12), tap the virtual switch that's associated with the Use iCloud feature to turn on the auto file syncing feature with iCloud that kicks in each time the Pages app is launched. Repeat steps 6 and 7 for the Numbers and Keynote apps, if applicable.

8. Repeat this process on each of your other iOS devices that you have Pages, Numbers, and Keynote installed on, including your iPhone and your iPod touch.

9. On your Mac, launch System Preferences.

10. From the System Preferences menu, click the iCloud icon (displayed under the Internet & Wireless heading).

11. When the iCloud window appears, make sure you sign into iCloud using the same account username and password as you used on your iPad (and other iOS devices).

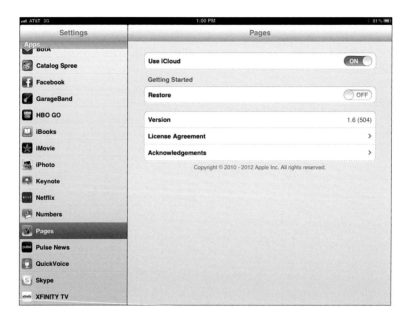

FIGURE 10.12

In addition to turning on the Documents & Data feature from the iCloud menu screen within Settings, you also need to turn on the iCloud feature for Pages, Numbers, or Keynote separately.

12. On the right side of the iCloud window (on your Mac), add a check mark to the checkbox associated with the Documents & Data option.

13. Within the Pages, Numbers, and Keynote software running on your Mac, turn on the iCloud functionality for each program.

When you begin experiencing the word processing capabilities of Pages, the number-crunching functionality of Numbers, and the digital-slide creation and viewing tools offered by Keynote on your iPad, and combine these capabilities with your iPad's 10-hour battery life and other functionality, you'll see why so many businesspeople are incorporating the iPad into their daily work lives instead of using laptop computers or netbooks.

IN THIS CHAPTER

■ Apps that enable you to view, create, edit, print, and share Microsoft Office–compatible documents and files that can be shared with a PC or Mac

■ Remotely access files on your PC or Mac from your iPad

11

THIRD-PARTY APPS THAT OFFER MICROSOFT OFFICE COMPATIBILITY TO iPAD

One of the key features that enables many business people to use their iPads as a powerful tool in their everyday work lives is the ability to view, create, edit, print, and share Microsoft Office documents and files on their iPads. This includes using the iPad to access documents and files created on a PC or Mac using Microsoft Word, Microsoft Excel, and Microsoft PowerPoint, and sharing documents and files created from scratch on the tablet with a PC or Mac.

The most popular apps for achieving Word, Excel and PowerPoint compatibility are the iWork collection of iPad apps from Apple—including Pages, Numbers, and Keynote (available for $9.99 each from the App Store). These three apps (refer to Chapter 10, "Working with Pages, Numbers, and

Keynote") enable iPad users to import and export Microsoft Office files so those files can be viewed, edited, printed, and shared using the iPad. The iWork apps also allow documents and files to be exported in the popular PDF file format.

> **NOTE** The iWork apps for iPad are also fully compatible with the Pages, Numbers, and Keynote apps for the Mac (sold separately from the Mac App Store). These three apps on a Mac are also used for word processing, spreadsheet management, and digital slide presentations, respectively.

As you'll discover from this chapter, in addition to the iWork apps for iPad, there are a handful of third-party apps, including Documents To Go and Quickoffice that offer Microsoft Office document and file compatibility as well as file-sharing options and other features that are not offered by the iWork apps.

In addition, when an iPad is connected to the Internet, there are third-party apps that enable you to easily connect to and take control of your PC or Mac computer and actually run software remotely from it. So, while you're on the go, you can use your iPad to control Microsoft Word on your desktop computer and see everything from your tablet's screen. Thus, file compatibility is no longer an issue, and you have full access to all of the Microsoft Office features and functions you need because you're actually controlling the Microsoft Office software from your iPad.

> **NOTE** Microsoft Corporation is believed to be working on an iPad edition of Microsoft Office, which will offer full compatibility with Word, PowerPoint, and Excel running on a PC or Mac. Currently available from the App Store is an iPad edition of Microsoft OneNote for iPad (free) and Microsoft Lync 2010 for iPad (free). OneNote is a powerful note-taking tool that is compatible with the PC and Mac versions of the software. Lync is a tool for communicating with co-workers or groups via the Web. Meanwhile, the free Microsoft SkyDrive app gives your iOS device access to Microsoft's cloud-based file-sharing service.
>
> To determine whether a Microsoft Office app (or suite of apps) has yet been released for the iPad, visit the App Store, and enter "Microsoft Office" in the Search field.

WORKING WITH MICROSOFT OFFICE DOCUMENTS AND FILES USING THE DOCUMENTS TO GO APP

The Documents To Go Premium – Office Suite app ($16.99) from DataViz, Inc. (www.dataviz.com) offers document and file compatibility with Microsoft Office. This single app offers the same core functionality and features you'd get using

Microsoft Office on a desktop or laptop computer, but it's designed for the iPad. This includes the ability to create, view, edit, print, and share Word, Excel, and PowerPoint documents and files.

This app also makes it easy to share (import/export) Office-compatible documents and files via email or one of several popular cloud-based file sharing services, including Google Docs and Dropbox. Documents To Go Premium – Office Suite comes with free software for a PC or Mac to make file syncing and transfers within a wireless network easy.

Documents To Go Premium – Office Suite has a unique user interface and menu layout. In other words, the available editing and formatting tools are similar to what's available from Microsoft Office running on a PC or Mac, but the app's menu structure and layout is vastly different. The app supports Office 2007, 2008, and 2010 version files and documents.

Documents To Go Premium – Office Suite also offers the proprietary "InTact Technology" feature, which helps automatically compensate for formatting incompatibility (font or type style incompatibility) when a file or document is transferred from a computer to an iPad (or from an iPad to a computer).

There are several versions of the Documents To Go app in the App Store. Only the Documents To Go Premium – Office Suite edition enables you to create, edit, and view Word, Excel, PowerPoint, and PDF documents and files as well as utilize a handful of cloud-based file sharing services. The less-expensive version of the app does not allow you to edit or create PowerPoint-compatible files, for example, and it also has other limitations. Both versions, however, are compatible with Apple's iWork software.

CAUTION Whether you're using the iWork apps, Documents To Go, Quickoffice, or another app to create or edit Microsoft Office files and documents, unless your iPad has the same library of fonts as your primary computer, you might discover minor font-compatibility issues as you're working.

Likewise, you might discover page-formatting issues or incompatibility with PowerPoint slide transitions and animations when you're using an iPad and attempting to work with files created on a PC or Mac (or you transfer an iPad-created file or document to a PC or Mac).

The Office-compatible app you're using often automatically compensates for minor compatibility issues. However, be sure to review documents or files carefully to make sure they've been handled correctly by the app.

For example, after transferring a PowerPoint presentation to your iPad, review it carefully yourself before presenting it to an audience. When you import or export

PDF files created from Office documents or files, all formatting and fonts are preserved perfectly, but your ability to edit the document or file in PDF format is limited based on which PDF reader app you're using. (You learn more about the PDFpen app for editing and annotating PDF files, for example, in Chapter 13, "Discovering 'Must-Have' Business Apps.")

WORKING WITH MICROSOFT OFFICE DOCUMENTS AND FILES USING THE QUICKOFFICE APP

The Quickoffice Pro HD app ($19.99) from Quickoffice, Inc. (www.quickoffice.com/ quickoffice_pro_hd_ipad) offers a comprehensive file and document creation and editing tool that is compatible with Word, Excel, and PowerPoint as well as a handful of cloud-based file sharing services and online-based software tools, such as Google Docs.

Using this app, you can import, view, edit, print, or share Microsoft Office–compatible files and documents with ease. You can also create documents or files from scratch on your tablet and then share them with other computers or mobile devices that are running Microsoft Office software.

Quickoffice Pro HD is one app with several distinct modules, used for word processing, managing spreadsheet, and working with digital slide presentations. The word processing module, however, is compatible with Microsoft Word (.doc and .docx) files, and the spreadsheet module is compatible with Excel (.xls and .xlsx) files. The digital slide presentation tools built into the app are compatible with PowerPoint (.ppt and .pptx) files.

All three Quickoffice Pro HD modules can export files or documents into PDF format, and all offer AirPrint wireless printing capabilities. You can also use the app as a PDF file viewer.

When it comes to creating or editing Microsoft Office–compatible files and documents, the Quickoffice Pro HD app offers robust formatting tools that enable you to easily control fonts, type styles, page and paragraph formatting, and other elements of a file or document. The app also works nicely when the iPad is in either portrait or landscape mode, and it supports a variety of iOS features, such as select, copy, cut, and paste.

When using Quickoffice Pro HD on an iPad, you'll discover that the app offers many of the same features and functions built in to Microsoft Office, but the user interface and menu layout of the app are vastly different from what running Microsoft Office software on a laptop or desktop computer looks like. However, once you get used to working with Quickoffice Pro HD, you'll find that it offers the features and functionality you need to get work done while on the go, yet still be able to maintain file compatibility with other Windows PC or Mac OS X Microsoft Office users.

Like its competitors, Quickoffice enables you to import or export documents and files via email or sync documents and files using a handful of cloud-based file sharing services, including Evernote, Dropbox, Google Docs, Huddle, SugarSync, Egnyte, and Catch. You can also publish content to Facebook, Twitter, LinkedIn, and other online social networking sites directly from the app.

> **TIP** Beyond Documents To Go and Quickoffice, there are a handful of other third-party apps available from the App Store, such as Smart Office ($9.99), that offer Microsoft Office compatibility. To find these apps, visit the App Store and search for "Microsoft Office."
>
> One difference between these apps is how you can share documents and files with other computers or users. All the apps enable you to email documents and files (or receive documents and files via email), but each works with a different selection of cloud-based file sharing services. They are not all compatible with iCloud, Dropbox (www.dropbox.com), or Microsoft's SkyDrive (http://explore.live.com/skydrive-mobile), for example.
>
> Be sure to choose a solution that not only allows you to create and/or edit the Microsoft Office–compatible documents and files you need, but also choose one that meets your needs in terms of wireless file syncing and sharing with your primary computer and your co-workers.

ACCESSING YOUR PRIMARY COMPUTER REMOTELY WITH YOUR iPAD

When you use Apple's iWork apps or a third-party app to view, create, edit, print, or share Word, Excel, PowerPoint, and PDF files and documents, you have to worry about minor font and formatting compatibility issues. You also need to successfully sync or transfer files and documents between your computer and tablet.

If your iPad has continuous Internet access, another option for working with truly compatible Microsoft Office files and documents is to utilize a remote desktop app, which enables you to wirelessly access and control your PC or Mac directly from your tablet via the Internet or a wireless network.

After establishing a remote connection between your iPad and PC or Mac, whatever would be seen on your computer's monitor is displayed in almost real-time on your tablet's screen.

Figure 11.1 shows an iPad remotely running Microsoft Word on a Mac using the Splashtop app. On the Mac, the free Splashtop Streamer software is running simultaneously so there is a secure connection between the computer and tablet.

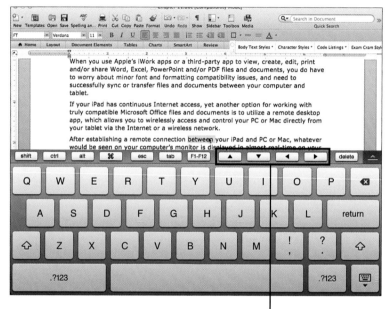

Directional Arrow (Navigation) Keys

FIGURE 11.1

Splashtop is one of the least expensive, yet easiest remote desktop apps available for the iPad.

One nice feature of Splashtop is that when the iPad's virtual keyboard is being used, directional arrow keys are available just above the keyboard to make navigating within a document faster and more precise. Additional navigational arrow buttons can also be displayed on the screen without the iPad's virtual keyboard (as shown in Figure 11.2).

Thus, you can run software (including Word, Excel, or PowerPoint) on your computer, but view what's happening on your iPad's screen from almost any remote location.

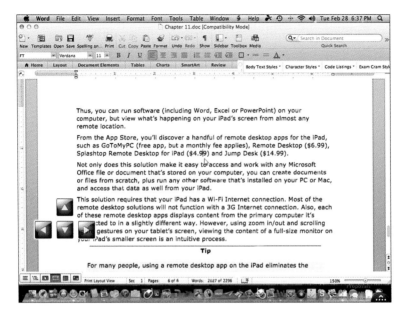

FIGURE 11.2

Using Splashtop, directional navigation arrows can be displayed above the virtual keyboard or separately from the keyboard.

> **TIP** For many people, using a remote desktop app on the iPad eliminates the need to travel with a notebook or netbook computer because their iPad can meet their mobile computing needs.

In the App Store, you can find a handful of remote desktop apps for the iPad, such as GoToMyPC (a free app, but there's a monthly fee), Remote Desktop ($6.99), Splashtop Remote Desktop for iPad ($4.99), and Jump Desk ($14.99).

Not only does solution remote desktop app make it easy to use your iPad to access and work with any Microsoft Office file or document that's stored on your computer, you can create documents or files from scratch, run any other software that's installed on your PC or Mac, and access data that's stored on your other computer.

This solution requires that your iPad has a Wi-Fi Internet connection. Most of the remote desktop solutions do not function with a 3G Internet connection. Also, each of these remote desktop apps displays content from the primary computer it's connected to in a slightly different way. However, viewing the content of a full-size monitor on your iPad's smaller screen is an intuitive process.

NOTE   When you install a remote desktop app on your iPad, additional software (supplied for free) must also be installed and run on your PC or Mac whenever you want a secure connection to be made between your computer and tablet. Plus, for this solution to work, your primary computer must be left turned on while you're away. After the remote desktop software is set up (a process that takes just minutes), taking control over your PC or Mac from your iPad is an easy process that enables you to access documents, files, and data, plus run software on your computer with very little lag time.

12

CONDUCTING VIDEO CONFERENCES AND VIRTUAL MEETINGS

Although the iPad isn't designed to work as a cell phone, when it's connected to the Internet, you can use the iPad as a Voice-Over-IP (VoIP) telephone or speakerphone when you use a third-party app, such as Skype or Line2 (see Chapter 13, "Discovering 'Must-Have' Business Apps," for more information on these apps, which enable you to make and receive free or low-cost calls from your tablet).

Thanks to the tablet's built-in camera, microphone, and speaker, you can also use the iPad as a video-conferencing tool when an Internet connection is available. The FaceTime app that came preinstalled on your iPad 2 or new iPad is designed specifically for video conferencing (for free) with other Mac, iPad, iPhone, and iPod touch users.

> **TIP** Mac users can download the FaceTime software ($.99) from the online-based Mac App Store. It comes preinstalled on all Apple iOS devices with both front- and rear-facing cameras built-in, including the more recent iPad, iPhone, and iPod touch models. Using the FaceTime service is free of charge for unlimited use.

To easily video conference with PCs, Macs, or other web-enabled mobile devices, the Skype app offers an easy alternative that's also free, unless you utilize the service's premium features.

You can also use your tablet for video conferencing and to attend virtual meetings using GoToMeeting or WebEx, for example, when you download apps that enable you to connect to these fee-based services from the App Store.

> **NOTE** In some cases, it's possible to participate in video conferences using a 3G or 4G Internet connection. However, to experience the highest quality video and the clearest possible connections without quickly using up your monthly wireless data allocation, you should use a Wi-Fi Internet connection. In fact, a Wi-Fi connection is required for using certain services, such as FaceTime.

> **NOTE** Another way to communicate with fellow Mac and iOS device users is via text messaging or Instant Messaging using Apple's newly enhanced iMessage service and the Messages app on your iPad. You find out how to use this text messaging app later in this chapter. Instead of using a cellular network for text messaging (from your cell phone), the Messages app on your iPad uses Apple's own, Internet-based iMessage text messaging/instant messaging service.

USING FACETIME FOR VIDEO CONFERENCING

The first time you launch the FaceTime app, you need to set up a free Apple ID account or enter your existing Apple ID username and password. You are also asked to enter an email address that will be associated with your FaceTime account.

Either your Apple ID or the email address you provide becomes your unique FaceTime identifier (which acts just like a phone number), so others can initiate connections with you when you both have FaceTime running on your devices.

When you want to call another FaceTime user, you must know the other person's email address (the one associated with his or her FaceTime account) or iPhone phone number.

After you complete the initial FaceTime set-up process (it takes less than a minute), as long as you have FaceTime running on your tablet and it's connected to the Internet through a Wi-Fi connection, you are able to initiate or receive calls and participate in video conferences.

> **NOTE** Users of FaceTime on an iPad 2 or new iPad, iPod touch, or Mac utilize an Apple ID or email address as their identifier when making connections using the FaceTime app or software. However, if you're making contact with an iPhone 4/4s user via FaceTime, use the iPhone's mobile phone number.

After your iPad is connected to a Wi-Fi network, launch the FaceTime app. As soon as it's launched, the tablet's front-facing camera turns on automatically, and you should see yourself on the iPad's screen.

On the right side of the screen is a window requesting that you sign in with your Apple ID username and password (shown in Figure 12.1). Enter this information and then tap the Sign In button.

FIGURE 12.1
Use your Apple ID to log into the FaceTime service.

You're now ready to initiate or receive FaceTime calls and participate in a video conference via the Web. Displayed near the lower-right corner of this app screen are three buttons: Favorites, Recents, and Contacts (see Figure 12.2).

FIGURE 12.2

When FaceTime is running on your iPad, you see three buttons near the lower-right corner of the screen.

CREATING A FACETIME FAVORITES LIST

A Favorites list within FaceTime is a list you can customize to include the people with whom you plan to FaceTime video conference the most. In essence, this Favorites option serves as a one-touch speed dial list.

To add a contact, tap the plus sign in the upper-right corner of the Favorites window and then select people from your established contacts database.

In the Contacts entry for each person, if the person is an iPhone 4/4s user, be sure to associate the mobile phone number with the iPhone label rather than the Mobile phone label. Doing so helps the FaceTime app easily identify and connect with that person.

USING FACETIME'S AUTOMATIC RECENTS LIST

When you tap the Recents icon while using FaceTime, you see a list of people with whom you've already communicated using FaceTime. Tap any of the contacts in this list to video conference again with that person.

If this is the first time you're using the FaceTime app, this window is empty except for the All and Missed tabs displayed at the top of the window.

After you begin using the app, the All tab displays all FaceTime video conferences you've participated in, as well as any incoming missed calls. Tap the Missed tab to see a list of only the incoming FaceTime calls you didn't answer.

CHOOSING PREFERRED FACETIME CONTACTS

The Contacts icon that's displayed near the lower-right corner of the FaceTime screen enables you to select any person listed in your Contacts database to call using this app.

To initiate a call with someone who also has FaceTime installed and operating on their computer or iOS mobile device, select that person from your Contacts list and tap on the email address or iPhone phone number that was used to register with

FaceTime. If a connection can be made, a FaceTime icon automatically appears next to the person's name within the FaceTime app.

When you initiate a call, at the bottom center of the screen, the FaceTime With message and the person's name are displayed. Next to this label is the End button, which you can tap at any time to terminate the connection (see Figure 12.3).

FIGURE 12.3

As soon as you tap someone's name to call from within FaceTime, the app attempts to initiate a video conference connection with that person.

PARTICIPATING IN A FACETIME CALL

If the person you're calling with the FaceTime app answers, your own image that was displayed in full-screen mode on the tablet's screen shrinks. It is now displayed in the upper-left corner of the screen. The rest of the iPad's screen displays the person you're connected with using FaceTime (as shown in Figure 12.4).

> **NOTE**   If you initiate a FaceTime call but the person you're calling does not answer, after a minute or so, you see the "FaceTime Unavailable. [Insert Name] is not available for FaceTime." message.

FIGURE 12.4

When you're participating in a video conference with someone using FaceTime, this is what your tablet's screen looks like.

As you participate in a video conference, notice that near the bottom of the FaceTime screen are three command buttons: Mute, End Call, and Switch Camera. Use them for the following purposes:

■ Tap the Mute button to continue the video connection, but mute the iPad's built-in microphone so the person you're communicating with is able to see you but not hear you.

■ Tap the End Call button to terminate the FaceTime connection and promptly end the call.

■ Tap the Switch Camera button to alternate between the two cameras built in to your iPad. The front-facing camera is facing toward you, whereas the camera on the back of the iPad shows off whatever it's pointing at.

The FaceTime app is pretty simple to use, and it is a powerful tool for video conferencing. The best thing about using FaceTime is that it's free, and you can communicate with anyone in the world that also uses the FaceTime app or software.

In other words, you never have to pay long-distance phone charges, international calling fees, or cell phone roaming charges when using FaceTime. Nor do you have to worry about using up your cell phone minutes or your monthly 3G/4G wireless data usage allocation. And, the biggest benefit to using FaceTime is that you can actually see *and* hear the person you're communicating with.

PARTICIPATING IN VIRTUAL MEETINGS FROM ANYWHERE

If your company uses fee-based virtual meeting software, such as GoToMeeting or WebEx, there are apps that enable you to participate in these meetings using your iPad from anywhere an Internet connection is available (such as from your home, hotel room, poolside at a resort, or from a client's office.)

Web conferences or virtual meetings involve using the Internet to connect people at different locations, enabling them to talk while simultaneously sharing information on their computer screens in real time. This capability has changed the way many companies do business.

GOTOMEETING OFFERS VIRTUAL MEETING CAPABILITIES

One of the pioneers in the virtual meeting field is Citrix Systems, Inc., with its GoToMeeting software for PCs and Macs. For iPad users, a free iPad app that enables people to attend online-based virtual meetings that are hosted by others using GoToMeeting or GoToWebinar is available from the App Store.

> TIP   The host of a virtual meeting that utilizes GoToMeeting or GoToWebinar pays a flat monthly fee, starting at $49.00 per month, to host an unlimited number of meetings with up to 15 attendees each. You cannot host virtual meetings from an iPad, but you can attend them.

Attendees using a PC or Mac to participate in a meeting can utilize audio conferencing via Voice-Over-IP service, using their computer's microphone and speakers, while simultaneously being able to view whatever the meeting host is showcasing on his computer screen, such as a PowerPoint presentation or a spreadsheet report. People can also collaborate on Word documents, for example.

Thanks to the GoToMeeting app for iPad (shown in Figure 12.5), tablet users can do everything a meeting attendee using a PC or Mac can do, such as see who is presenting, who's talking at any given moment, and who else is attending the meeting.

Using the GoToMeeting app, meeting attendees can also view exactly what is on the presenter's screen, and simultaneously join a voice conversation via a VoIP connection (using the iPad's built-in microphone and speaker or a headset that's connected to the tablet).

FIGURE 12.5

When attending a virtual meeting on a iPad using GoToMeeting, you can see and hear other participants, plus share what's displayed on the host's computer screen.

The GoToMeeting app was designed to utilize some of the tablet's key features, such as its touch-screen interface, so you can zoom in on content being showcased during a meeting.

If you're a mobile executive who wants or needs to "attend" meetings or webinars from a location outside your office, this app is ideal. When you're invited to a virtual meeting via email, from the iPad simply tap the link embedded within the invitation email to connect to a meeting and automatically launch the GoToMeeting app. From within the app you can manually enter a meeting ID and your username to be connected to a meeting within seconds.

> **TIP** To view a free demo showcasing how GoToMeeting works on an iPad, visit www.gotomeeting.com/iPad.

ANOTHER VIRTUAL MEETING OPTION: THE WEBEX PLATFORM

In addition to utilizing Citrix's GoToMeeting software and iPad app, similar functionality is provided by Cisco Systems, via its popular WebEx virtual meeting solution (www.webex.com).

For businesses, consultants, or entrepreneurs who already use WebEx to host meetings, the company offers a free iPad app that enables people to attend virtual meetings from their Apple mobile devices. Users connect via a Wi-Fi hotspot or through a 3G/4G web connection.

> **CAUTION** Participating in a virtual meeting requires a significant amount of wireless data usage, and it quickly depletes your monthly 3G or 4G wireless data allocation. To avoid surcharges for additional wireless data usage, consider using a free and unlimited Wi-Fi connection to participate in virtual meetings using the GoToMeeting or WebEx app.

To schedule and host a meeting using Cisco's WebEx, the host must be using the WebEx software from a Mac or PC and be a paid subscriber to the service. Pricing starts at $49.00 per month to host an unlimited number of meetings that can be attended by up to 25 people. A free 14-day trial of the service (for hosting purposes) is available.

Attending meetings, however, is free and does not require a WebEx membership (but the free WebEx software for the PC, Mac, iPhone, or iPad is required). You can download WebEx for iPad free from the App Store.

MAKING AND RECEIVING PHONE CALLS OR VIDEO CONFERENCING WITH SKYPE

Skype is a VoIP phone service that enables you to make and receive phone calls over the Web (as opposed to a cellular phone network or traditional telephone landline). When used with an iPad or a smartphone or computer with a built-in camera, it also allows for free video conferencing using a 3G, 4G, or Wi-Fi Internet connection.

In addition to being a powerful and cost-effective communications tool for PC and Mac users, thanks to the Skype for iPad app, the service is fully functional on the iPad 2 or new iPad for both VoIP phone calls and video conferencing.

The Skype app uses your iPad's built-in microphone, speaker (or headphone jack), and camera(s) to enable you to hear and be heard during calls, and be heard and seen during video conferences.

Making unlimited Skype-to-Skype calls is always free. However, there is a very low per-minute fee to make calls to a landline or cellular telephone from your iPad using Skype (shown in Figure 12.6). This per-minute fee is typically only pennies per minute, even if you're traveling overseas and make a call to the United States. You can also save a fortune on international calling from the U.S. when making calls to any other country.

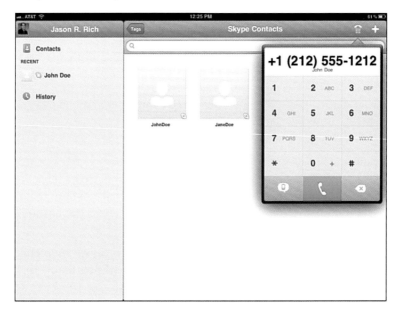

FIGURE 12.6

You can make and receive voice calls using the Skype for iPad app, or use it for video conferencing.

The video-conferencing functionality of Skype is similar to using FaceTime, but it is compatible with Skype software or apps running on any other devices, including PCs, Macs, and mobile devices (including smartphones and tablets from many different manufacturers).

Through Skype, you can obtain your own unique telephone number (for an additional fee of $6.00 per month), which comes with call forwarding, voice mail, and other calling features.

With your own phone number you can manage incoming calls whether or not Skype is activated and your iPad is connected to the Web. You can also receive calls on your iPad from people calling from a landline who do not use Skype.

Thus, people are able to reach you inexpensively by dialing a local phone number regardless of where you're traveling. However, you can initiate calls (and receive calls from fellow Skype users) without paying for a unique local phone number.

When traveling abroad, making and receiving calls on a cell phone (such as an iPhone) costs anywhere from $.50 to $3.00 per minute because international roaming fees apply. With Skype, that same call costs just a little more than $.02 per minute. Alternatively, you can pay a flat fee of less than $20.00 per month to make and receive unlimited domestic and international calls from your iPad.

In terms of call quality, as long as you're within a 3G/4G coverage area or Wi-Fi hotspot and your iPad has a strong Web connection, calls are crystal clear. The Skype app is easy to use, and it enables you to maintain a contact list of frequently called people, dial out using a familiar telephone touchpad display, and maintain a detailed call history that lists incoming, outgoing, and missed calls.

If you opt to establish a paid Skype account (to have your own unique phone number and be able to make non-Skype-to-Skype calls), setting up the account takes just minutes when you visit www.Skype.com. All charges are billed to a major credit card or debit card.

SENDING AND RECEIVING TEXT MESSAGES WITH iMESSAGE

If you use a cell phone or smartphone, such as the iPhone 4/4s, you're probably familiar with the concept of text messaging. Through your cell phone service provider, you can use your phone to send a private text message to a recipient's phone. This text message can include a photo, short video clip, or another data attachment. Within a second or two after sending your text message, the recipient receives the message and can reply to it, which enables you to conduct a text-based conversation.

The primary drawback to text messaging via your cell phone is that your cell phone service provider typically charges extra for this feature, and/or allows only a predetermined number of text messages to be sent or received as part of your service plan per month.

Apple's iMessage service allows any Mac or iOS device that's connected to the Web to send and receive unlimited text messages (or instant massages) using the free Messages app that comes preinstalled on all iPads running iOS 5.1 or later. Messages software for the Mac is currently freely available from the Apple website, and as of summer 2012 it is preinstalled as part of the OS X Mountain Lion operating system for Mac.

iMessage has some pros and cons. On the plus side, this is a totally free service. You can send and receive as many text messages or instant messages as you want. On the negative side, this service only works with other Mac and iOS devices.

Like any text messaging app, Messages for use with Apple's iMessage service, enables you to participate in multiple text message "conversations" simultaneously, but each one is kept separate. As you participate in a text-based dialogue, the text messages you send are displayed in a different color than the messages you receive from the recipient, so tracking the progression of a dialogue is easy.

To initiate an iMessage conversation or receive text messages, you must associate an email address with your free iMessage account. This email address serves as your unique identifier (like a phone number). You can use your Apple ID or any other existing email address. The email address you plan to use must be added to the Receive At option within the Messages screen of the Settings app.

When you launch the Messages app you can compose a new outgoing text message or respond to an incoming message using the iPad's virtual keyboard. To create and send a new text message, fill in the To field in the New Message window (see Figure 12.7).

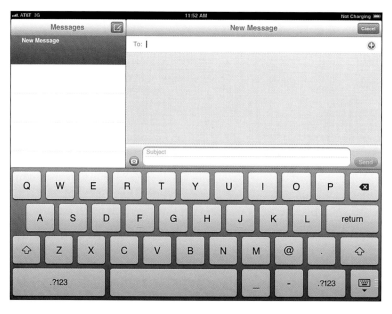

FIGURE 12.7

To create a new text message, begin by filling in the To field of the New Message window. (Shown here on an iPad 2.)

TIP   On the new iPad, you can use the Dictation feature to compose an outgoing message instead of typing it on the virtual keyboard. To do this, tap the Dictate button displayed on the virtual keyboard and begin speaking when prompted.

In the To field, you can manually enter the email address that the recipient has associated with his iMessage account. Alternatively, you can select this information from your Contacts database by typing the recipient's name in the To field, and then selecting the appropriate email address from the Contacts listing.

NOTE   If you're sending a message to an iPhone user, use her iPhone's phone number in the To field of your message.

To manually search your Contacts database, tap the blue-and-white plus sign that's located to the right of the To field. After filling in the To field, you have the option of tapping the empty Subject window and filling it in, or you can simply compose your text-based message in the appropriate field.

To attach a digital photo or short movie clip to the outgoing text message, tap the camera icon to the left of the Subject window and select the Take Photo or Video option or the Choose Existing option.

If you select Take Photo or Video, the iPad's Camera app launches. If you select the Choose Existing option, the Photos app launches, and you can choose a digital photo or video clip that's stored on your iPad.

After composing your message, tap the blue-and-white Send icon to send the message via the Internet to its intended recipient.

NOTE   To use the Messages app to send and receive text messages via Apple's iMessage service, your iPad must have access to the Internet via a Wi-Fi or 3G/4G connection.

If you're a Mac, iPad, or iPhone user, as long as the Messages app on each computer and device is initially set up with the same iMessage account information, you can begin a conversation on one computer or device, but switch to another, and pick up exactly where you left off.

When the recipient of your message responds, her incoming message is displayed in the window on the right side of the screen if her conversation is open. Otherwise, an incoming message alert displays on the left side of the screen (as well as within the Notification Center window). You can tap each conversation listed on the left side of the screen, one at a time, to read incoming messages from different people and respond to them.

If you send a message to someone who isn't currently online, the message is received when he again accesses his Messages app or uses his iOS device to access the Web. Likewise, when you turn on your iPad and reconnect it to the Web, your missed incoming messages are displayed in the Notification Center window and on the left side of the Messages app screen when you re-launch the app.

13

DISCOVERING "MUST-HAVE" BUSINESS APPS

Right out of the box, the iPad is a powerful tool that includes a handful of useful, preinstalled apps. However, by finding, purchasing, and installing third-party apps, you can truly customize the tablet. You can also add a range of additional functionality to the mobile device.

This chapter showcases a small handful of general business-related apps and describes some special-interest apps that can save you time and money, boost your productivity, and enhance your organization when traveling, participating in meetings, or juggling the many tasks and responsibilities you handle throughout your day.

> **TIP**   The apps featured here have general appeal among business profession-
> als, salespeople, freelancers, and consultants, but this is just a small sampling
> of the apps available from the App Store in the Business, Finance, Productivity,
> Reference, and Social Networking categories.
>
> Even if some of the apps described in this chapter are not directly relevant to your
> needs, they might help you understand the many different ways you can use your
> tablet for handling tasks you might not have realized were possible.

To find any of the apps described in this chapter, launch the App Store app on your
tablet and then enter the app's title in the Search field that's displayed near the
upper-right corner of the screen (see Figure 13.1).

FIGURE 13.1

Use the Search field within the App Store to find specific apps based on their title or a keyword.

After entering the app's title, tap the Search key on the virtual keyboard and then
tap the search result that matches the specific app you're looking for (shown in
Figure 13.2). A detailed Description screen for the app displays. You can then purchase, download, and install the app.

FIGURE 13.2

Upon executing a search, related listings for apps are displayed. Tap any app listing to reveal its Description screen.

To browse for apps in a specific category, follow these steps:

1. Launch the App Store app on your iPad when it's connected to the Internet.

2. At the bottom of the screen, tap the Categories command icon. A listing of 22 app categories displays.

3. Tap a category, such as Business or Finance.

4. When the listing of category-specific apps is displayed, tap the Sort By icon that's displayed near the upper-right corner of the screen to sort and display the individual app listings by Release Date (with the newest apps displayed first), Most Popular (with the bestselling apps displayed first), or alphabetically by name.

You can also view a list of bestselling apps in each category by tapping the Top Charts command icon that's displayed near the bottom-center of the main App Store screen. Then, tap the Categories command icon that's displayed near the upper-right corner of the screen to select a category. App listings for the Top Paid iPad Apps for the selected category are displayed on the left side of the screen, and a listing of the Top Free iPad Apps is displayed on the right side of the screen.

Tap any app listing within the App Store to reveal a detailed description for that app (see Figure 13.3). From an app's Description screen, you can download and install the app by tapping the Price icon (or the Free icon) that's displayed.

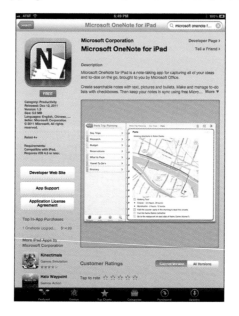

FIGURE 13.3

An app's Description screen displays details about the app, its price, ratings, reviews, and related screen shots. Tap the price (or Free) icon to purchase, download, and install the app.

25 BUSINESS APPS THAT ENHANCE THE CAPABILITIES OF YOUR iPAD

The following is just a sampling of the business apps available from the App Store. Many of these apps, listed in alphabetical order, introduce you to new tasks above and beyond what's possible using the preinstalled apps that come with iOS 5.1.

Often, as you browse the App Store, you'll discover multiple apps that are designed to handle the same functions or tasks but that offer slightly different features or a unique user interface. For example, PDFpen is one of several dozen apps that allow you to view, edit, annotate, print, and share PDF files on the iPad.

With each app described within this section, similar apps are also listed. As you review app descriptions as you browse the App Store, pay attention to its average rating, detailed reviews, listing of features, and sample screen shots to help you choose which app is best suited to meet your personal needs.

> **TIP** If a free version of an app is available, consider downloading it on a trial basis before you invest in the paid version of the app.

> **NOTE** In addition to using the App Store app on your iPad, it's possible to access the App Store and purchase iPad apps using iTunes on a PC or Mac, and then sync your tablet with your primary computer or transfer your purchased apps to your iPad via iCloud. An Apple ID is required to purchase apps from the App Store. From any web browser, you can also research apps by visiting the App Store's website (http://itunes.apple.com), but you can't purchase apps through the website.

> **TIP** Whenever possible, choose the iPad-specific version of an app because it is designed to fully utilize your tablet. Remember, however, that iPad-specific apps do not run on iPhones or other iOS devices. If you also use an iPhone, unless you want to purchase two different versions of the same app, select the hybrid or iPhone version of the app to install on both your tablet and phone.

1PASSWORD PRO

One of the many challenges people face is the need to memorize dozens of passwords, ID numbers, usernames, and other confidential pieces of information related to their personal identification, banking, favorite websites, and group or association memberships. Using an app such as 1Password for iPad ($9.99), it's possible to create and manage an easily accessible but secure database that contains all of your usernames, passwords, ID numbers, and related information.

What's useful about 1Password Pro is that your personalized database can be synced with a PC or Mac (using optional Windows or OS X software). You can also customize the database to store specific types of information, such as website URLs and their related usernames and passwords or credit cards with their related account numbers, PINs, expiration dates, and contact information for the issuing bank or financial institution.

You can set up separate sections within the database to store bank account details, credit card information, personal ID information (driver's license, passport, Social Security, and so on), membership information, and frequently visited websites, for example.

1Password Pro uses a simple and intuitive user interface but encrypts and password protects all data. The app includes a nice collection of features designed to make it easy to keep track of important, highly confidential information.

Similar apps available from the App Store: My Secret Folder, mSecure, one-Safe, eWallet, Password Wallet, Private Photo Vault, My Secret Apps, and Keeper Password & Data Vault.

DROPBOX

As an iPad user, you're probably already familiar with Apple's iCloud service and the tasks that a cloud-based file-sharing service can be used for, such as backing up or synchronizing data wirelessly with other computers, mobile devices, and users.

In addition to iCloud, there are many other cloud-based file-sharing services that provide similar functionality and that offer free accounts with a predetermined amount of online storage space. These services make it easy for iPad users to share data, documents, photos, and files; back up information remotely; collaborate with other users; and transfer important information between a tablet and other computers or mobile devices.

Many of the popular cloud-based services now support the iPad, including Dropbox. Dropbox functionality has also been seamlessly incorporated into hundreds of third-party iPad apps. The Dropbox app allows an iPad that's connected to the Web to easily import files from a cloud-based Dropbox account, or export files to a Dropbox account with a few taps on the tablet's screen. Dropbox is fully compatible with PCs, Macs, and most other mobile devices that can access the Internet.

Similar apps available from the App Store: Box, Evernote, CloudOn, Onebox, and Microsoft SkyDrive.

EFAX MOBILE

Your iPad is capable of helping you communicate with other people in many ways. For example, use the Mail app to send and receive email or the Messages app to send and receive text messages. You can use FaceTime, Skype, or WebEx for iPad for video conferencing. You can also make and receive telephone calls via Voice-Over-IP (VoIP) using the Skype, Line2, Talkatone, or CallTime apps.

With a third-party app, you can transform your iPad into a feature-packed fax machine that sends and receives faxes wirelessly via the Web. The eFax app nicely integrates with Contacts and enables you to add a digital signature to outgoing documents. You can also create custom cover sheets and view or search through sent or received faxes.

The eFax Mobile app is free, but you must have a paid eFax account to use it. The monthly $16.95 eFax plan includes a personal fax number (either a toll-free or local phone number). You can send 150 pages per month and receive 150 pages per month. To set up an account, visit www.eFax.com.

Similar apps available from the App Store: Fax It, iFax Pro, JotNot Fax, FAX, and Pocket Fax.

EVERNOTE

If you want to use your iPad for word processing, Apple's own Pages app (see Chapter 10, "Working with Pages, Numbers, and Keynote") enables you to create Microsoft Word-compatible documents from scratch on your tablet and then share them with other computers or devices via email, iCloud, or a few other file-sharing services. You can also import Word or Pages documents created elsewhere into your iPad for use with the Pages app.

The free Evernote app is a powerful note-taking app that you can use to compose documents and detailed lists. Within each document, you can record and attach audio clips, or you can attach digital images (photos). What's useful about Evernote is that you can then store and organize your documents, lists, and notes into separate virtual notebooks, which can easily be synced with a desktop or notebook computer or other mobile devices using email or a variety of popular cloud-based services.

Versions of Evernote are available for PCs, Macs, all iOS devices, and other mobile operating systems, so regardless of what other equipment you use, your Evernote documents and files can remain synced. To learn about or acquire other versions of Evernote, visit www.evernote.com.

Although Evernote does not offer the robust formatting capabilities of a full-featured word processor, it does offer a plethora of tools for organizing, managing, and sharing documents and lists. After you've stored content within Evernote, you can easily search and access it.

Similar apps available from the App Store: Simplenote, Microsoft OneNote, JotAgent, Note+, Awesome Note HD, Notes Plus, Note Taker HD, Ghostwriter Notes, Note!, Super Note, Penultimate, Easy Note + To Do, and Noteability.

FILEMAKER GO FOR iPAD

For many businesses, having an app created (see Chapter 17, "Creating and Distributing Content on the iPad") provides a customized solution for making a wide range of tasks manageable via an iPad. For independent business professionals, entrepreneurs, or small business operators, though, it's too costly to develop a custom app. Fortunately, there are a variety of much more affordable solutions.

FileMaker continues to be one of the most powerful and robust database management tools on the market. Using this PC, Mac, or network-based software, you can create and deploy highly complex and extremely customized database applications. The FileMaker Go app makes these interactive custom databases accessible from the iPad.

This $39.99 app enables users to access and utilize FileMaker databases from anywhere an iPad can connect to the Internet via a Wi-Fi, 3G, or 4G connection. Using FileMaker Go, signatures can be captured in the field; inventory or customer data can be searched, accessed, viewed, and printed wirelessly; or information can be collected or disseminated between a centralized database and the iPad.

A custom database must be created with FileMaker Pro or FileMaker Pro Advanced before it can be accessed with FileMaker Go for iPad. For many businesses, FileMaker Pro and FileMaker Go provides the perfect tool set for creating the closest thing to an iPad proprietary app possible, without incurring the time and expense of actually programming, testing, and deploying the app. Using FileMaker, no programming is required.

To learn more about how FileMaker is being used for highly customized mobile applications in a wide range of industries, visit www.filemaker.com/products/milemaker-go. For less sophisticated database applications that can also be customized, the Bento for iPad or Things apps can also be utilized with their respective PC or Mac versions.

Similar apps available from the App Store: Bento for iPad and Things.

FLIGHTTRACK PRO

Out of all the apps created for travelers, many iPad users who are frequent fliers believe that FlightTrack Pro ($9.99) is the best designed and most feature packed. In addition to helping you manage your travel itinerary, it automatically syncs data with the Calendar app and keeps you informed, in real time, of flight delays, cancellations, gate changes, and other details pertinent to your trip. FlightTrack Pro (see Figure 13.4) works with every major airline and contains information about virtually all major airports throughout the world.

Using this app, you can track any flight in real time, plus access information based on the flight's past history to determine the chances of it arriving on time. This information is useful if you're picking up someone at the airport, or you need to coordinate ground transportation upon your arrival.

FIGURE 13.4
FlightTrack Pro handles a wide range of tasks related to flying, and helps you more efficiently manage your travel itinerary.

If a flight gets canceled, this app helps you quickly find an alternative flight online. You can also share your itinerary via email, determine at which baggage claim carousel your luggage can be retrieved when you land, and be able to view the extended local weather forecast for your destination.

FlightTrack Pro uses the wireless web to keep you well informed, plus it's designed to work seamlessly with TripIt.com, so you don't even need to enter your travel itinerary manually. Just forward your emailed flight confirmation from any airline to plans@TripIt.com, and your itinerary information is automatically synced with the FlightTrack Pro app and the Calendar app.

This is truly an indispensable app for frequent travelers. It goes well beyond being an organizational tool, and it can actually take some of the stress out of flying on any commercial airline, anywhere in the world.

Similar apps available from the App Store: FlightTrack Live, US Flights, FlightAware Flight Tracker, KAYAK Mobile Pro, TripAssist by Expedia, FlightBoard, TripIt – Travel Organizer, Skyscanner, Flight Update, and Flight Status.

GRUBHUB

Whether you're a frequent business traveler who constantly orders room service from hotels, you're often forced to work late at the office, or you're too tired to cook a healthy meal when you get home, the free GrubHub app offers an affordable dining solution.

The GrubHub service has teamed up with more than 25,000 restaurants within major cities to make each restaurant's entire menu available for delivery, often for no extra charge. So, if you live in or are visiting any of more than 300 cities, you can use this app to automatically pinpoint your location and find local participating restaurants, view their menus, place an order, pay by credit card or PayPal, and have your food delivered to your home, office, or hotel room—often within 30 to 60 minutes.

Instead of being limited to fast food, GrubHub offers delivery from top-rated, fine-dining restaurants (as well as less costly dining options). The choices are not only plentiful; they can be healthy as well.

GrubHub offers a cost-effective alternative to hotel room service, which often features a limited menu and charges a 15 to 25 percent premium to have food delivered.

Similar apps available from the App Store: Many of your favorite chain restaurants, such as Starbucks, McDonald's, Pizza Hut, Chipotle, Papa John's, Ruth's Chris Steakhouse, Outback Steakhouse, The Capital Grille, Subway, and Baja Fresh have their own custom apps that can help you find the closest location to wherever you happen to be.

INVOICE2GO FOR iPAD

For small business operators, consultants, and freelancers, the need to generate and send invoices in a timely and efficient manner in order is essential. Using the Invoice2Go software on a PC or Mac ($99.00 to $149.00 per year), in conjunction with the Invoice2Go for iPad app ($14.99), you have the ability to create professional-looking, customized invoices that you can design from scratch or adapt from more than 300 invoice templates offered with the software and app.

A free Invoice2Go Lite for iPad version is available. It includes 20 built-in invoice templates. This is a slightly scaled down version of the paid app, but it is still highly functional and useful.

Finding and generating the perfect invoice to bill a customer or client for your products, services, or time is possible using this app. For invoices sent electronically, you can add an interactive PayPal button, so you can be paid with a click of the mouse by the recipient. As you're generating the invoice, subtotals, sales tax, and totals are automatically calculated.

> **NOTE** Use the Invoice2Go for iPad app to create and generate personalized purchase orders, estimates, and credit memos that can contain all of your company information, including your logo.

In addition to simply generating the invoices, this app generates sales and business reports in 16 different formats, enabling you to email invoices directly to clients or customers from your iPad and track incoming payments. You can print invoices and reports wirelessly from the iPad, or you can transfer all data and sync it with Invoice2Go on your computer. Data from Invoice2go can also be exported for use in Intuit's QuickBooks accounting and bookkeeping software that's running on your primary computer or network.

Invoice2Go can meet all of your customer and client invoicing needs, yet the software and app (either of which you can use as a standalone product) are extremely user friendly and require no accounting knowledge to fully utilize. For more information, go to www.Invoice2go.com.

Similar apps available from the App Store: invoiceASAP, Quick Sale for iPad, Invoice Robot, Invoice, iQuote, Simple Invoices – Services, Invoice Studio, Invoice Generator HD, and TapInvoice.

LINE2

Thanks to the Line2 app, your iPad can be transformed into a powerful business telephone as long you're connected to the Internet. The app not only gives you your own telephone number, but it enables you to use VoIP technology to make and receive calls from your tablet wherever you happen to be (including overseas).

Although a free version of Line2 is offered, to fully utilize the app you must subscribe to a monthly service plan, which starts at $9.99. This includes a unique phone number, the ability to make and receive unlimited calls within the U.S. and Canada, call forwarding, voice mail, the ability to establish conference calls, as well as other useful phone features (such as Caller ID, call waiting, and hold).

Line2 (shown in Figure 13.5) integrates nicely with the Contacts app and uses the iPad's built in microphone and speaker to transform the tablet into a speakerphone. Users can pay for one month at a time; no long-term service contract is required. Using this app, it's not only possible to use the iPad to make and receive calls from an iPad, it's also cost effective and convenient. As long as a good quality Internet connection is available, calls are crystal clear, and you never have to worry about using peak versus off-peak cellular minutes, long distance charges, or (international) roaming charges.

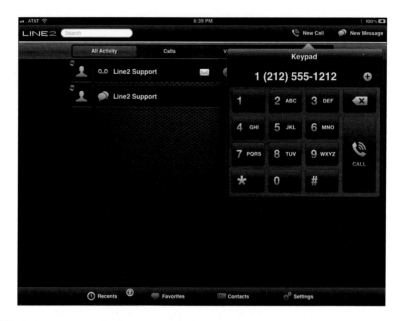

FIGURE 13.5

You can use Line2 as a standalone telephone (speakerphone) for making and receiving calls from a unique phone number when your iPad is connected to the Internet.

Similar apps available from the App Store: Skype, secondLine, Takeatone, NorthEast Voip Phone, VOIP, and FreePhoo.

MICROSOFT ONENOTE FOR iPAD

Based on the Microsoft OneNote software for desktop and laptop computers, the iPad edition is designed for capturing ideas, taking notes, and managing to-do lists while on the go. The free app enables you to create notes that incorporate text, pictures, or bulleted items that are searchable, as well as to-do lists complete with checkboxes.

The OneNote app is also Microsoft SkyDrive compatible, so you can back up your documents and notes online, share them with others, or synchronize them with computers or mobile devices running the OneNote software or app. Using the free edition of OneNote, you can create up to 500 notes. Beyond that, it's necessary to upgrade to the unlimited edition of the app for $14.99 via an in-app purchase.

By combining elements of a text editor and to-do list manager, but not the full functionality of a word processor, OneNote offers a customizable way to create, manage, and share information and lists. The functionality of the app is somewhat similar to Evernote.

Similar apps available from the App Store: Evernote, Text Writer, Note Taker HD, Notes Plus, Noteshelf, iA Writer, and WritePad for iPad.

> NOTE   Microsoft is currently believed to be working on an iPad edition of Microsoft Office, which will include full word processing, spreadsheet management, and digital slide show presentation capabilities either through a single app or suite of apps that will be fully compatible with Microsoft Office for PCs and Macs.

MONSTER.COM JOBS FOR iPAD

In addition to serving as a powerful communications, organizational, and productivity tool while you're on-the-job, your iPad can be a powerful job search tool and help you find and land your dream job.

This app enables you to connect via the Internet to the popular Monster.com online service in order to create customizable online resumes and cover letters and then search and apply for jobs. Monster.com maintains a vast database of job openings available in virtually all industries. The app can also be used to alert you as new job openings that you're qualified for become available in your immediate geographic area or anywhere in the world.

Using this app, you can manage all aspects of your job search process and use the tools of Monster.com to help you pinpoint and then apply for positions that you're most qualified to fill.

Monster.com Jobs for iPad works nicely with the free Monster.com Interviews by Monster app, which serves as an interactive coach to help you prepare for and ace job interviews. In the App Store there are other apps to help you manage specific aspects of the job search process, such as creating your resume or searching through published job listings. The Monster.com Jobs for iPad app, however, offers a more comprehensive set of job search tools than many of the available apps.

Similar apps available from the App Store: Job Finder for iPad, Job Search, Dice Job Search, Job Search XL, Interview Questions Pro, Resume Templates App, JobAnimal.com, My Resume, Easy Resume, IT Jobs+, and aVirtualInterview.

PDFPEN

Simply by visiting the App Store and entering the phrase "PDF" into the Search field, you'll discover dozens of iPad apps that enable you to create, view, annotate, print, organize, store, and share PDF files. Some of these apps have very specific purposes. For example, Adobe Reader simply enables you to view PDF files that are already created and stored on your tablet.

Many apps, such as Pages, Numbers, and Keynote, also enable you to create PDF files that you can share. The PDFpen app ($9.99) is one of the more powerful apps for working with PDF files because it enables you to view, edit, annotate, print, organize, and share them with ease. It's designed to be a full-featured PDF editor that is compatible with iCloud, Dropbox, Evernote, and Google Docs. This makes sharing PDF files with PCs, Macs, and other mobile devices easy.

> **NOTE** PDF (Portable Document Format) files are an industry standard file type that was originally created by Adobe almost two decades ago. With this file format, you can save a file or document that can easily be viewed on any computer, web browser, or mobile device while its appearance, fonts, and formatting remain intact. The PDF format provides a convenient way to share information between PCs and Macs or other devices, and insure full compatibility regardless of what software is being used to create or view the PDF file.
>
> For a long time, after a PDF file was created, it could be viewed, but it couldn't be edited or annotated. The PDFpen app for iPad enables PDF files to be edited or annotated after they've been created. Thus, you can add a digital signature to a document (shown in Figure 13.6 using PDFpen) or alter the document on your tablet, regardless of where or how it was originally created.
>
> You can export virtually any type of file or document that can be printed—no matter what software it was created with—into the PDF file format using the proper tools (which are built into some software packages and apps or are available using additional software or apps).

The ability to create, view, edit, annotate, print, organize and share PDF files is a must for most mobile executives. By adding these capabilities to an iPad, it further reduces the need for a notebook or netbook computer while you're on the go.

Similar apps available from the App Store: Adobe Reader, PDF Reader Pro, SignMyPad, iAnnotate PDF, and UPad.

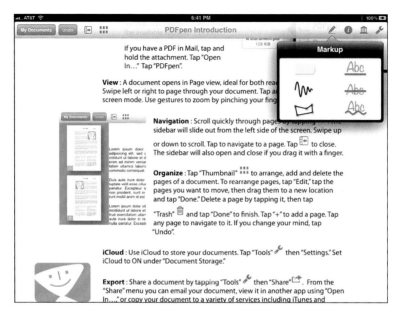

FIGURE 13.6

Using PDFpen, you can mark up or annotate a contract, letter, or document that's transferred to or created on your iPad in PDF format. Then you can email it to others (or upload it to a cloud-based file-sharing service).

PHOTON FLASH WEB BROWSER

The Safari web browser that comes preinstalled on all iOS mobile devices, including the iPad, is a feature-packed and powerful app used for surfing the Web. Although new features continue to be added to this web browser with each new version of the iOS that Apple releases, one feature that remains absent is the ability to display Adobe Flash animations and graphics.

Until recently, when surfing the Web, most of the animations on websites were created using a programming language called Flash. To view these animations, a Flash plug-in for your web browser is required. Apple has never made a Flash plug-in available for the iOS version of Safari. As a result, it's not possible to fully access any websites that utilize Flash programming.

With the ever-growing popularity of iOS devices, many website developers and programmers have turned away from utilizing Flash animations within their sites. However, as an iPad user, if you absolutely need to visit websites that utilize Flash, you have two solutions.

The Photon Flash Web Browser ($4.99) is a full-featured web browser app for the iPad that serves as an alternative to using Safari when surfing the Web. This web browser is compatible with most Flash-based websites and can display their Flash-based animations and graphics.

A second alternative for viewing Flash-based graphics while surfing the Web on an iPad is to use a remote desktop application to access and control a PC or Mac remotely. (See "Splashtop" later in this chapter.) When your iPad has control over your primary computer via the Internet or a wireless network, you can run any web browser and surf the Web via your computer and see everything on your tablet's screen (with a slight lag time).

Similar apps available from the App Store: Skyfire Web Browser for iPad, Flash Web Brower- Splashtop Remote Browser, and FlashIE.

PULSE

The Pulse News app (free) is a fully customizable news reader that enables you to pick and choose from a vast selection of news and special interest websites to monitor. It also monitors your Facebook and Twitter accounts and presents new content in a filmstrip-like format on a single, scrollable screen.

After installing the iPad-specific Pulse app on your tablet, it automatically begins monitoring a handful of news websites, including *USA Today,* on your behalf. Each news source or website has its own horizontal column comprised of individual story-squares.

Scroll left or right along each column to view headlines from that news source or website, or tap a specific headline to read a news story or article in full (or access related photos, videos, or audio content). Likewise, scroll up or down on the screen to quickly view content from other news sources or websites.

What makes Pulse News a powerful and useful app is that you can fully customize which news sources and websites it monitors, and then you can select the order in which that information is displayed. To begin customizing the app, tap the gear-shaped icon that's displayed in the upper-left corner of the main Pulse News screen.

News sources your iPad can monitor using Pulse are divided into a handful of subject categories, such as Social, Art & Design, Business, Entertainment, Food, Fun & Humor, Lifestyle, News, Politics, Science, Sports, and Technology. Below each category heading are at least a dozen websites or news sources you can have the Pulse News app monitor for you. This can include local, national, international, or industry-oriented news, or it can be content related to a specific topic or subject matter.

The Pulse News app also enables you to group websites and news sources by subject matter, and then display those subjects as "Packs" on separate pages.

The content displayed by Pulse News (shown in Figure 13.7) utilizes text-based headlines and full-color photos. Each link can lead to a text-based article, video, photo collection, audio clip, or multimedia web content, for example.

FIGURE 13.7

Using Pulse, you can easily monitor multiple online news sources and view only articles, photos, news stories, multimedia content, or videos that are of direct interest to you.

By visiting www.pulse.me and setting up a free account, you can set your Pulse content preferences once and then view that content using Pulse apps on your other iOS, Windows Phone, and Android mobile devices.

Similar apps available from the App Store: Flipboard.

QUICKVOICE RECORDER

Using the microphone that's built in to your iPad, you can use the tablet as a full-featured digital audio recorder. You can use this functionality as a dictation tool or to record meetings, for example. Some digital recording apps, such as Apple's Garage Band, can transform the iPad into a multi-track digital recording studio.

The QuickVoice Recorder is one of the easier-to-use digital recording apps. It is ideal for recording dictation, voice memos, lectures, classes, or meetings. You can play the recordings on the iPad or transfer (synced) them with a computer, cloud-based file-sharing service, or another mobile device. A version of QuickVoice is also available for PCs and Macs.

The user interface used by QuickVoice Recorder is very straightforward and simple. To record, simply tap the large red Record button. You can name your recordings, and play them back by tapping the large green Play button. It's also possible to pause and resume a recording.

TIP If the quality of the microphone that's built in to your iPad isn't good enough to meet your needs, several third-party companies offer external micro-phones that plug into the tablet's headphones jack and offer significantly higher recording quality. For example, Mic-W (www.mic-w.com) offers its i-Series of professional-quality microphones for the iPad, which include a high sensitivity car-dioid microphone, a professional Class 2 microphone, and a lavaliere microphone.

Similar apps available from the App Store: Smart Recorder, Audio Memos, QuickVoice2Text Email, Voice Recorder HD, Voice Memos for iPad, iRecorder Pro, AudioNote, Smart Recorder, Super Note: Voice Recorder, Recorder HD, and Mobile Recorder HD.

REMEMBER THE MILK

When Apple released iOS 5 for the iPad, the operating system included a new, pre-installed app called Reminders, which is a powerful to-do list manager. For some people, however, Reminders doesn't meet their needs when it comes to managing lists, organizing information, or prioritizing tasks.

The Remember the Milk app (free) offers a feature-packed alternative to the Reminders app. It enables you to easily sync data between this app and Outlook, iCal, Gmail, Google Calendar, Twitter, and other services, apps, and software.

To fully utilize this app, you should upgrade to the Pro edition, which costs $2.99 per month or $24.99 per year. It allows for unlimited auto-syncing with Remember the Milk Online, as well as with multiple mobile devices and computers. It also offers Push Notification reminders and badge updates on your tablet, as well as Notification Center compatibility.

As you'd expect from a to-do list manager, Remember the Milk enables you to cre-ate an unlimited number of separate to-do-style lists and then prioritize the lists, as well as each item within each list. Each to-do list item can also be accompanied by notes or photos, and all items are fully searchable.

The user interface and some of the core features of Remember the Milk are different than the Reminders app, although you can use either to successfully manage a vast amount of information in the form of to-do lists.

Similar apps available from the App Store: Post-It PopNotes, Wunderlist HD, To+Do, Errands To-Do List, Toodledo, Task PRO, 2Do, Awesome Lists, Easy Note + To Do, iReminder, and Evernote.

SEESMIC PING

Hundreds of millions of people all over the world have become active on the various online social networking sites, such as Facebook, Twitter, and LinkedIn. When you become active on a new site, however, you have to post updates and content to each account separately. So, if you have multiple accounts on separate services, staying active online can become a time-consuming task.

Seesmic Ping (free) automates the process of updating your status and adding content to the various online social networking services by enabling you to create one update and simultaneously post (publish) it to multiple accounts on the same service or to separate services. Using this app, you can add URL links, photos, and your location to each update. Plus, you can create updates but schedule specific times in advance for them to be published online.

Composing a post using Seesmic Ping is as easy as using the compose post feature of the Facebook or Twitter app, for example. This app, however, automatically saves all of your posts and lets you know on which services each post was published to.

If you're active on Facebook, Twitter, LinkedIn, or on other online social networking sites, the Seesmic Ping app can save you time and make it easier to post content and updates to all of your accounts simultaneously.

Similar apps available from the App Store: iSocial Connect, Hellotxt, HootSuite, and Yoono.

SPLASHTOP

Imagine being able to access and run any software or utilize any files, documents or data that are stored on your desktop computer (at home or your office) from your iPad—anytime and anywhere. This is possible using a remote desktop app, such as Splashtop (see Figure 13.8).

FIGURE 13.8

Shown here, Microsoft Word, Adobe Photoshop Elements, and Microsoft PowerPoint are running simultaneously on a Mac, but being controlled from an iPad.

As long as your primary computer is turned on and running free companion software to Splashtop, you can use your iPad to remotely access your computer from anywhere and then run software or access files from it. The display on your iPad shows everything on your primary computer's screen and enables you to control PC or Mac software, for example, using the tablet's touch screen.

To make navigating around your primary computer's full-size screen from your iPad's smaller size screen easier, the Splashtop app adds navigational arrow keys to your tablet's virtual keyboard, plus uses a proprietary interface to reduce the amount of scrolling that would otherwise be necessary.

Instead of using Pages for word processing on your iPad, having to export your Pages document to Microsoft Word format, and then somehow transferring or syncing the document to your computer, with Splashtop you can run the PC or Mac version of Microsoft Word (or any software for that matter) directly from your iPad so that you have full control over your primary computer.

The basic Splashtop app is free. However, the developer also offers the fee-based Splashtop Pro app (www.splashtop.com/pro), which is designed for corporate use. In addition to being able to access and utilize files, data, and documents, when you use your iPad to run software from your primary computer, you can also play games, view Flash-based websites, or watch multimedia content that's stored on your computer (without transferring it to your iPad first).

For Splashtop to work, your iPad must have access to a Wi-Fi Internet connection, and your primary computer must also be turned on and connected to the Web. Depending on the software you're running, you might experience a slight lag, but for most applications, this is acceptable.

Using a remote desktop solution such as Splashtop, you no longer have to worry about transferring to your tablet the files, documents, or data that you need while you're on the go because everything that's stored on your primary computer (as well as external storage devices connected to your computer) is readily available.

Similar apps available from the App Store: Remote Desktop, GoToMyPC, iRemoteDesktop, and Jump Desktop.

SQUARE

Whether you're a small business, consultant, freelancer, or even an artisan showcasing your work at a local crafts show, one of the easiest ways to set up a merchant account and be able to accept credit card payments within a few minutes is to use the Square app and credit card processing service.

Begin by visiting http://squareup.com to set up a free account. Next, from the App Store, download the free Square app. To use the Square service in order to accept and process credit card transactions, there are no upfront costs, no contracts to sign, no recurring monthly fees, and no hidden charges. You simply pay a flat 2.75% fee per transaction (as long as you swipe the customer's credit card). Without the card swipe, each transaction costs $.15 plus 3.5% of the transaction.

Square even provides a free, and extremely small, credit card swiper that attaches to the iPad through the unit's headphones jack. Use it to swipe credit cards and process transactions, or you can manually enter credit card information from your customers or clients.

The free Square app accepts an on-screen signature from your customer, processes the transaction, and promptly emails your customer a detailed receipt. The proceeds from the transaction are transferred directly to the checking or savings account you have linked to your Square account.

Within minutes of setting up a Square merchant account you are able to accept Visa, MasterCard, American Express, Discover, and debit card payments using your iPad.

Before using the app for the first time to process credit card transactions, you can set up onscreen icons that represent each item you're selling. You can include the item name, price, applicable sales tax, and a brief item description. You also can attach a photo of that item.

When you're ready to accept a credit card payment, simply launch the Square app, enter the transaction amount or tap a preprogrammed Item icon (based on what's being purchased), swipe the customer's credit card, and have the customer sign your iPad's screen. The app connects to the Internet and securely processes the transaction within seconds.

Being able to accept major credit cards and debit cards, especially while working offsite, offers a huge advantage to small businesses, consultants, freelancers, and entrepreneurs while also offering added convenience to customers.

Square offers an efficient and low-cost way to be able to handle credit card transactions from any location and automatically maintain detailed records of each transaction that you can later export to bookkeeping or inventory management software on a primary computer.

Similar apps available from the App Store: Intuit GoPayment Credit Card Terminal and Phone Swipe.

THE WEATHER CHANNEL

As you're preparing for a trip and deciding what to pack or determining what to do each day when you arrive at your destination, knowing the local weather forecast is extremely useful. The free Weather Channel Max for iPad app enables you to pick any city in the world and obtain a detailed current weather report, as well as an extended weather forecast. Plus, you can watch streaming Weather Channel television reports, view animated weather radar maps, and use other features within this colorful app as you monitor the weather in one or more cities.

Use this app as you're packing to figure out the average daily temperature at your destination so you know in advance whether to pack extra sweaters, jackets, hats, and gloves, for example. There are many weather-related apps available for the iPad; however, the Weather Channel Max for iPad app is created specifically for the iPad and offers forecast information and weather reports from a reliable and well-respected source.

Similar apps available from the App Store: Weather+, Weather HD, MyRadar Weather Radar, Weather Live, Nightstand Central for iPad, WeatherBug for iPad, and Fahrenheit Free Weather and Temperature.

THINGS FOR iPAD

Things for iPad ($19.99) combines functionality of a highly customizable database manager app with a to-do list manager and scheduling app, allowing it to be used to gather, organize, prioritize, display, and share a wide range of information. By more effectively managing to-do lists, due dates, and data related to projects, it's easier to become more efficient during your work day.

Things for iPad nicely combines functionality found in Calendars, Reminders, and Notification Center, for example, into a single customizable app. A version of Things (sold separately) is also available for the Mac and iPhone, so your personalized data can easily be synced and utilized on multiple computers and devices.

Similar apps available from the App Store: FileMaker Go and Bento for iPad.

TIME MASTER + BILLING

If you need to track your time and bill customers or clients for it, the Time Master + Billing app ($9.99) is one of several apps that offer this capability using an iPad. Whether you're a lawyer, accountant, contractor, consultant, or freelancer, the Time Master + Billing app is an easy way to track your time (down to the second, if necessary), and expenses, plus generate invoices from virtually anywhere. The app enables you to run multiple timers simultaneously, start and stop timers as needed, and display or export reports that you can share via email or syncing.

Paid upgrades to the Time Master + Billing app are required to generate invoices from the app, synchronize data, and or export data to Quickbooks. Using the core version of the app, however, you can export timesheet data to other formats, such as CSV or HTML.

The user interface of this app isn't slick, but the functionality built into the app is impressive and versatile, making it ideal for use by professionals working in a variety of industries.

Similar apps available from the App Store: eBility Time Tracker for Intuit Quickbooks and TimeTracker – Time Sheet.

WORLD CLOCK

Traveling between time zones and keeping track of the current time where you are as well as in your home time zone is a constant challenge for many travelers. Plus, many frequent travelers have learned the hard way that you shouldn't rely solely on a hotel wake-up call service.

The World Clock app ($1.99) enables you to display between 1 and 24 clocks that are programmed to show the current time in specific cities of your choice. You can also set alarms and wake-up calls. The app enables you to manually set the current time wherever you are, or can automatically determine the exact time and date by accessing the Internet.

This particular clock app enables you to select from five different clock face designs and offers a handful of useful features that are ideal for world travelers.

Similar apps available from the App Store: Clock, Clock+, Alarm Clock HD, Night Stand for iPad, World Clock Pro, Clock Pro HD, The World Clock, and My Alarm Clock.

XPENSETRACKER

People who are on the go, who travel for business, or who entertain or service customers or clients often need to accurately and efficiently keep track of personal or business-related expenses. The XpenseTracker app ($4.99) is one of several available from the App Store designed specifically for this purpose.

Using this app, you can customize how you keep track of expenses—by category or customer, for example—and create as many categories and subcategories as needed. For each expense, you can store details about payment type and include a related time, date, or other notes and details.

In addition to enabling you to create detailed expense reports, the app tracks which expenses have been submitted for reimbursement, and which expenses have already been repaid. You can also track vehicle miles and calculate currency exchange rates, as needed.

You can export expense reports and data to Microsoft Excel or Numbers, for example, or you can synchronize them with your primary computer. In-app add-ons include Dropbox support and OCR scanner support (allowing for printed receipts to be scanned directly into the app using an optional scanner).

> TIP   For QuickBooks users, there are a variety of apps that enable you to gather financial data on an iPad and export it into QuickBooks running on a PC or Mac (of the QuickBooks Online edition). The qBooks app, for example enables you to access and manipulate QuickBooks data and files from your tablet. You can also use your iPad to access Intuit's fee-based QuickBooks Online service (http://quickbooks.intuit.com). Using Intuit's fee-based GoPayment Credit Card Processing app, you can use your iPad as a wireless credit card terminal, and you can sync related data directly with QuickBooks.

Similar apps available from the App Store: Concur, Expensify, BizXPenseTracker, Expense Tablet for iPad, Visual Budget: Expense Tracker, Office Time – Time & Expense Tracking, and Pocket Expense.

YELP

Ideal for business travelers, Yelp (free) helps you quickly locate the businesses, restaurants, or services you want or need, in virtually any city. In addition to simply displaying an address and phone number for the desired listing, Yelp offers customer reviews and ratings, plus directions from your current location.

When it comes to finding restaurants, for example, you can search by geographic region, price, or food type, and you can make reservations for participating restaurants from within the app. You can also use Yelp to publish where you are and what you're doing on Facebook or Twitter or quickly share your own reviews about a business, restaurant, or bar you're visiting.

Yelp is an easy-to-use app that provides far more information than a typical Yellow Pages or phone directory app. It works seamlessly with the Maps and Contacts apps, for example, and often utilizes photos within business or restaurant listings. Using details from your Contacts app and Facebook account (if applicable), Yelp can share details about who you know that's nearby, as well as the ratings and bookmarked Yelp listings from others.

Use Yelp to easily find nearby restaurants, bars, coffee shops, gas stations, drugstores, retail shopping, salons/spas, nightlife, theaters, professional services, hotels, houses of worship, or hospitals, for example, whether you're in your home city or traveling virtually anywhere in the world.

Similar apps available from the App Store: AroundMe!, Zagats To Go, and OpenTable.

DISCOVERING WHAT TRAVEL APPS CAN DO FOR YOU

Here's a rundown of the different types of travel-related apps you can find listed under the Travel category of the App Store:

- Apps, such as Travelocity, Kayak HD, or Priceline, are designed to help you find and book the best deals on airfares, hotels, and rental cars.

- Just about every major airline (American Airlines, Delta, JetBlue, and Southwest, to name a few), hotel chain, and rental car company has its own proprietary app that enables you to book travel, review your reservations, make last-minute changes to your itinerary, and manage your frequent flier (or customer reward membership) points/miles.

TIP The AwardWallet app (free) enables you to create and manage a centralized and auto-updating database of your airline frequent flier accounts and easily view balances, recent activity, and other pertinent data. It can also be used for other travel-related hotel or rental car reward programs or to manage credit card-related award points.

NOTE Some of the airline apps even enable you to check-in for an upcoming flight via the Internet, choose your seat assignment, pre-check your luggage, and generate your boarding pass, which can be scanned by the airline from your iPad's screen as you board the aircraft.

- As you're making travel arrangements, use free apps, such as Trip Advisor: Hotels, Flights, Restaurants, to read detailed reviews of thousands of travel service providers, hotels, airlines, and restaurants that were written by fellow travelers. Discover the best and worst of what a particular travel destination has to offer.

- Use apps such as FlightTrack Pro (described earlier in this chapter) to manage every aspect of your travel itinerary after you've booked it. For example, you can track flights in real time and have the app alert you of last-minute gate changes, flight cancellations, or other problems. If such problems occur, you can use the app to find alternative flights and notify the people expecting you if your itinerary changes via email or text message. When you land, the app directs you to the correct baggage claim conveyor belt to retrieve your checked luggage, provides a detailed map of the destination airport, and offers a multiday weather forecast for your destination city.

- Instead of using a traditionally printed travel guide to help you navigate your way around a city, most popular travel destinations have interactive travel guide apps. These apps utilize the GPS feature of your tablet to help you navigate your way around a city, as well as share information about the best hotels, attractions, sights, and restaurants. You can also obtain apps for specific cities that contain interactive subway maps and schedules that help you utilize the city's public transportation system.

- The App Store includes a collection of travel-related apps that pinpoint your exact location and instantly locate a local town car, limousine, or taxi company, enabling you to schedule a pick-up in any city, at any time, with a few taps on your iPad's screen. Call A Taxi, Taxi, or GetLimo are three such apps.

- While traveling, there are also apps that help you find the best restaurants to dine at (such as Yelp, AroundMe, or Zagat to Go) and other apps that enable you to book your restaurant reservation directly from your iPad (such as OpenTable).

- If you're traveling abroad, the Skype app enables you to make voice-over-IP phone calls whenever you're within range of a Wi-Fi hotspot.

- Many different currency conversion apps are available to help you accurately convert the U.S. dollar to other currencies and quickly figure out how much things actually cost wherever in the world you are. When choosing one of these apps, select one that does not require constant access to the Web; otherwise, you wind up paying high international wireless data roaming charges.

> **TIP**   Don't forget, you can also use your iPad to watch TV shows and movies, serve as an eBook reader, and play exciting games, which helps you pass the time during long flights (or during flight delays when you're stuck at an airport). Of course, you can also use your tablet with apps such as Pages, Numbers, Keynote, and FileMaker Go to get work done during a flight.
>
> If you need to extend the battery life of your iPad while you're on the go, a handful of external rechargeable battery packs are available, such as the RichardSolo 9000 ($69.95 USD, www.RichardSolo.com), which can add upward of 10 hours to the life of your tablet's battery on a single charge. The RichardSolo 1000 battery pack is smaller than a pack of cigarettes, so it's portable. You can recharge it from any electrical outlet.

ONLINE BANKING MADE EASY ON YOUR iPAD

Many major banks, financial institutions and credit card issuers, such as Bank of America, Chase, Citibank, Fidelity, Schwab, Capital One, PNC, Citizens Bank, Amex, and TD Bank now offer specialized apps for handling your online banking and money management from the iPad. You can easily and securely check your balances, transfer money between accounts, pay bills online, manage credit cards, and more using these free, bank-specific iPad apps.

SAVING TIME IN YOUR EVERYDAY LIFE

Beyond apps that are strictly for business, you can find a plethora of apps within the App Store that can save you time in your personal life. For example, there's the Walgreen's app, which enables you to manage your prescription medications and order refills from anywhere.

Many of your favorite chain stores also have their own apps, enabling you to shop online or find the store's nearest retail location. If you're a business professional who's constantly on the go, the FedEx Mobile app helps you ship and track packages, but it also helps you find the nearest FedEx location wherever you happen to be. To order office supplies or find the closest Staples location, the free Staples app can prove helpful.

Or, if you're in need of a jolt of caffeine, the MyStarbucks app helps you find the nearest Starbucks location and decide what you want to order. You can use the Starbucks Mobile Card app to actually pay for your in-store purchases.

14

STAYING INFORMED USING THE iBOOKS AND NEWSSTAND APPS

By downloading the free iBooks 2 app from the App Store (which replaces the original iBooks app and offers more features), you can transform your iPad into a powerful eBook reader, purchase eBooks from Apple's online-based iBookstore, and view PDF files imported into your tablet.

> **TIP** To install iBooks for the first time on your iPad, launch the App Store app. Type "iBooks" into the Search field that's displayed in the upper-right corner of the screen, and then tap the Search key on the virtual keyboard. When the iBooks listing appears, tap it. Next, from the iBooks 2 Description page, tap the Free icon to download and install the app.

To make sure you're using the latest version of the iBooks 2 app (version 2.1 or later), launch the App Store app and tap the Updates command icon that's displayed at the bottom of the screen. If necessary, you will be able to update the iBooks app for free by tapping the Update icon.

However, if you already have an eBook reader, such as Amazon's Kindle or Barnes & Noble's NOOK, in addition to the iBooks app, you can download the free Kindle or NOOK app from the App Store. Using one of these other eBook reader apps, you can then download and read eBooks formatted for the Kindle or NOOK, respectively. You also can access your personal library of eBooks that you've already acquired for your other eBook reader without having to repurchase them.

Each eBook reader, such as the iPad, Kindle, or NOOK, formats eBook files differently and features a different interface for reading eBooks. In addition, each of the different online-based eBook stores offers a different selection of eBooks titles and charges different prices to purchase eBooks. What's available from Apple's own iBookstore via the iBooks app is only one option when it comes to shopping for, purchasing, and adding eBooks to your iPad.

Regardless of which eBook reader you use with your iPad, you have access to millions of eBook titles published by the world's leading publishers. You also have access to electronically published works from self-published authors, as well as free eBook content that's in the public domain. Chapter 17, "Creating and Distributing Content on the iPad," covers how you can use the free iBooks Author software on a Mac to create and distribute your own eBook content for the iPad.

NOTE   To download and read a digital edition of a magazine or newspaper on your iPad and manage your digital subscriptions, use the Newsstand app. For many digital publications, you also need a free and proprietary app (downloadable from within Newsstand and/or the App Store).

SELECTING AND DOWNLOADING EBOOKS

The free iBooks 2 app has two distinct, but related, purposes. It serves as a conduit for accessing Apple's online-based iBookstore, from which you can find, purchase, and download eBooks from publishers, as well as download free eBooks that are in the public domain.

After you have used iBooks to load eBook content onto your iPad, this same app is used to read eBooks (see Figure 14.1) using a customizable user interface that enables you to personalize how the pages of your eBook appear on the screen.

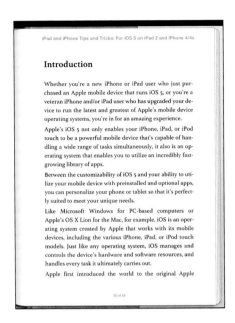

FIGURE 14.1

As you read a text-based eBook, your iPad's screen will look like the pages of a traditionally printed hardcover or paperback book. However, you can adjust the appearance of the text on the screen, making it larger or smaller, for example.

iBooks 2 offers the ability to view enhanced interactive eBooks, which can include text, photos, animated graphics, audio and other interactive elements. Textbooks, children's books, cookbooks, and photo books are among the types of books that offer the enhanced, multi-touch reading experience available exclusively on an iPad.

ACCESSING THE iBOOKSTORE

From the main iBooks Library screen, which looks like a virtual bookshelf (see Figure 14.2), tap the Store icon near the upper-left corner of the screen to access the online-based iBookstore.

Your tablet must have access to the Internet to find, download, and purchase eBooks from iBookstore. However, you don't need Internet access to read eBooks after you've loaded them into your iPad.

FIGURE 14.2

The main Library screen of iBooks. From here, you can access iBookstore or read an eBook by tapping its cover graphic.

After you access iBookstore, at the bottom of the screen are six command icons. They're labeled Featured, NY Times, Top Charts, Categories, Browse, and Purchased. These six buttons, the Search field, the Library button in the upper-left corner of the screen, and the Featured and Release Date tabs enable you to quickly search the iBookstore's multimillion title eBook selection to find exactly what you are looking for.

Here's a rundown of how you can use these iBookstore command buttons and tabs:

- **Featured:** Titles in this category are eBooks featured by Apple that include new titles by best-selling authors. When you select this search option, you see two tabs near the top center of the screen: Featured and Release Date. When you select the Featured tab a listing of Apple-recommended eBook titles displays. When you select the Release Date tab, the recommended eBooks are sorted based on their release date, with the newest eBooks listed first.

- **NY Times:** Taken from the weekly *New York Times* bestsellers list, these are the books from the newspaper's Fiction and Non-Fiction lists that are available in eBook form from iBookstore. Keep in mind that not all books that appear on the published *New York Times* bestseller lists are available in eBook form or are sold through Apple's iBookstore.

- **Top Charts:** Based on sales of eBooks through iBookstore, the Top Charts category lists the current most popular titles. Here, you find a master list of popular books from all categories, plus individual Top Charts lists within specific categories, such as Business & Personal Finance, Fiction & Literature, Professional & Technical, and Reference. These lists change frequently.

- **Categories:** iBookstore sorts its eBook offerings into 25 categories, such as Arts & Entertainment, Fiction & Literature, Computers & Internet, and Reference to make browsing for books about a specific topic easier.

- **Browse:** This search feature enables you to find eBook titles based on keywords, an author's name, a publisher, a subject matter, or other search criteria.

- **Purchased:** iBookstore automatically keeps track of all your eBook purchases and downloads. Thus, if you delete an eBook from your tablet's internal storage, you can download it again later at no charge. All of your online purchases are tracked by iBookstore and also stored on iCloud, so you never have to worry about accidentally purchasing the same eBook twice. An eBook purchased from iBookstore becomes readable on all of your iOS devices.

UNDERSTANDING iBOOKSTORE'S EBOOK LISTINGS

While browsing iBookstore, you see individual eBook listings for titles that relate to what you are looking for. As you can see in Figure 14.3, a typical eBook listing includes a graphic of the eBook's cover, along with its title, author, category, star-based rating, and price icon.

FIGURE 14.3
An eBook listing offers a quick summary of a book title. As you're browsing iBookstore, you can simultaneously view many eBook listings.

Tap a book's title or cover artwork to access a detailed description of that eBook, which includes the capability to download and read a free sample of most eBook titles. Alternatively, to quickly purchase and download an eBook, tap the Price button within its listing or its Description window. When you tap a Price button, it changes to a Purchase button.

As soon as an eBook is downloaded and ready to read, the book's front cover artwork displays as part of the iBook app's Library screen.

> **NOTE** Some eBooks are freely available from iBookstore. In this case, the Price button displays the word Free. When you tap this button, it is replaced by a Download button. You still need to enter your Apple ID password to confirm your download request, but you are not charged to download free eBook content.

REVIEWING EBOOK DESCRIPTIONS

When you're looking at an eBook listing, if you tap the book's title or cover thumbnail image, a new and detailed eBook Description screen is displayed. This screen is divided into several sections.

For example, there's a Get Sample button, which you can tap to download a free sample of the eBook. Below the cover thumbnail is the eBook's Price button. Tap this button to purchase the book and download it.

The Description screen also displays the eBook's star-based rating. Here, you can view an overall average rating for the eBook. Five stars is the highest rating possible. Scroll down the Description window to read reviews written by others who have purchased, downloaded, and presumably read the eBook.

CUSTOMIZING iBOOKS SETTINGS

From the Library screen of iBooks, tap a book cover thumbnail to open that eBook and start reading it. While you're reading most eBooks, you can hold the iPad in portrait or landscape mode. If you're reading a digital edition of a traditional paperback or hardcover book your reading experience is more authentic if you hold the iPad in portrait mode (vertically).

As you're reading an eBook, tap once anywhere on the screen to make the various command icons, buttons, and options appear. The Library button is displayed near the upper-left corner of the screen. Tap it to return to iBook's Library screen.

To the right of the Library button is the Table of Contents button (shown in Figure 14.4). Tap it to display an interactive Table of Contents for the eBook you're reading.

FIGURE 14.4

The Table of Contents screen for every eBook is interactive. Tap the chapter number or chapter title to jump to the appropriate page.

As you're looking at a Table of Contents, tap any chapter number or title to immediately jump to that location in the book. Alternatively, tap the Bookmarks button to see a list of bookmarks you have previously saved as you were reading that eBook. You'll find out how to set a bookmark later in this section.

As you're reading an eBook, you'll notice several additional command buttons and options near the upper-right corner of the screen. Shown in Figure 14.5, tap the aA icon to adjust the screen brightness, change the font size of the text displayed on the screen, change the font used to display the text, or switch between the Normal, Sepia, and Night visual themes (shown in Figure 14.6). You can also turn on Full Screen mode to fully utilize the iPad's screen while you're reading, and remove the clutter created by the various command icons.

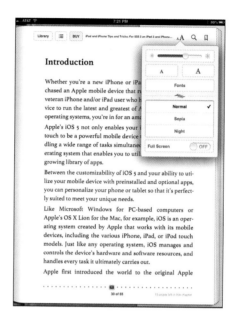

FIGURE 14.5

The aA command icon offers a menu that allows you to fully customize the appearance of an eBook's text on the iPad's screen.

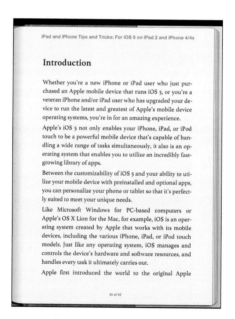

FIGURE 14.6

Themes are a relatively new feature added to the iBooks 2 app. With a touch of an icon, you can change the appearance of an eBook's text.

> **TIP** After tapping the aA icon, tap the small "a" button under the brightness slider to shrink the onscreen font size. Or, tap the "A" button to increase the font size. The changes take effect immediately. Choose a font size and font that is the most visually appealing to you.

Also displayed near the top-right corner of the screen is a magnifying glass icon. Tap this to access a Search field and quickly locate any keyword or search phrase that appears in the eBook you are currently reading.

The Bookmark button is located near the extreme upper-right corner of the iBooks screen. When you tap this button, you add a red bookmark to the page you're reading. Any time you exit out of iBooks, the page number you're currently on is automatically saved, so when you return to reading the eBook later, you can immediately pick up where you left off. However, adding a red bookmark to a page also stores that page. You can later access your list of saved bookmarks from the Table of Contents page, so you can instantly jump to any bookmarked page to refer to it.

> **TIP** To access your list of bookmarks, tap the Table of Contents button. Near the top center of the screen, tap the Bookmarks icon to display the list of bookmarks that you've saved in the eBook you are currently reading. Tap any bookmark listing to jump to that page.

Displayed near the bottom center of the screen is the page number in the eBook you're currently reading, as well as the total number of pages in the eBook. The number of pages remaining in the current chapter is displayed to the right of the page number.

As you're reading, hold your finger on any single word (shown in Figure 14.7) to look up its definition instantly, begin highlighting text, add a note to the margin, or search the text for a specific keyword or phrase.

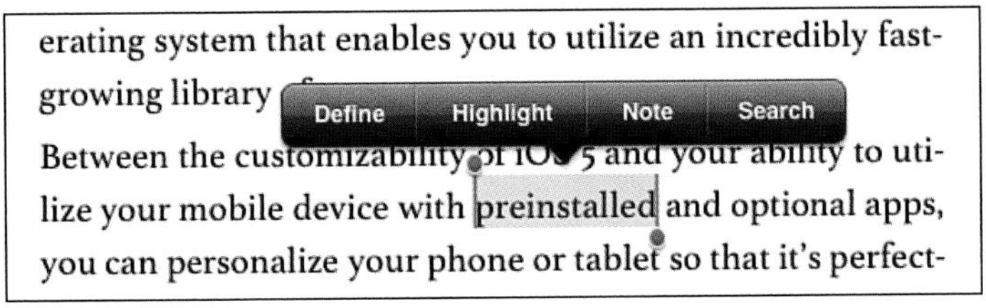

erating system that enables you to utilize an incredibly fast-growing library of iOS 5 and your ability to utilize your mobile device with preinstalled and optional apps, you can personalize your phone or tablet so that it's perfect-

Define **Highlight** **Note** **Search**

FIGURE 14.7

Hold your finger briefly on a word to make a pop-up menu appear that includes the Define, Highlight, Note, and Search commands.

If you tap the Highlight command that appears after holding your finder on a word, you'll be able to select surrounding text and choose from five highlight colors. You can also underline text in red.

Or, if you tap on the Note command, a pop-up sticky note window displays along with the virtual keyboard. You can then enter notes that will be saved within the text, allowing you to refer back to them later.

READING PDF FILES USING THE iBOOKS APP

In addition to reading eBooks, you can use the iBooks 2 app to read (not edit or annotate) PDF files you download or transfer to your iPad. This can include a wide range of business-related documents that vary in length from a single page to a book-length manuscript.

When you receive an email with a PDF file as an attachment, tap and hold your finger on the email's PDF file attachment thumbnail for a few seconds to download and open it.

When a menu window appears, you have several options that depend on which PDF reader apps you have installed on your iPad. In Figure 14.8, the available options are Quick Look, Open in "iBooks," and Open In. If you also have other PDF reader apps installed on your iPad, such as Evernote, PDFpen, or GoodReader for iPad, those apps are listed here as well because you can use them to open and read (as well as edit or annotate) PDF files.

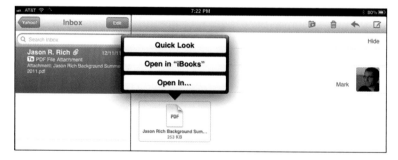

FIGURE 14.8

From the Mail app, you can open and read a PDF file that is an attachment in an incoming email using the iBooks app.

Quick Look enables you to view a PDF document on your iPad's screen. Using the buttons in the upper-right corner of the document preview window, you can then open the PDF file in iBooks, or print the file if you have your iPad configured to work with a wireless printer.

The Open in iBooks command automatically launches the iBooks 2 app and enables you to read the PDF document as if you're reading an eBook you downloaded from iBookstore.

When a PDF file opens in iBooks 2, you see command buttons along the top of the screen and small thumbnails of the PDF document's pages displayed along the bottom of the screen.

Tap the Library button to return to iBook's main Library screen. Notice when you do this that the Library displays all the PDF files stored on your iPad, not only eBooks you downloaded from iBookstore. To access your eBooks, tap the Collections button in the upper-left corner of the iBooks Library screen, and tap the Books option.

As you're viewing a PDF file from within iBooks, next to the Library button is the Table of Contents button. Tap it to display larger thumbnails of each page in your PDF document, and then tap any of the thumbnails to jump to that page. Alternatively, tap the Resume button to return to the main view of your PDF file.

NOTE If you want to be able to edit or annotate a PDF file, you should download and install a third-party app, such as PDFpen on Evernote. See Chapter 13, "Discovering 'Must-Have' Business Apps," for more information about various apps that you can use for working with PDF files.

READING NEWSPAPERS AND MAGAZINES ON YOUR iPAD

Many local, regional, and national newspapers, as well as popular consumer and industry-oriented magazines, are now available in digital form and accessible from your iPad via the Newsstand app that comes preinstalled with iOS 5.1 (or later).

WORKING WITH THE NEWSSTAND APP

Not to be confused with the iBooks app (which is used for finding, purchasing, downloading, and reading eBooks), the Newsstand app is used to manage and access all of your digital newspaper and magazine subscriptions in one place. However, the iBooks and Newsstand apps have a similar user interface, so after you learn how to use one, you'll have no trouble using the other.

NOTE Many of the world's most popular newspapers, including *The New York Times*, *The Wall Street Journal*, *Barron's*, and *USA Today* are now published in digital form, as are popular business-oriented magazines, such as *Inc. Magazine*, *TIME*, *Newsweek*, *FORTUNE Magazine*, *Bloomberg BusinessWeek*, *Harvard Business Review*, *The Economist*, and *Fast Company*.

After you launch Newsstand (shown in Figure 14.9), tap the Store icon and browse through the ever-growing selection of digital newspapers and magazines that are available for the iPad. With the tap of an icon, you can subscribe to any publication, or in some instances, purchase a single current or back issue.

FIGURE 14.9

The main Newsstand screen displays thumbnails for all newspaper and magazine issues currently stored on your iPad.

All purchases you make are automatically billed to the credit card you have on file with your Apple ID account, or you can pay using iTunes gift cards.

TIP To entice you to become a paid subscriber, some publishers offer free issues of their digital newspaper or magazine that you can download and read before actually paying for a subscription.

Some publications give away the digital edition of their publication for free to paid subscribers of the print edition.

After you purchase a digital newspaper or magazine subscription (or a single issue of a publication), it appears on your Newsstand shelf in the Newsstand app. Tap the publication's cover thumbnail to access the available issue(s).

If you've subscribed to a digital publication, Newsstand automatically downloads the most current issue as soon as it's published (assuming your tablet has a Wi-Fi Internet connection available), so when you wake your tablet from Sleep Mode each morning, the latest edition of your favorite newspaper can be waiting for you.

TIP To use a 3G or 4G wireless data network to automatically download digital publications, you must turn on this feature from within the Settings app. Launch Settings, select the Store menu option from the left side of the screen, and then turn on the virtual switch associated with the Use Cellular Data option.

You also need to turn on the virtual switches associated with each specific newspaper or magazine subscription that's listed. Downloading digital publications using a cellular data network quickly uses up your monthly data allocation and could ultimately result in additional charges if you're not on an unlimited data plan.

Using a Wi-Fi connection, your iPad automatically downloads all new publication content when it becomes available, without you having to worry about using up your monthly wireless data allocation.

A Home screen icon badge and the Notification Center notify you immediately whenever a new issue of a digital publication is automatically downloaded to your iPad and is ready for reading. When you access Newsstand, you also see a thumbnail of that publication's cover on the main Newsstand shelf screen.

TIP Shop for digital newspapers or magazines from within the Newsstand app by tapping the Store icon. Alternatively, you can find and purchase digital newspapers and magazines from within the App Store. However, all new purchases are sent directly to your tablet's Newsstand folder for easy access within the Newsstand app.

Although most digital publications allow you to view the newspaper or magazine's content from within the Newsstand app, some digital publications are designed to be more interactive and have their own proprietary app. You can still find these publications using the Newsstand app (or the App Store app), however, you are prompted to download and install the proprietary app in order to view a publication's content.

READING PUBLICATIONS USING NEWSSTAND

Every publisher utilizes the iPad's vibrant touch screen in a different way in order to transform a traditionally printed newspaper or magazine into an engaging and interactive reading experience on the tablet. Thus, each publication has its own user interface.

In most cases, a digital edition of a publication faithfully reproduces the printed edition and features the same content. However, you'll often discover that the digital edition of a publication that's accessible from your iPad offers bonus content, such as links to websites, video clips, animated slide shows, or interactive elements not offered by the printed edition.

As you'll discover, reading a digital publication is very much like reading an eBook. Figure 14.10 shows the digital edition of *GQ*. Use a finger swipe motion to turn the pages, or to scroll up or down on a page. Tap the Table of Contents icon to view an interactive table of contents for each issue of the publication. When viewing some publications, you can also use a reverse pinch, pinch, or double-tap finger motion to zoom in or zoom out on specific content.

Depending on the publisher, you might be able to access past issues of a publication at any given time in addition to the current issue.

FIGURE 14.10

Each page of GQ magazine's digital edition looks very much like the printed edition.

MANAGING YOUR NEWSPAPER AND MAGAZINE SUBSCRIPTIONS

If you opt to subscribe to a digital publication, you often need to select a duration for your subscription, such as one year. However, almost all digital subscriptions acquired through the Newsstand app are auto-renewing. Thus, when the subscription ends, unless you manually cancel it, Newsstand automatically renews your subscription and bills your credit card accordingly.

To manage your recurring subscriptions, launch the Newsstand app and tap the Store icon. From the Newsstand store, tap the Featured command icon near the bottom of the screen. Scroll to the bottom of the screen and tap the Apple ID icon. When prompted, enter your Apple ID password.

Next, from the Account Settings window that appears (shown in Figure 14.11), tap the Manage icon displayed under the Subscriptions heading. Displayed on the Subscriptions screen is a listing of all publications you've subscribed to. Tap any publication's listing to see the expiration date of your subscription, to cancel a subscription, or to renew your subscription.

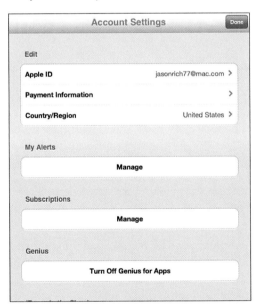

FIGURE 14.11

From within the Newsstand app, you can manage your subscriptions as long as your iPad has access to the Internet.

IN THIS CHAPTER

- The difference between download-ing and streaming web content
- How to acquire and download content from iTunes
- Sources for streaming audio and video content

15

DOWNLOADING VERSUS STREAMING ONLINE CONTENT

In addition to using apps on your iPad to accomplish various tasks, you can experience content on your tablet in the form of music, eBooks, audiobooks, TV show episodes, movies, music videos, digital editions of newspapers and magazines, and YouTube videos, for example.

NOTE To learn more about finding, downloading and installing apps, see Chapter 6, "Finding and Installing Apps from the App Store."

To learn more about downloading and reading eBooks and digital newspapers/magazines on your iPad, see Chapter 14, "Staying Informed Using the iBooks and Newsstand Apps."

Each type of media requires you to utilize a specific app to experience it. However, you also have the option to download, store, and experience content on your iPad, or simply stream content from the Internet to your iPad.

Whether you're taking an airplane or train ride, commuting to work, traveling on vacation, or simply relaxing by watching your favorite TV show or movie on demand, your iPad offers a handful of ways you can download or stream content from the Internet.

> **TIP** From your iPad, you can stay current on late-breaking national, international, business, and financial news from virtually anywhere and at any time when you access or stream programming from TV news stations or news radio broadcasts.

UNDERSTANDING THE DIFFERENCE BETWEEN DOWNLOADING AND STREAMING CONTENT

Content you download from the Internet is stored in your tablet's internal memory. It then becomes available to you any time you want to experience it. Keep in mind that when it comes to acquiring media to enjoy on your tablet, you typically must pay a fee to purchase and download a TV show episode or movie (or to rent a movie).

The alternative is to stream content from the Internet. In this case, no content is actually saved on your iPad, and you can often stream content for free (or pay a low monthly fee for unlimited access to content).

> **CAUTION** The ability to stream content from the Web and experience it on your iPad gives you free access to a wide range of programming. However, whenever you stream audio or video content from the Web you are transferring a tremendous amount of data to your tablet. Thus, if you use a 3G or 4G connection, you quickly use your monthly wireless data allocation. So, when streaming web content, it's best to use a Wi-Fi connection.
>
> Not only does a Wi-Fi connection allow data to be transferred to your tablet at much faster speeds, there's also no limit as to how much data you can send or receive. Plus, when streaming video content, you are often able to view it at a higher resolution when you use a Wi-Fi connection, and none of your iPad's internal storage space is needed.

WHAT YOU SHOULD KNOW ABOUT DOWNLOADING CONTENT

To download content, you must be connected to the Internet. However, after the content is stored on your tablet, you can enjoy it again and again without having an Internet connection (such as while your iPad is in Airplane Mode, when you're out of a Wi-Fi hotspot's radius, or there's no wireless data signal available).

NOTE Depending on the type of media you're downloading, you might need a Wi-Fi connection rather than a 3G (4G) connection. For music, eBooks, and digital editions of newspapers or magazines (which have smaller files), a 3G connection is typically sufficient to download content from the Web or from the iTunes Store. However, you need a Wi-Fi or 4G connection for larger files (larger than 50MB), such as TV show episodes, movies, or audiobooks.

TIP Instead of downloading media directly from your iPad via the iTunes Store, iBookstore, Newsstand, or the App Store, you can use the free iTunes software on your PC or Mac computer to initially purchase and download the content and then sync it to your iPad later using iTunes Sync or transfer it from iCloud.

With the exception of rented movies, content you download and acquire from the Internet is then owned by you. Thus, you have the right to experience it as often as you'd like on your iPad. Or, if it's iTunes content, you can also experience it on your primary computer(s), iPhone, iPod touch, and Apple TV as long as the devices are linked to the same iCloud account.

NOTE All content you purchase or acquire from iTunes is automatically saved within your free Apple iCloud account and becomes accessible from all your computers and iOS mobile devices that are linked to the same iCloud account. Apple provides you with unlimited free online storage space in your iCloud account for content you purchase from iTunes, the App Store, Newsstand, or iBookstore. Refer to Chapter 9, "Syncing Your iPad via iTunes or iCloud," for more information about the iCloud service.

Rented movies from iTunes also are temporarily stored on your iPad (and take up internal storage space), and remain there for up to 30 days before they're automatically deleted. However, after you begin playing a rented movie from iTunes, you have 24 hours to watch it as often as you'd like before it is automatically deleted from your tablet.

You pay for content you purchase from iTunes at the time you download it. You pay a one-time fee for unlimited use of that content in terms of how frequently you can experience it. Some content that's available from iTunes, iBookstore, Newsstand, or the App Store is also offered for free. This is treated, however, as purchased content by your iPad, but you are not charged for it.

> **NOTE** Purchases made from the iTunes Store, iBookstore, Newsstand, or the App Store are automatically billed to the credit card or debit card you have linked to your Apple ID account. You can also redeem iTunes Gift Cards to make purchases.

THE COST OF DOWNLOADING CONTENT TO YOUR iPAD

The cost of downloading content to your iPad varies based on the type of content. Although some content is free from the iTunes Store, iBookstore, Newsstand, and App Store, you typically have to purchase downloadable content outright. Table 15.1 lists the typical fees for downloading media from the iTunes Store and Apple's other online ventures.

Table 15.1   The Price of iTunes Content

Content Type	Standard Definition	High Definition
Purchase Music Single (One Song)	$.99 to $1.29	N/A
Purchase Music Album	$7.99 to $15.99	N/A
Purchase Music Video	$1.99	N/A
Purchase TV Show Episode	$1.99	$2.99
Purchase Made-for-TV Movie	$3.99	$4.99
Purchase Entire Season of a TV Show	Price varies, based on TV series and number of episodes. It's always cheaper to purchase an entire season, as opposed to separately purchasing all episodes in a season.	Price varies, based on TV series and number of episodes. It's always cheaper to purchase an entire season, as opposed to all episodes in a season separately.
Purchase Movie	$.99 to $14.99	$.99 to $19.99

Content Type	Standard Definition	High Definition
Rent Movie	$.99 to $3.99 (New releases start at $3.99, with library titles available for as little as $.99 per rental.)	$1.99 to $4.99 (New releases start at $4.99, with library titles available for as little as $1.99 per rental.)
Audiobooks from iTunes or Audible.com	$.95 to $41.95 (Unabridged audiobooks of current bestsellers tend to be among the higher priced titles. These tend to range from $14.95 to $26.95.)	N/A

TIP To save money downloading and listening to audiobooks, sign up for an optional membership to the Audible.com service. A monthly fee of $14.95 applies, but you receive one free, full-length audiobook of your choice per month, plus a significant discount on additional audiobook purchases throughout the month. Use the free Audible app on your iPad to listen to audiobooks you purchase from Audible.com.

TIP When shopping for music or TV show episodes from iTunes, you can save money by utilizing the Complete My Album or Complete My Season feature. If you purchase one or more songs from a single album (or one or more episodes from a TV series), you can go back at anytime and download the entire album or a complete TV series season at a discounted rate. To learn more about the iTunes Complete My Album feature, visit http://support.apple.com/kb/HT1849. To learn more about the iTunes Complete My Season feature, visit http://support.apple.com/kb/HT5070.

YOU CAN ALSO STREAM CONTENT FROM THE INTERNET

The alternative to downloading content to experience on your tablet is to stream it directly from the Internet. Content such as TV show episodes, videos, music, and movies can be streamed from various sources on the Internet, such as Netflix, Hulu Plus, and using dozens of other specialized apps from radio stations and TV networks, for example. These apps are explained shortly.

When you stream content directly from the Internet, it is not stored on your iPad. Instead, a special media player app plays the content on your iPad directly from the Web. Thus, you need a constant Internet connection to experience the content. If you don't have an Internet connection, you are not able to access streaming content.

APPS FOR STREAMING WEB CONTENT

The type of content you want to experience on your iPad determines which apps you use. The following sections help you select the most appropriate app for acquiring and then experiencing specific types of content.

DOWNLOADABLE iPAD CONTENT

There are many different types of content you can download, acquire, or stream from the Internet. Table 15.2 explains which iPad app you'll need to utilize, access, or exerience that content.

Table 15.2   Choose the Right App to Access Specific Content

Content Type	App Needed to Acquire Content	App Needed to Experience Content	Notes
Music	iTunes	Music	From the iTunes Store, you can purchase individual songs or entire albums.
Audiobooks	iTunes or Audible.com	Music or Audible*	Use the Music app to listen to audiobooks acquired from iTunes. Use the Audible app to listen to audiobooks acquired from the Audible.com service.
TV Show Episodes	iTunes	Videos	From the iTunes Store, you can purchase individual TV show episodes or entire seasons of a TV show.
Movies	iTunes	Videos	You can either rent or purchase movies from iTunes.
Movies Shot Yourself (Using Your iPad or Another Video Camera)	Camera	Photos or iMovie**	You can shoot movies using the Camera app or another photography app on your iPad, or you can transfer them to your iPad via iTunes Sync.

Content Type	App Needed to Acquire Content	App Needed to Experience Content	Notes
eBooks	iBooks	iBooks	Use iBooks to acquire and read eBooks from Apple's online-based iBookstore. You can also use a third-party app, such as Kindle or NOOK, to read eBooks acquired from Amazon.com or BN.com, respectively.
Digital Edition of a Newspaper or Magazine	Newsstand	Newsstand or a publication's proprietary app	Some digital publications require a proprietary app that's available from the App Store.
Podcasts	iTunes	Music	Download podcasts for free from the iTunes Store.
Apps	App Store	The app itself that you download and install	Apps for the iPad are available from Apple's App Store. See Chapter 7 for more information about apps.

* Audible is a third-party app that's a free download from the App Store. You use it to experience content purchased or downloaded from Audible.com's online store.

** iMovie is an optional app from Apple that you use to edit and play movies you shot yourself or that are not copyrighted or copy protected.

Using a specialized app that serves as an audio or video player, you can stream a wide range of content directly from the Internet. Often, streamed content is free of charge. In some cases, you can pay a flat monthly fee to experience unlimited content from a specific online-based content-streaming service, such as Netflix or Sirius/XM.

TIP   In addition to the apps used for streaming specific TV networks or programming from cable service providers, many television stations (including network affiliates) throughout the country have their own proprietary apps for streaming local news and other programming. In addition, some individual network and cable TV shows also have their own proprietary apps, which feature interactive content in addition to the ability to watch clips from that specific TV show or to view entire episodes.

ABC News, CBS News, NBC Nightly News, CBS Sunday Morning, 60 Minutes, Good Morning America, and The Today Show all have their own apps for streaming free national news broadcasts from the respective network or show.

STREAMING TV AND MOVIE PROGRAMMING

Table 15.3 is just a sampling of the video content that can be streamed directly from the Internet to your iPad, including full-length TV show episodes and movies. The majority of these services work exclusively within the United States and won't work while you're traveling abroad.

When traveling overseas, you can download TV show episodes and/or movies from iTunes and store them on your tablet. You can do this before you leave home or while traveling abroad; you simply must have a Wi-Fi Internet connection.

Table 15.3   Access Content from Specific TV Networks

Content Type	App Needed to Play Content	Notes
ABC Television Network Programming	ABC Player	Free.
Bloomberg TV	Bloomberg TV+	This app gives you free access to Bloomberg Television programming, whereas the Bloomberg Anywhere and Bloomberg for iPad apps offer financial data.
CBS News Programming	CBS News for iPad	Free.
Cinemax Programming	MAX Go	Free if you're already a paid Cinemax subscriber.
CNN Programming	CNN App for iPad	Free.
ESPN TV Programming	WatchESPN	Free.
FOX News Programming	Fox News for iPad	Free.
FOX Business News Programming	Fox Business for iPad	Free.
HBO Programming	HBO Go	Free if you're already a paid HBO subscriber.
Hulu Plus TV Shows and Movies	Hulu Plus	A monthly $8.00 fee applies for unlimited access.
NBC Television Network Programming	NBC	Free.
Netflix TV Shows and Movies	Netflix	A monthly $8.00 fee applies for unlimited access.
On-Demand COX Cable TV Programming	Cox TV Connect for iPad	Free for paid Cox TV subscribers.
On-Demand DirectTV TV Programming	DirectTV App for iPad	Free for paid DirectTV subscribers.

Content Type	App Needed to Play Content	Notes
On-Demand Time Warner Cable TV Programming	TWC TV	Free for paid Time Warner Cable subscribers.
On-Demand Xfinity (Comcast) Cable TV Programming	Xfinity	Free for paid Xfinity subscribers.
Showtime Programming	Showtime Anytime	Free for paid Showtime subscribers.
Stream shows from CBS, The CW, Showtime, CNet and Other Cable Networks	TV.com	Free.
Stream shows from The CW Television Network	The CW	Free.
Wall Street Journal Live	WSJ Live	Free.
Weather Channel Programming	The Weather Channel for iPad	Free.
YouTube Videos	YouTube	Preinstalled on your iPad. The YouTube service is free.

TIP   With any app that's used for streaming TV shows and/or movies, you can watch your favorite programming on demand as long as your iPad has access to the Web. You never have to worry about missing the scheduled air time for a show or movie on TV again because you decide what to watch and when it begins. You can also pause, fast forward, or rewind streaming content. With some apps you can stop the program altogether, use your iPad for something else, and then pick up where you left off later.

Plus, instead of paying $15.00 or more for a pay-per-view movie while staying at a hotel while you're traveling, you can simply stream a movie on your iPad and enjoy a high-definition video experience, with amazing sound quality (if you attach optional headphones to the tablet's headphones jack). See Chapter 18, "Must-Have Accessories," for information about top-quality headphones that are perfect for use with the iPad.

STREAMING AUDIO CONTENT

Table 15.4 lists just some of the apps you can use to stream audio programming and/or music directly from the Internet.

Table 15.4   Radio and Audio Program You Can Stream from the Web

Content Type	App Needed to Play Content	Notes
Conservative Talk Radio	iTalk Conservative Talk Radio ($2.99)	Purchase the app once, and then freely listen to unlimited programming from well-known conservative talk radio personalities, such as Rush Limbaugh, Michael Savage, Don Imus, Glen Beck, and Sean Hannity.
ESPN Radio Programming	ESPN Radio	Purchase the app for $2.99, and then stream free and unlimited programming from ESPN radio station affiliates throughout the country.
Internet Radio Programming	Internet Online Radio ($3.99)	After purchasing the app once, listen to more than 48,000 Internet-based radio stations for free, including programming from 184 countries.
Music Programming	Pandora Radio	Free.
Music Programming	iHeartRadio for iPad	Free.
NPR Radio Programming	NPR for iPad	Free.
Radio and Podcast Programming	Pocket Tunes Radio ($4.99)	Stream content from hundreds of commercial radio stations as well as listen to podcasts. No monthly fees apply after you purchase the app once.
SiriusXM Radio Programming	SiriusXM Internet Radio	A monthly fee is required for unlimited access to hundreds of satellite radio stations.

NOTE One other difference between paying for and downloading iTunes TV show and movie content versus streaming similar content is that when you stream free video content, it often includes commercials. For example, if you watch a TV show using ABC Player or the NBC app, you must watch commercials as part of the programming, just as if you're watching television. However, if you purchase those same shows from iTunes, they are commercial free. Streaming "premium" content from networks such as Showtime or HBO also is commercial free because you must already be a paid Showtime or HBO subscriber to access it. Also, because you're paying a monthly fee to access Netflix or Hulu Plus programming, it is commercial free.

16

PROTECTING YOUR iPAD AND ITS DATA

Your iPad is designed to be taken with you and used throughout the day in a variety of settings and conditions. However, you need to make sure to protect the tablet as you carry it with you. In addition to keeping the battery charged, it's also important to protect the iPad's screen against accidental scratches and to safeguard the entire tablet from accidents, such as being dropped or having some type of liquid spilled on it.

After you have made sure the iPad itself is well protected, you should focus on your important and potentially confidential data to make sure it too is safe. Finally, you might also consider purchasing optional insurance for your tablet in case it does get damaged, lost, or stolen.

With the new iPad, Apple now offers its AppleCare+ coverage, which recently has been enhanced. Priced at $99.00 for two years, AppleCare+ covers the tablet against certain types of problems and accidental damage and grants you unlimited

access to Apple's superior technical support in-person at Apple Stores or on the telephone. If a repair needs to be made, however, a $49 service fee applies. AppleCare+ does not cover the tablet against loss or theft.

Another alternative is to purchase third-party insurance, which does not include technical support but does offer comprehensive coverage against damage, loss, or theft.

PROTECTING YOUR iPAD FROM PHYSICAL DAMAGE

Your iPad's slick modern exterior covers a powerful but nonetheless delicate electronic device. Apple designed the tablet to be held and touched, but even the hardiest of gadgets can be damaged by heavy use and the accidents of everyday life. To provide sufficient physical protection for your iPad, you can start at the screen level and build layers of defense until your tablet is well armored against harm.

The options you choose should depend on the risks you expect your iPad to encounter and the amount of money you're willing to spend to defend it from those hazards. The following sections work from the lowest level outward, starting with a clear, essentially invisible film that protects the touch screen from the oils in your skin and the occasional raindrop, and working all the way out to slipcovers and carriers for the entire iPad.

TOUCHSCREEN FILMS

There are a handful of ways you can protect your iPad's screen against cracks, scratches, minor water damage, glare, and excessive smudges (due to fingerprints). The easiest thing to do is purchase a clear, thin, highly durable protective film that fits over the screen (or the entire tablet). Although these films are easily removable, they're meant to be kept on the tablet permanently.

Created from incredibly strong, military-grade material, these protective films, which are offered by a variety of companies, help protect your tablet's screen and keep it clean. They're typically less than one or two millimeters thick, and are virtually invisible after you apply them to the tablet's screen or body.

> TIP   When purchasing a clear, protective film for your iPad, make sure you choose one that's been custom-shaped for the iPad model you own, especially if you're purchasing a full-body protective film for your tablet. There are minor differences between the various iPad models.

Zagg (www.zagg.com) is one of dozens of companies that offer protective films for the various iPad models. The company's InvisibleSHIELD for iPad, for example, offers an incredibly strong protective film for just the front of your tablet ($29.99) or the entire iPad ($39.99).

In addition to offering a thin but strong layer of protection, glare-resistance, and scratch-resistance, the full-body InvisibleSHIELD makes the iPad less slippery to hold. InvisibleSHIELD is also designed to reduce fingerprint smudges on the screen, and it can be easily cleaned.

The Zagg InvisibleSHIELD (shown in Figure 16.1), and other protective films like it, are available from any store that sells Apple products, including many consumer electronics stores, such as Best Buy.

FIGURE 16.1

Zagg.com's InvisibleSHIELD offers a thin, clear protective film covering to the iPad's screen, as well as its entire body.

After you've attached the film, it is almost invisible. It does not negatively affect the sensitivity, clarity, or functionality of the iPad's touch screen in any way.

Within many shopping malls across the U.S., you'll find specialized kiosks that sell similar protective film products for your iPad (and other devices). In some cases, these companies will apply the protective film to your device for you. Removing the protective film, however, takes just seconds, and it leaves no sticky residue.

> **TIP** 3M offers a special Screen Protector film for the various iPad models that also includes the company's patented Privacy Screen feature. When installed over your tablet's screen, if you're looking at the screen head-on, you see everything with complete clarity. However, if someone attempts to look over your shoulder, all he sees on your iPad is a dark, blank screen.
>
> This Privacy Screen technology can help you keep your data or whatever you're working on private, and it also protects your screen against scratches. To purchase an optional 3M Privacy Screen protector film for your iPad model ($39.99), visit www.Shop3M.com.

PROTECTIVE SKINS FOR YOUR iPAD

To protect the back of your iPad, several companies, including SkinIt (www.skinit.com), Decal Girl (www.decalgirl.com), and GelaSkins (www.gelaskins.com), offer protective skins made from the same highly durable, ultra-thin material as the protective screen films, but they are imprinted with decorative graphics or can be printed with your own digital photo or company logo.

A skin offers a way to protect your tablet while also customizing and personalizing its exterior look. Skins for the iPad are priced at less than $20.00 each. There are hundreds of available design choices.

You can apply the skin to the tablet in minutes, and it is meant to remain attached permanently. However, it is easily removable in seconds. A protective skin adds less than one millimeter of thickness to the tablet, and can be used with any other screen cover, case, or stand.

SCREEN COVERS AND CASES

Adding a clear protective film to your iPad is certainly a good strategy to help protect your tablet when it's being used or transported. In addition to this optional protection, however, seriously consider investing in a screen cover for your iPad. A screen cover is used to protect the screen when the device is not in use, such as when you're transporting it.

While designing the iPad 2, Apple created a special screen cover for it, called the Smart Cover, which protects the tablet's screen when it's not in use. In addition, as you're using the iPad, the Smart Cover doubles as a stand (adjustable into two different positions). The Smart Cover also works perfectly with the new iPad.

Made from either leather ($69.00) or polyurethane ($39.00), these interchangeable Apple Smart Covers quickly attach and detach from your tablet using magnets.

When placed over the screen, a Smart Cover automatically places your iPad 2 or new iPad into Sleep Mode. When removed, it wakes the device.

When you fold back the Smart Cover, it can serve as a stand that enables you to position your tablet horizontally on a flat surface, which is ideal for watching a movie. You can also arrange the Smart Cover into a position that's more suitable for typing.

> CAUTION You cannot use an Apple Smart Cover as a stand to hold your iPad 2 or new iPad in a portrait (vertical) position. Also, these covers are not designed for use with the original iPad.

Apple's Smart Covers come in 10 colors. The leather versions offer a more conservative color selection and have a classier look that's better suited to business professionals. Smart Covers are available wherever Apple products are sold, including from Apple Stores and Apple.com. For more information, visit www.apple.com/ipad/accessories.

Several companies that manufacture cases and accessories for the various iPad models have also released their own versions of the Smart Cover. Some add slightly different functionality or a different color selection.

> TIP When choosing any type of screen cover or case for your iPad, make sure that it offers ample protection but also keeps all the tablet's buttons and ports easily accessible without requiring that you remove the iPad from the case. Depending on your needs, you might also want a case that looks stylish but also easily fits in your briefcase, purse, backpack, or messenger bag.
>
> Keep in mind that how much you pay for a "designer" iPad screen cover or case often has little relevance to its quality, functionality, or stylish design. Be sure to choose a screen cover or case for your tablet that's well made.

FULL-BODY CASES

Some cases for the iPad are designed to protect the entire tablet (front and back) when it's not in use. These cases come in a variety of designs and are made from many different types of materials.

A handful of full-body cases for the iPad have a flap that covers the tablet's screen when it's not in use that also folds back to offer some type of stand functionality.

The benefit to a full-body case is that when you transport your tablet, or even when it's in use, the entire unit is protected against scratches if you accidentally drop it or if the iPad is exposed to a small amount of liquid. You can safely place an iPad that's fully protected by a case in a briefcase, purse, backpack, or messenger bag without fear of damaging or scuffing the unit.

Many companies offer full-body cases. When shopping for this type of case, it's essential that you choose one that's designed for the iPad model you own. In addition to selecting a case to protect your tablet, the appearance of the case is important from a style standpoint, but more important is its craftsmanship and quality.

Plan on spending anywhere from $19.95 to $199.00 for a full-body case for your tablet. With so many cases to choose from, you can easily find one that perfectly fits your needs and sense of style.

One example of a handcrafted and extremely durable full-body leather case for the iPad 2 or new iPad, which also doubles as a stand, is available from Saddleback Leather Company ($104.00, www.saddlebackleather.com). Available in four stylish colors, these 100% leather cases (see Figure 16.2) engulf the entire tablet, but all of the iPad's buttons and ports are still readily accessible.

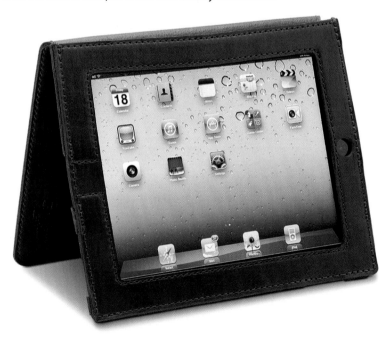

FIGURE 16.2

The handcrafted leather iPad 2 case from Saddleback Leather Company is durable and stylish, and it has a sophisticated look.

When closed, the Saddleback Leather Company's iPad case protects the tablet's screen. However, when its front flap is flipped back, the case can serve as stand that holds your iPad in a horizontal or vertical position, or in a position that's conducive to typing.

The iPad case available from Saddleback Leather Company is so well made, using premium-quality leather and superior craftsmanship, it's designed to last for decades (long after your tablet has become outdated and you have replaced it). Saddleback Leather Company also offers a gorgeous line of handcrafted leather satchels and shoulder bags that contain an interior compartment that perfectly holds the iPad.

Lusso Cartella (www.lussocartella.com) is another company that offers a hand-crafted, portfolio-style leather case for the iPad 2 or new iPad. The case has an exterior pocket that can hold a smartphone, pens, business cards, and small iPad accessories (such as the USB cable and AC plug). Designed for a mobile executive, the Mobile Office iPad case ($199.00) comes in several colors, is suitable (from a style standpoint) for men or women, is extremely durable, and is exceptionally well made. It's shown in Figure 16.3.

FIGURE 16.3

The handcrafted Lusso Cartella Mobile Office iPad case offers both elegance and protection.

> **TIP** To find other full-body cases for the iPad, enter the search phrase "iPad Case" in any search engine or visit any consumer electronics retailer that sells Apple products. Many of these retail stores, however, don't offer the higher-quality, designer cases that many business professionals seek. Those types of cases are more readily available from the Web.
>
> For example, you'll find a nice selection of quality leather iPad cases and screen covers that offer a sophisticated and conservative look from Sena Cases (www.senacases.com). These cases range in price from $75.00 to $125.00.
>
> Brookstone (www.brookstone.com) also offers a selection of full-body leather cases for the various iPad models.

Another extremely elegant iPad cover solution that's suitable for business executives comes from J.W. Hulme Company (www.jwhulmeco.com). It's a handcrafted iPad 2/new iPad Smart Cover and stand combo that's made from high-quality leather.

Unlike Apple's Smart Cover (which only covers the iPad's screen), the iPad Smart Cover & Sleeve ($295.00) from J.W. Hulme Company (shown in Figure 16.4) encases the entire iPad and serves as a Smart Cover to protect the screen. When in use, the leather Smart Cover can be folded back to be used as a stand with two position options.

FIGURE 16.4

Priced at $295, the iPad Smart Cover & Sleeve from J.W. Hulme Company isn't cheap, but it's extremely elegant.

The iPad Smart Cover & Sleeve offers easy access to all of the iPad's buttons and ports but provides a luxurious way to protect the tablet both while you're using it and while you're transporting it.

SLIPCOVERS, SLEEVES, AND POUCHES

Designed for those times when you're transporting your tablet, a handful of companies make custom-shaped, padded slip covers, sleeves, and pouches. Whether you're carrying your iPad alone or inserting the tablet into a briefcase, purse, backpack, or messenger bag, you'll know the padded case, sleeve, or pouch is keeping the entire tablet well protected.

Many companies, including those in the following list, offer iPad slip covers, sleeves, and pouches in a wide range of colors and styles:

■ **WaterField Designs** (http://sfbags.com/products/ipad-cases/ipad-cases.php): This company offers multiple iPad 2 and new iPad-specific cases and covers, each of which comes in a variety of colors. The company also offers messenger-style bags with built-in, padded compartments designed for the iPad. Figure 16.5 shows the iPad Travel Express case for the iPad ($69.99). It comes in a variety of colors and is made from durable Ballistic nylon.

FIGURE 16.5

The iPad Travel Express case for iPad covers the entire tablet when it's being transported, and can also be used with a Smart Cover.

- **Timbuk2** (www.timbuk2.com): This San Francisco-based company's large selection of messenger bags and backpacks are made from extremely durable ballistic nylon and have strong hook-and-loop closures. The bags offer compartments for an iPad, or stand-alone, custom-fitted padded slip cases for the tablet (sold separately).

- **BoxWave** (www.boxwave.com): In addition to offering a handful of different cases and covers for the various iPad models, the company offers the Manila iPad Leather Envelope (from $29.95), which looks like a traditional manila envelope. In reality, it's a well-made, custom-fit, padded slipcover for your iPad. This is a slim and lightweight slipcover that also offers a soft interior to keep your tablet from getting scuffed during transport.

SECURING YOUR DATA

Throughout this book, you've read about a handful of ways to protect the data stored on your tablet. For example, you can use the passcode protection feature that's built in to the iOS. When activated, you must enter the correct passcode (which you preset) before you can get past the iPad's Lock screen whenever the tablet is turned on or awakened from Sleep Mode.

To recap, you can activate the iPad's Passcode option by tapping the Settings app icon from the Home screen and then selecting the General option from the left side of the Settings screen.

With the General option highlighted, select the Passcode Lock feature that's displayed on the right side of the screen. When the Passcode Lock window appears, tap the Turn Passcode On tab near the top of the screen (see Figure 16.6), and then enter and confirm a custom four-digit numeric passcode when prompted.

For added protection, you can turn on the Erase Data option (also found in the Passcode Lock screen of the Settings app). When this additional feature is active, if someone enters the wrong passcode 10 times, all data on your tablet is deleted.

Figure 16.7 shows what the Lock screen looks like when the Passcode feature is turned on. However, if you're concerned that a four-digit passcode doesn't offer ample protection, you can turn off the Simple Passcode option (also found in the Passcode Lock window of the Settings app). This enables you to create and use a longer, alphanumeric password.

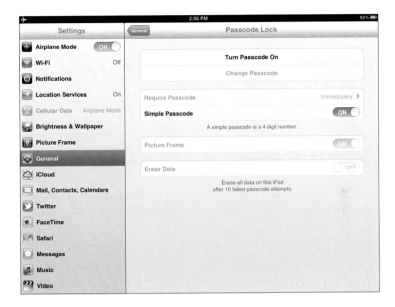

FIGURE 16.6

From the Passcode Lock window of the Settings app, you can set and activate either a four-digit passcode or an alphanumeric password of any length to help keep unauthorized people from accessing your tablet and its data.

FIGURE 16.7

When turned on, an iPad user must enter the correct passcode before being allowed to progress past the tablet's Lock screen.

TIP   If you're using your iPad to access your company's network, your company can implement additional security software onto the network itself that ensures a secure wireless connection whenever you access it with an iPad. Based on the type of network you'll be accessing, the steps for establishing this secure connection vary. To learn more, visit www.apple.com/ipad/business/integration.

NOTE   If you use your iPad to connect to a corporate intranet, Juniper Networks offers its proprietary Junos Pulse Mobile Security Suite (888-586-4737, www.juniper.net/pulse). It provides instant and secure connectivity to your corporate intranet from anywhere. This includes secure remote access to corporate email, applications, and intranet resources providing that the corporate intranet itself utilizes the Juniper Networks Secure Access SSL VPN Appliance.

PROTECTING YOUR iPAD FROM THEFT OR LOSS

If your iPad is lost or stolen, Apple offers its powerful Find My iPad feature via iCloud, which enables you to pinpoint the tablet's exact location on a map as long as it's turned on and able to connect to the Internet. If the tablet is turned off, you can set the Find My iPad feature to keep trying to locate the iPad if it is later turned on.

To utilize Find My iPad, you must set up your device in advance (prior to it being lost or stolen). To do this on an iPad running iOS 5.1 or later, access the Home screen and tap the Settings icon.

Next, select iCloud menu option and either create a free iCloud account (using your Apple ID) or access your existing iCloud account. If you're creating a new iCloud account, it must be verified before the Find My iPad service can work.

From the iCloud account screen, scroll down and turn on the Find My iPad feature by tapping the virtual On/Off switch associated with it so that the switch is in the On position. This enables Apple to locate your iPad whenever it's turned on (and not in Airplane Mode).

After you have activated Find My iPad, if you misplace your iPad or the tablet is stolen then you can access the iCloud website (www.iCloud.com/#find) from any computer or wireless Internet device and have the Find My iPad service quickly pinpoint the exact location of your device.

TIP   If you're also an iPhone user, you can download the free Find My iPhone app from the App Store, which enables you to locate your iPhone, iPad, iMac, or MacBook using this free service. Or, you can install the Find My iPhone app on your iPad to locate your various other Apple devices from your tablet.

Using the Find My iPad feature (as long as the tablet is connected to the Internet using a Wi-Fi, 3G, or 4G connection), you can remotely type a message that displays on your tablet's screen (asking for the iPad to be returned), or you can force the device to emit a sound (so you can more easily find it if it's lost in the same location where you are, such as if it's under the sofa cushion).

You can also remotely lock the device using a password, or you can wipe out and delete the contents of your iPad, which ensures that your sensitive data doesn't fall into the wrong hands. You can always restore your data from an iTunes or iCloud backup after the unit has been retrieved.

Although this is a useful tool for securing your iPad, it's not foolproof. If the iPad is not turned on or is in Airplane Mode, for example, the Find My iPad features won't work. However, when you use this tool with the tablet's Passcode feature, it does provide an added level of security that helps to keep your data safe if your iPad gets lost or stolen.

INSURING YOUR iPAD

If something were to go wrong with your iPad, you would either have to pay to replace the unit outright if it's been lost or stolen, or you might have to pay a hefty repair bill for damages that aren't covered by the warrantee.

The four most common mishaps people have with their iPads are that the unit gets lost, stolen, damaged by liquid, or accidentally dropped. Unfortunately, not all of these problems are covered by Apple's 90-day warranty or AppleCare+.

You can gamble on the fact that you won't encounter any of these problems. If you do have problems, you could potentially purchase a used or refurbished iPad as a replacement for your original device instead of buying a new one.

To guard against troubles, the optional AppleCare+ extended warranty plan ($99.00) for the iPad 2 or new iPad has a few advantages, especially for non-tech-savvy people. For two years, AppleCare+ offers unlimited and extemporary technical support in person at any Apple Store or by telephone. Plus, the optional AppleCare+ plan offers hardware coverage of the iPad itself, as well as its battery, earphones, and included accessories.

The AppleCare+ coverage now protects your iPad against accidental damage, however, a $49.00 service fee for repairs, as well as other conditions apply. This optional coverage does not offer protection against loss or theft.

For full insurance coverage for an iPad against loss, theft, or accidental damage you can acquire third-party insurance, which is offered by a handful of companies. This third-party insurance, however, does not offer technical support or offer any assistance when it comes to using your tablet.

> **TIP**   Enter the search phrase, "iPad insurance," into any search engine to find insurance companies that offer optional coverage for Apple mobile devices.

Two companies that offer comprehensive iPad 2 and new iPad insurance coverage are SquareTrade (www.squaretrade.com) and Worth Ave. Group (www.worthavegroup.com). Both of these companies offer two-year insurance coverage for between $79.00 and $100.00. However, what's covered under each policy varies. In many cases, a $50.00 deductible applies per claim.

As you evaluate the various insurance policies and extended warranty programs, determine what's covered and what's not, how much of a deductible you'll be charged per claim, and how repairs or product replacements are handled. Ideally, you want a policy that offers next-day equipment replacement.

Purchasing insurance or an extended warrantee for your iPad is optional. Like any type of insurance, it offers you peace of mind and financial protection should something go wrong. If you're a person who is extremely reliant on your Apple tablet, having this added protection could save you a lot of frustration and stress, and it can provide you with quick equipment replacement.

> **TIP**   Regardless of whether you opt to protect your Apple hardware, it's essential that you regularly back up your apps and data. Using iOS 5.1, you can do this in a variety of ways using the iTunes sync process or wirelessly via iCloud. See Chapter 9, "Syncing Your iPad via iTunes or iCloud," for details on backing up your iPad data.

IN THIS CHAPTER

- Self-publish and distribute interactive eBooks using Apple's iBooks Author software on a Mac
- Create and sell eBooks using Blurb.com
- Commission a custom iPad app to be developed

17

CREATING AND DISTRIBUTING CONTENT ON THE iPAD

Until recently, if you or your company wanted to create an app or distribute proprietary content via the iPad, a costly custom app needed to be created. However, to cater to the needs of businesses and entrepreneurs who want to utilize the iPad as an interactive tool for disseminating information, Apple has created several low-cost and easy solutions that require no programming skills and that can be utilized in-house in a fraction of the time needed to create a custom iPad app.

Using any Mac and the free iBooks Author software available from Apple (www.apple.com/ibooks-author), anyone who knows how to use a word processor can now create professional-quality and highly interactive eBooks for the iPad that can incorporate text, photos, video clips, audio, other multimedia content, interactive diagrams, 3D objects, voice overs, and quizzes.

eBooks created using the iBooks Author software can be distributed to employees, customers, and clients or distributed (sold) to the public via Apple's iBookstore. Using the iBooks Author software, a company can easily adapt any printed materials, such as catalogs, annual reports, user manuals, training guides (and training videos), marketing materials, or other documents into eBooks for viewing on an iPad.

If a company's needs involve gathering data via an iPad, streamlining the process of filling out forms, or accessing database content remotely from a tablet, using the FileMaker Pro 12 database software with the FileMaker Go iPad app serves as a low-cost, extremely customizable option.

From this chapter, you'll discover more about how to utilize the iBooks Author software, learn about a similar eBook publishing solution from Blurb.com, and learn more about what's involved in having an iPad app created from scratch.

> **TIP** Does your company have dozens or hundreds of iPads that need to be charged and synchronized simultaneously from a single iTunes source? Parat Solutions (866-647-5976, www.paratsolutions.com) has solved this problem with its ParaSync system, a proprietary docking station that allows up to 10 iPads to be charged and synced from one iTunes library. Using this system, multiple ParaSync docking stations can be linked together, so you can charge and sync 20, 30, 40, or more iPads at the same time. No special software or cable connections are required.
>
> The ParaSync system includes a docking station that connects to a host computer via a USB cable connection for syncing. For charging, a single electrical plug from a wall outlet is needed. The system includes custom-designed iPad cases that not only protect the tablets while they're in use, but also protect the iPad's Dock connector port during the charging process.
>
> Custom solutions for charging and syncing any number of iPads are available. These solutions can include lockable, steel enclosures for the ParaSync charging stations.

CREATING INTERACTIVE EBOOKS FOR iPAD USING iBOOKS AUTHOR

If you use a Mac, and you know how to use a word processor, you already have the knowledge needed to create visually compelling, professional-quality, and highly interactive eBooks for use with an iPad.

As you'll soon discover when you use Apple's iBooks Author software, any printed materials, as well as photos, graphics, illustrations, video clips, audio, or other multimedia content, can be incorporated into an interactive eBook that also utilizes the touch screen on the iPad.

iBooks Author is a free Mac software application that's available from the Mac App Store. Using this software, you can custom create compelling eBook content using templates and a simple-to-learn, drag-and-drop interface.

> **TIP** In addition to the eBook templates that come bundled with the iBooks Author software, a variety of third-party companies have released additional templates for creating specific types of eBooks.
>
> Jumsoft has introduced Book Palette 1.0 for the Mac ($2.99) that includes 10 eBook templates designed for use with iBook Author. You can also find additional free and fee-based templates by visiting www.iBookAuthorTemplates.com or by entering the search phrase "iBook Author Templates" into any Internet search engine.

When you select a template within the iBook Author software, you can import and format content from a word processor (such as Pages or Microsoft Word) within the eBook that's being created. You can then import images or other pre-created multimedia content, and the iBooks Author software auto-formats the text around the photos or content.

Instead of having to program interactive elements into the eBook, from within iBooks Author, you can import and customize pre-created widgets, so it's easy to incorporate an interactive table of contents, glossary, or quiz, for example.

After you've created an eBook using the iBooks Author software, you can transfer it to an iPad and read it using the free iBooks 2 app that is available from the App Store. Using the iBooks Author software, you can also publish your eBook using Apple's iBookstore service and then distribute the eBook for free or sell it online.

Self-published authors, entrepreneurs, small business operators, educators, and public speakers, for example, have discovered a wide range of innovative ways to use iBooks Author to create and distribute compelling iPad content for employees, customers, and clients.

For example, traditionally printed catalogs and sales materials can become interactive and highly engaging when created into an eBook. Product user manuals can be created for the iPad that utilize more than just text and graphics to teach customers how to use a new product. Boring employee training manuals can be transformed into interactive training tools that can be utilized anywhere. Presentation handouts or reports can be published in eBook form and presented in ways not possible on a traditionally printed page. The possibilities are truly limitless.

> **NOTE** eBooks created using iBooks Author are viewable on any iPad running iOS 5.0 (or later) and the latest version of the iBooks 2 app (version 2.0.1 or later).

iBooks Author runs exclusively on Mac computers and can create eBooks compatible exclusively for the iPad. (The eBooks are not viewable on an iPhone or iPod touch running the iBooks 2 app.) However, if you're a Windows PC user, a similar eBook creation and publishing tool (albeit with fewer features) is available, also for free, from Blurb.com.

BLURB.COM'S EBOOK PUBLISHING SOLUTION

For PC or Mac users interested in creating, publishing, and distributing non-interactive photo eBooks viewable on an iPhone, iPod touch, or iPad, Blurb.com (www.blurb.com) offers an inexpensive, easy-to-use eBook publishing option.

By downloading the free Blurb BookSmart software (www.blurb.com), PC or Mac users can easily create and publish professionally printed photo books in both hardcover and softcover formats. The books are created by dragging and dropping photos into a template, adding text and other graphic elements, and then uploading the book to the Blurb service to be traditionally printed.

Photo books created using Blurb on a PC or Mac can be printed one copy at a time or can be sold directly through the Blurb.com online store. By selecting the eBook publishing option, a photo book created and published using Blurb can also be created into an iPhone or iPad-compatible eBook and then downloaded directly to the iOS mobile device and viewed using iBooks for just $1.99 per digital copy.

You can use the Blurb software to create photo books, cookbooks, children's books, or any content that includes photos and text. The software's capabilities are not as advanced or robust as what's possible using iBook Author. However, any book created using the Blurb software can be printed in hardcover or softcover in any quantity and also published in eBook form. The quality is extremely impressive, but the cost is highly competitive.

DOES YOUR COMPANY NEED A CUSTOM APP?

There are currently more than 600,000 iPad-specific apps available from the App Store, in addition to more than 600,000 iPhone and hybrid apps that run on an iPad. If one or more of these apps do not meet the needs of your company, having a custom app created may be a viable option.

Many custom apps have been created by mid- to large-size companies in an effort to better cater to the needs of their customers or to serve as a marketing tool to increase business. Another portion of these apps were custom designed for specific companies to be used in-house by employees in an effort to streamline or automate specific tasks or give people access to company resources while they're in the field.

Every day companies in all different industries are discovering innovative ways to utilize the iPad. Some of these uses, however, require that a custom app be created.

> **NOTE** Before investing the time, money, and resources needed to create a vertical market app or proprietary enterprise solution involving the iPad, see whether a customizable app has already been created. Marketcircle, Inc. (www.marketcircle.com), for example, offers a handful of highly customizable iPad apps for billing, invoicing, time tracking/billing, and scheduling that have been created for use in specific industries, such as film and video, photography, print and design, real estate, sales, legal, recruiting, and software development.
>
> From other app developers, there are also countless industry-oriented, vertical market or specialty apps for those working in hundreds of industries, including medical, manufacturing, retail sales, telemarketing, event planning, and education. Be sure to research what's currently available before incurring the cost of re-creating something from scratch that already exists.

WHAT TO CONSIDER FIRST WHEN DEVELOPING AN APP

If you're thinking about having a custom app developed for the iPad, first carefully define the purpose for the app and determine exactly what you want it to do.

Next, sketch out or create a detailed outline for the app. For example, figure out what options should appear on the various screens and decide what features and functions the app needs to include. This includes determining your target audience for the app. For this step, absolutely no programming knowledge is required, but considering these things gives you, and the programmers you ultimately hire to develop your app, a clear understanding of your goals.

> **TIP** Based on your company's needs, determine whether an iPad-specific app is more appropriate or if your app development budget is best spent on an app that runs on all iOS devices, including the various iPhones, iPads, and iPods. Making an app available to all users of iOS devices dramatically increases the potential audience for an app, which might be important if the app will cater to your customers or clients.

Before proceeding further, visit the App Store to determine whether an iOS app already exists that meets your needs. If similar apps already exist, determine whether you can use one, or what your intended app needs to do differently or better. It's essential that you understand, from day one, how the app will be used and how it will fit into your company's established workflow and overall business objectives.

CAUTION   If you hire an app developer to begin work on a custom app, but you have only a vague idea about what the app should do, how it will be used, and who it will be used by, in the result will be a variety of potentially costly problems.

At the very least, having a clearly defined one- or two-page summary of what you want the iOS app to do helps a developer dramatically when it comes to designing and programming the app you envision.

Remember, the app developer you hire is most likely an expert at designing apps and programming, but he probably does not understand your business, industry, customers, or the unique needs for the app. Thus, it's your company's responsibility to bring this knowledge to the table and stay active in the development process for your app.

If your app developer doesn't understand your needs or isn't listening to you during development meetings, find a new developer. Otherwise, you'll wind up paying a fortune for a custom app that doesn't meet your needs or expectations, that is confusing to use, and that is actually detrimental to your business because the end result will be an app that does not achieve its objectives.

Next, invest $99.00 (per year) and join Apple's iOS Development Program (http://developer.apple.com) to learn more about what's possible in terms of having a custom app created, plus gain access to the resources and tools available directly from Apple.

HAVING A CUSTOM APP CREATED

After determining that your company does want to pursue developing a custom app, you need to hire experienced and knowledgeable app designers and programmers (unless you already have someone on staff). It's important to understand that developing a custom app is a time-consuming and potentially costly process that requires a clear understanding of what's possible and what you're trying to accomplish.

By hiring an independent iOS app developer, companies are creating innovative, proprietary, and highly specialized apps for use in house. An app that gives a sales force a streamlined method for entering and processing orders while on the road and grants them full access to an online inventory database or catalog from their mobile devices is an example of a custom app.

In some situations, cutting-edge companies are developing custom apps for their customers and clients as a way to boost sales, distribute marketing or promotional content, improve customer service, increase brand awareness, or build customer loyalty.

Thanks to the GPS capabilities and Maps app that is built in to the iPad, a custom app can determine where a customer is located at any given moment and direct her to a company's nearest retail location. This same customized app can enable a customer to place an order online from her mobile device and have it waiting for her upon her arrival at her destination. In the case of Pizza Hut or GrubHub, for example, a customer can arrange for food delivery with a few taps on her mobile device's screen.

The cost of developing a custom app is becoming far more economical than it was just a year or two ago, in part due to increased competition among independent software and app developers.

One of the biggest challenges you face after you decide to have a custom app developed is not determining what the app should do or how it will be used; it's finding and hiring an independent app developer that's capable of creating an app that perfectly caters to the intended audience by offering the end user value, simplicity, security, and intuitive functionality.

It's important to realize up front that having a custom iOS app created is very much like having customized software developed for any other platform. Having a well-designed, highly functional, and bug-free app developed that includes a slick user interface and the back-end functionality you need is going to be a costly and time-consuming endeavor that should include involvement from various departments within your company.

One problem that many companies encounter is that they hire a low-cost app development company or team of programmers. Companies that do this wind up with an inferior result that is riddled with problems. It's important to choose an app development company that's stable because you want the same company to be around in the future to support the app and make enhancements or bug fixes.

Speaking of app development problems, to save money, some businesses opt to outsource their work to small, overseas app development companies. Common problems with this solution include dealing with time zone differences, which causes delays in communication, and significant language barriers. If you're unable to easily communicate with your app developer, explain your needs, and closely follow the app's development, the end result will often not be what you anticipated.

Ultimately, your goal should be to establish a long-term relationship with the app developer you hire. Even if you choose not to add new features or functions to the app down the road, as Apple releases new versions of the iOS operating system, you might need to have the app updated to keep it functional.

NOTE As a general rule, when it comes to hiring an app development company, you generally get what you pay for. A single freelancer or a small development company might be able to create the initial app for you, but if you want or need the app to be updated or expanded with new features in the future, that same freelancer or small development company might not be available or might have gone out of business.

Before hiring an app developer, look at the company's portfolio of work. Carefully evaluate the quality of its apps, including the user interfaces and functionality. Also, keep in mind that many different factors go into calculating development costs and the amount of time the development process will take.

Development costs for most good-quality apps, created by an experienced and competent development company, run between $5,000 and $50,000. Realistically the development, programming, and testing process typically takes between 12 and 16 weeks.

The more detailed your company's initial outline or plan for the app is, the easier it is for the app development company you hire to offer you a reliable price quote. How much you wind up paying for the app's development is in part based on the complexity of the app itself.

TIP As you're sketching your app on paper and brainstorming about what the app should be able to do, start with what you envision the app's home screen and main menu will look like. Then work your way out from there, focusing on one page or screen of the proposed app at a time. This helps you create a more comprehensive plan for your app.

To help you sketch a map or detailed plan for your app, consider using easy-to-use flowcharting or diagramming software on your primary computer, such as Microsoft Visio (www.microsoft.com), SmartDraw (www.smartdraw.com), or OmniGraffle (www.omnigroup.com/products/omnigraffle).

To keep things simple, start by developing an app with the core features and functionality you want or need. Work with your app development team to get the core app up and running so you can release it to your workforce or customers.

You can later revise the app to add new features and functions after the initial app has proven itself to be a success. After launching your app, solicit feedback from its audience to discover ways to improve upon its interface, features, and functionality.

Hiring a programmer, as opposed to a full-service app development company, is a low-cost option for small to mid-size businesses. You can find iOS app programmers using an online service, such as eLance.com or guru.com. Alternatively, use a search engine to enter the search phrase "iOS app developer" to find links to app developer websites.

Another method for finding a well-qualified developer is to search the App Store for apps you like and then make contact with those developers. Part of every app's description in the App Store includes the developer's name and a link to the developer's website.

TIP It's a good idea to have a lawyer who represents your company create a contract between your organization and the app developer. The contract should clearly state who will ultimately own the programming code and indicate that your company will also receive the source code associated with the app, not just the finished app.

In addition to indicating who owns the code, the contract should give you the right to modify the code as needed in the future and ensure that the code contains no backdoor access that could later be used by the app developer for unauthorized purposes.

Also, if your company will own the code, by purchasing it outright from the developer, the contract should stipulate what rights the developer has to reuse or resell the source code (or portions of it) to develop future applications.

OTHER POTENTIAL LOW-COST CUSTOM APP SOLUTIONS

If you're thinking about having a proprietary app developed for in-house use to handle specialized tasks, determine whether it would be less expensive to have a developer create a mobile website that your iPad-using employees could access. Another alternative might be to have a custom database application created using FileMaker Pro and then use the FileMaker Go app for iPad to allow for remote access to that custom database.

Often, having a custom FileMaker Pro database created is significantly less expensive and much faster than having a iOS custom app developed, yet the functionality could be very similar, depending on your company's needs. To learn more about the FileMaker Pro and FileMaker Go options, visit www.filemaker.com/products/filemaker-go.

> **TIP**   To learn more about having a custom iOS app developed for your business, visit Apple's iOS In Business website at www.apple.com/business/accelerator.

iPAD CUSTOM APP DEVELOPMENT STRATEGIES

When you decide to move forward with a custom app, follow these strategies to help insure the successful planning, development, and deployment of the app:

- Do your research to determine what's possible and then decide exactly what you want your custom app to do. As you do this, put yourself in the app user's shoes. Determine their wants, needs, and level of expertise using the iPad and then cater to the intended user every step of the way.

- Develop a specific plan for your app, outlining the overall goal or objective of the app, as well as each feature or function you want to include within it.

- Plan the development process in a realistic way, making sure you have the budget and resources in place to handle the process appropriately. The main stages of an app's development include Planning, Design, Coding/Programming, Debugging, Testing, and Deployment/Implementation. Each of these steps require planning, time, resources, and money. Cutting corners during any of these steps could result in costly problems, development delays, or unanticipated results.

- Be sure to put together the most knowledgeable and experienced app development team possible, starting with people within your business or organization who clearly understand how your business operates, the needs of those who will ultimately be using the app, and the ultimate goal for the app itself. Pair this in-house team with skilled and experienced programmers and app testers.

- For apps being developed from scratch, start by incorporating the core functionality that's wanted and needed, and make sure that it works properly and has an intuitive user interface. Then, over time, add additional features and functions. Not only will this save time and money, it will also keep the app's development easier to manage.

- Before releasing the app to your employees, customers, or clients, be sure it's been properly tested and is 100 percent bug-free and that it functions exactly how it should. The easiest way to alienate your customers or annoy those who will ultimately be using the app is to release an app that contains bugs, is unstable and crashes, that doesn't handle the intended objectives properly, or that is unintuitive to use.

■ The app should also function using the latest version of the iOS operating system and fully utilizes the capabilities of the iPad. If the app ultimately doesn't serve a defined purpose, successfully address a need, solve a problem, or provide value to the user, it will not be embraced and adopted by its intended users.

> **NOTE** After your custom app is created and ready for distribution, you have several options, based on the target audience for your app. An iPad app can be distributed through the App Store and made available to the general public, or your company can work with Apple to utilize other enterprise solutions for distributing an app in house. To learn more about custom app development and distribution (deployment) options, visit www.apple.com/business/accelerator.

> **NOTE** According to AppleInsider, a website that follows the latest Apple-related news, Apple is apparently working on Mac software, similar to iBooks Author, that will enable people to develop their own iPhone or iPad apps, without needing any programming skills or knowledge whatsoever. To learn more about this software, visit www.appleinsider.com/articles/12/04/12/apple_wants_to_make_it_easy_for_non_programmers_to_build_ios_apps.html.

18

MUST-HAVE ACCESSORIES

The iPad has become popular in the business world because it is sleek, lightweight, and has up to 10 hours of battery life. Plus, it's customizable and can be used for a wide range of tasks. By adding optional accessories to your tablet, you can further personalize the device, and, at the same time, enhance its capabilities in order to broaden its functionality.

> **TIP** See Chapter 8, "Wireless Printing and Scanning via Your iPad," for information about printing directly from the iPad (even if your existing printer is not AirPrint compatible). The chapter also covers optional scanners that can be connected to the tablet.

EXTERNAL KEYBOARDS FOR YOUR TABLET

Many iPad users have discovered that the tablet's on-screen virtual keyboard is ideal for composing short email messages or performing a limited amount of data entry, but it's not ideal for touch-typing and creating long documents. By adding an external keyboard to your iPad, you can utilize a full-size keyboard or a portable keyboard that has actual keyboard keys (as opposed to flat icons displayed on the tablet's flat screen).

TIP   Some iPad cases have external Bluetooth keyboards built into them. Others protect the tablet while it's being transported but also serve as a stand while it's in use. For more information about iPad covers and cases, see Chapter 16, "Protecting Your iPad and Its Data."

A handful of companies offer iPad-compatible keyboards. Some connect to the tablet via its Dock Connector port, whereas others utilize a Bluetooth wireless connection. Some optional external keyboards are full size, and others are more compact and designed with portability in mind.

The Apple Wireless Keyboard ($69.00 USD) is a full-size keyboard for the iPad that uses a Bluetooth connection. This keyboard is ideal for touch-typing or data entry, and is the same keyboard that comes with most iMac computers (so it can serve double duty, depending on which device you're using). The keyboard operates using two AA batteries. It's ideal for working with your iPad at a desk when portability is not important.

The iKeyboard ($35.00, www.iKeyboard.com) is an overlay accessory that you place directly over the iPad's virtual keyboard when you need it to give the keys a more tactile feel (see Figure 18.1).

iKeyboard adds practically no thickness to the tablet, so you can use it with most covers and cases, but it helps improve your ability to accurately touch-type using the iPad's virtual keyboard. iKeyboard is made from a durable plastic and has an everlasting sticky backing that allows it to be stuck on and removed from the tablet's screen thousands of times with no residue left on the iPad. It's available in black or white, and, unlike other keyboards, it requires no batteries.

For people on the go, the Logitech Keyboard Case by Zagg for iPad ($99.99 USD, www.zagg.com/accessories/logitech-ipad-2-keyboard-case) is a traditional style, wireless (Bluetooth) keyboard that's slightly more compact than a full-size keyboard, but it offers real keyboard keys that enable touch-typing and quick data entry.

FIGURE 18.1

The iKeyboard is an inexpensive accessory that sticks onto the iPad's screen and adds a tactile feel to the keys displayed on the virtual keyboard.

NOTE The benefit to the Logitech Keyboard Case by Zagg is that you can touch-type on a traditional external keyboard that also serves as an iPad stand and hard shell case. It's great for getting work done on an airplane, for example.

The footprint of this keyboard is about the same as the iPad itself. The only drawback is that the keys are slightly smaller than a full-size keyboard, so they take some getting used to. For someone who is used to typing on a traditional keyboard, this external iPad keyboard is an ideal alternative to the tablet's on-screen virtual keyboard.

What's great about the Logitech Keyboard Case (shown in Figure 18.2) is that it doubles as a hard shell case for your iPad while you're on the go, adding just a little bit of thickness to the tablet as you transport it. This keyboard serves as a stand for the iPad, and it holds the tablet in either a portrait or landscape position. The keyboard itself is powered by a built-in rechargeable battery.

FIGURE 18.2

The Logitech Keyboard Case is a perfect solution for someone who needs portability, but who also wants a traditional-style keyboard for use with the iPad.

Another external keyboard that's compatible with the various iPad models (as well as other iOS mobile devices, including the iPhone and iPod touch) is the iType keyboard from Ion Audio ($119.95, www.ionaudio.com/products/details/itype). This is a handheld, wireless (Bluetooth), 49-key QWERTY keyboard that makes typing with your thumbs a quick and easy process, which, for some, is much faster and more efficient than using the iPad's on-screen virtual keyboard. You actually hold this keyboard in your hands while you're using it, so it's not like using a full-size keyboard. With practice, the end result is fast data entry on your tablet.

The Brookstone Roll-Up Keyboard ($49.99 USD, www.brookstone.com) offers a full-size keyboard that's compatible with the iPad; however, it's made from silicon rubber and actually rolls up into a compact package for easy transport. When you place it on a flat surface, you can utilize the full-size keyboard, but then you can roll it up and store it while you're on the go. The keyboard offers a wireless connection and full-size, "comfort-touch" keys, which make no clicking noise as you're typing.

Brookstone also offers a growing selection of other iPad external keyboards, as well as cases, external speakers, headphones, desktop stands, external battery packs, and chargers. These accessories are available from the company's chain of retail stores, via mail order, or from Brookstone's website.

The Verbatim Bluetooth Mobile Keyboard ($104.00, www.verbatim.com/prod/accessories/keyboards/wireless-mobile-keyboard) is a durable plastic keyboard that folds into a compact design for easy transport, but unfolds into a near-full-size wireless keyboard that you can use on any flat surface. The keyboard operates using two AAA batteries and includes directional arrow keys, a full QWERTY keyboard layout, plus additional function keys. It comes with its own case.

REPLACING FINGER MOTIONS WITH A STYLUS

Some apps enable you to write or draw directly on the iPad's screen, and others require precision tapping. Instead of using your finger, you can purchase an inexpensive stylus. A stylus is a pen-shaped device that has a soft tip that does not scratch or smudge the iPad's screen but offers a greater level of precision than your finger when writing or drawing on your iPad. You can also use a stylus to interact with your tablet's touch screen when you're wearing gloves.

A basic stylus costs anywhere between $15.00 and $30.00. The Bamboo Stylus from Wacom ($29.95 USD, http://wacom.com/en/Products/BambooStylus.aspx) was designed specifically for use with an iPad. This stylus feels like a pen in your hand but offers a narrow, soft tip that's ideal for apps that allow you to write or draw on the tablet's screen. Other companies offer similar stylus products; however, many offer thicker tips, which detracts from the accuracy of the iPad's touch screen, and some are not well-balanced or comfortable in your hand.

The Blue Tiger stylus from Ten One Designs (www.tenonedesign.com/bluetiger) is a pressure-sensitive stylus that communicates directly with the iPad via a Bluetooth 4.0 connection (so no pairing is required). It enables you to write on the tablet's screen and simultaneously rest your wrist on the screen, without it negatively affecting accuracy. Shown in Figure 18.3, the Blue Tiger stylus is a useful tool for handwriting on the iPad's screen, or it can be used in conjunction with compatible drawing or photo-editing apps that take advantage of its pressure sensitivity.

Many business professionals find it helpful to use an app that transforms their iPads into a traditional notepad so that they can handwrite notes directly on the screen as opposed to typing them using the iPad's virtual keyboard. This is just one type of application where using a stylus, instead of your finger, is helpful.

FIGURE 18.3

Instead of using your finger, the Blue Tiger stylus offers much greater accuracy when writing or drawing on the tablet's screen.

BATTERY OPTIONS

Depending on how it's being used, your iPad has an average battery life of 10 hours (less if you're doing a lot of web surfing via a 3G or 4G connection). Unfortunately, it's not always convenient to recharge your iPad by connecting it to your primary computer (via the supplied USB cable) or by plugging it into an electrical outlet. Fortunately, you can purchase optional battery packs and battery chargers to help you keep your iPad sufficiently powered.

BATTERY PACKS

A handful of companies offer external, rechargeable battery packs for the iPad that plug into the tablet via a cable that connects to its docking port. These optional battery packs come in different configurations and sizes, but most of them are smaller than a deck of cards.

The RichardSolo 9000 mAh Universal Mobile Charger ($69.95, www.RichardSolo. com) connects to your iPad via the supplied USB cable. It can dramatically extend the life of your tablet's battery power in between charges. Shown in Figure 18.4, this particular external rechargeable battery pack measures 3.76" × 1.57" × 1.57" and doubles the battery life of your iPad to about 20 hours per charge. It can also be used to recharge your iPhone or other battery powered devices with a USB port.

FIGURE 18.4

The RichardSolo 9000 is one of many external battery packs available for the iPad that can dramatically extend its battery life in between charges.

BATTERY CHARGERS

Your iPad comes with a white USB cable that you use to connect the tablet to your primary computer (unless you have an older computer that doesn't have a USB port that supplies ample power). The tablet uses the USB connection to charge its batteries while it's connected to the computer.

You can attach the AC adapter that comes with your iPad to the USB cable and charge your tablet by plugging the adapter into an electrical outlet. For those times when neither your primary computer nor an electrical outlet is available, you can purchase and use an optional car charger to plug the iPad into your car's 12v power outlet/cigarette lighter.

Car charger accessories are readily available from consumer electronics stores, mass market retailers, and office supply stores (such as Best Buy, Radio Shack, Staples, Walmart, and Target), as well as Apple stores and Brookstone.

When choosing a car charger adapter, make sure that it's been approved to work with your iPad model rather than an iPhone (which uses the same 30-pin dock connector).

TIP While driving in your car, you can use a car charger adapter to recharge the tablet's battery while it's also in use. Depending on your vehicle, however, the engine might need to be running for its 12v power outlet to operate.

DESKTOP STANDS FOR EASIER iPAD ACCESS

While you're sitting at your desk, there are a variety of ways to prop up your iPad for easy access and viewing. These desktop stands come in a range of styles. Some are designed exclusively to hold your tablet in only a portrait or landscape direction whereas others are more flexible. Ideally, you want a stand that's stylish and sturdy. It should also be able to hold your iPad in portrait or landscape mode, and potentially in a position that's conducive to typing.

Dozens of companies offer hundreds of general use and specialty iPad stands (designed for use in specific situations). For example, there are stands that attach to a refrigerator door or kitchen cabinets, music or microphone stands, car dashboards, or that are designed for use in a high traffic retail setting.

The easiest way to find a stand that best suits your needs is to use Google or Yahoo!, for example, and enter the search phrase "iPad Stand." Some of the companies that specialize in iPad stands, and offer a variety of designs, include:

- Belkin (www.belkin.com)
- Blue Lounge (www.bluelounge.com)
- Brookstone (www.brookstone.com)
- Griffin Technology (www.griffintechnology.com)
- HyperJuice (www.hypershop.com)
- IK Multimedia (www.ikmultimedia.com)
- Incase (www.goincase.com)
- Joby (www.joby.com)
- Levenger (www.levenger.com)
- Logitech (www.logitech.com)
- SwingHolder (www.standforstuff.com)
- Targus (www.targus.com)
- Twelve South (www.twelvesouth.com)

> **TIP** Villa ProCtrl (http://pro-ipad-stand.com/1/apple-ipad-floor-stand-wall-mount-counter-stand) offers a handful of ultra-contemporary looking, extremely durable iPad 2 and new iPad stands designed in Holland that are for use in high-traffic retail environments. The company's offerings include a stainless steel floor stand, wall-mount, and countertop stand. These stands include anti-theft locks and can be used in conjunction with an iPad for digital signage, interactive kiosks, touch panels. and tradeshow displays.

iPAD CAMERA CONNECTION KIT

If you have a separate digital camera (aside from what's built into your iPad), you can connect it directly to your tablet via a USB cable and Apple's iPad Camera Connection kit ($29.00). With the connection kit, you can quickly transfer your digital images from the camera's memory card to your tablet for viewing, editing, and sharing your photos.

Available from Apple Stores, Apple.com, or wherever Apple products are sold, the iPad Camera Connection Kit comes with two adapters that connect to the bottom of your iPad via the 30-pin Dock Connector port.

One of the adapters serves as an SD memory card reader. If your digital camera uses an SD memory card, you can insert the card directly into this memory card reader when it's attached to your iPad, and then quickly transfer its digital photo contents to your tablet. The second adapter is a standard USB port connector. You can use it to connect your digital camera (via its USB port) to your iPad (via this connection adapter and the USB cable that's supplied with your digital camera).

NOTE If your digital camera also shoots digital video, you can also transfer videos to your iPad using the iPad Camera Connection Kit.

After your photos are transferred from your digital camera, you can view and share them using the Photos app. You can also edit the photos using the optional Apple iPhone app, or a third-party app such as Photoshop Touch, Photogene, Luminance, Camera+, or CameraBag. You can view videos you transfer from your digital camera to your iPad using the Photos app, or you can view, edit, and share them with the iMovie app.

ENHANCE THE RECORDING CAPABILITIES OF YOUR iPAD

Whether you want to use your tablet to record dictation, meetings, lectures, workshops, or classes, you're a musician or singer who uses your tablet as a portable multi-track recording studio, or you have other work-related tasks that require high-quality digital recordings to be created, sometimes the microphone that's built into your iPad does not offer the recording quality that's needed.

Mic-W (www.mic-w.com) is one company that offers professional-quality, external microphones for the iPad that attach directly to the tablet's headphones jack. The company's iSeries of microphones are priced at less than $200.00, and each offers exceptional performance for audio measurement applications, recording, or even broadcast use. These mics require no additional power source.

The Mic-W Professional Class 2 Microphone is a calibrated measurement microphone that complies with the IEC 61672 Class 2 sound level meter standard. It can turn your iPad into a sound pressure level (SPL) meter or a real-time analyzer (RTA) for time and frequency domain measurement. The Cardioid Recording Microphone is ideal for recording vocals or acoustic instruments, as well as meetings, conferences, or interviews whereas the High Sensitivity Cardioid Microphone is also ideal for producing high-quality sound recordings suitable for broadcast. A lavaliere microphone is also available.

HEADPHONES AND EXTERNAL SPEAKERS

Whether you're listening to music, watching TV shows or movies, recording and then listening to important meetings, or streaming content from the Web, the speaker built in to your iPad has decent quality, but it's not good enough to satisfy a true audiophile. It's possible to dramatically improve the sound output of your tablet simply by plugging decent-quality stereo headphones into the iPad's headphone jack or by using good-quality external and wireless (Bluetooth) speakers.

When it comes to adding external speakers to your iPad, the choices are plentiful, and the price range is dramatic. You can spend between $50.00 and $100.00 for some decent external speakers, or you can invest hundreds in some top-of-the-line speakers from companies such as Bose (www.bose.com) or Bang & Olufsen (www.bang-olufsen.com).

> **NOTE** External speakers can connect to your iPad in a variety of ways: via the headphone jack, the 30-pin Dock Connector port, or a wireless Bluetooth connection (so no cables are required).

If you want awesome quality sound from an external speaker, but portability is important, Jawbone's Jambox Wireless Speaker ($199.99, www.jawbone.com) is the perfect companion for your tablet. This battery-powered speaker has an output capacity of 85 decibels and measures 6" × 1.5" × 2.25". It truly offers the power and sound quality you'd expect from an expensive home theater system. Because it's portable, battery-powered, and wireless (shown in Figure 18.5), you can use it virtually anywhere.

FIGURE 18.5
The Jawbone Jambox is the ideal portable speaker for the iPad.

iHome (www.ihomeaudio.com, from SDI Technologies) offers a complete line of external speakers with built-in connectors or docks for an iPad. These speakers are mid-priced and are ideal for at-home use. The iHome iA100 ($199.00), for example, is a feature-packed clock radio with a built-in iPad dock. It also offers wireless Bluetooth connectivity and a built-in AM/FM radio and clock display.

If you prefer to listen to high-quality audio in private, such as when you're on an airplane, consider investing in a pair of high-quality, noise-reduction stereo headphones. These range in price from $100.00 to $300.00, and are available from companies such as Bose, Monster Beats, Audio-Technica, Sony, and JVC.

In addition to full-size headphones that fit over your ears, you can achieve true portability and convenience without compromising sound quality with a pair of in-ear headphones. The Bose MIE2i mobile headset ($129.95, www.bose.com) is ideal for listening to audio or watching TV shows or movies in private on your iPad.

> **NOTE** As you discover later in this chapter, if you've already invested in a high-quality home theater system, there are multiple ways to connect your iPad to it, either using cables or a wireless connection. Connecting to your home theater system enables you to view content stored on your tablet on a large-screen HD television or listen to audio on your stereo surround-sound speakers.

Built in to iOS 5.1 are enhanced AirPlay features that support video mirroring. This feature enables you to wirelessly stream whatever audio or video content (as well as photos) is stored on your tablet directly to your HDTV by using an Apple TV device ($99.00).

EXTERNAL WIRELESS STORAGE FOR YOUR iPAD

Seagate, a well-known manufacturer of computer hard drives, offers its GoFlex Satellite mobile wireless storage drive that's designed to work with the iPad ($199.99, www.seagate.com/www/en-us/products/external/external-hard-drive/goflex-satellite).

Instead of utilizing your tablet's limited internal storage space to store multimedia content, including photos, music, movies, and TV show episodes, the GoFlex Satellite (shown in Figure 18.6) is a highly portable, 500GB external hard drive that can be accessed wirelessly via Wi-Fi from an iPad.

FIGURE 18.6

The GoFlex Satellite is a wireless hard drive that can stream multimedia content to your iPad via a Wi-Fi connection. Using it, you can access your entire multimedia library (music, videos, photos, and so on), wherever you happen to be.

The content stored on the GoFlex Satellite from your primary computer (a PC or Mac) can then be accessed simultaneously by up to three different devices wirelessly, and the drive itself can hold more than 300 full-length movies.

After you transfer your multimedia content to the GoFlex Satellite drive via a USB connection with your computer, you use the Safari web browser to stream (via a Wi-Fi connection) the content. The GoFlex Satellite is ideal for storing a vast amount of data, documents, or files that you want with you while on the go. The hard drive is battery powered (offering up to 5 hours of continuous data streaming or 25 hours of standby). It weighs less than .6 pounds and measures 4.72" × 3.54" × .87".

> **TIP** Sanho Corporation offers its HyperDrive Hard Drive for iPad ($99.95, www.hypershop.com) which is a hard drive with a USB connection that can connect directly to the bottom of the tablet using the USB port that comes with the optional Apple iPad Camera Connection Kit (sold separately).
>
> The company's HyperDrive iFlashDrive ($99.95 for 8GB, $149.95 for 16GB or $199.95 for 32GB) is a portable flash drive device that can connect directly to the iPad via it's Dock Connector, as well as to any PC or Mac via its USB connector. This provides an easy way to back up and transfer files, documents, or data, without the Internet or using a cloud-based service, such as iCloud.

USE YOUR iPAD TO PROCESS CREDIT CARD PAYMENTS

For small business operators and entrepreneurs, it's possible to quickly transform your iPad into a credit-card processing machine that works anywhere there's a Wi-Fi, 3G, or 4G Internet connection. Many credit-card merchant account providers and financial institutions now offer specialized iPad/iPhone apps that enable their clients to process credit-card transactions by attaching a tiny credit-card swiper to the tablet.

However, most credit-card merchant account providers charge an account set-up fee, monthly fee, and per-transaction fees, plus require the merchant to sign a one- or two-year service agreement.

Using the iPad, Square (www.squareup.com) and Intuit (www.intuit.com), both offer credit-card processing solutions for small businesses that have no monthly minimums, no monthly service charges, and no long-term commitments.

You can set up an account in minutes and begin processing credit-card payments. Both Square and Inuit offer proprietary iPhone/iPad apps, as well as their own credit-card swipers (supplied for free) that connect to the tablet via its headphone jack. Figure 18.7 shows the credit-card swiper provided by Intuit for its iPad-compatible GoPayment service.

FIGURE 18.7

Begin accepting credit-card payments from your customers or clients via your iPad using Intuit's GoPayment app.

After a merchant account is set up with either company, you pay a small percentage of each transaction total (2.75 percent with Square, 2.7 percent with Intuit GoPayment), but there are no other costs or recurring fees.

Using Square's iPad-specific app, for example, you can transform your tablet into a full-featured, mobile cash register (minus the cash draw) that's capable of processing Visa, MasterCard, Discover, or AmEx credit cards or debit cards. Your customer simply signs the tablet's screen after their credit card is swiped, and a detailed and customized receipt is emailed to them in seconds. The revenue you make from your sales is automatically deposited into your existing bank account within 24 hours.

CONNECTION OPTIONS: HD, VGA, HOME THEATER

When it comes to giving presentations or sharing multimedia content on your iPad with groups of people, you can easily connect your tablet to a HD television set or LCD projector using the right cables or adapters. Thanks to the AirPlay feature built into the iOS 5.1 operating system, you can also wirelessly stream content (movies, TV show episodes, photos, digital slide presentations, and so on) from your iPad to your HD television via a $99.00 Apple TV device.

CONNECTING TO AN HD MONITOR OR AN HDTV

If you have a high-definition television (HDTV) or monitor with an HDMI input, you can use Apple's Digital AV Adapter ($39.00) to connect your iPad to that monitor. After connecting, use the iOS's Video Mirroring feature so everything you see on your iPad's screen is also displayed on the monitor or television set.

This is a great way to showcase your Keynote presentations to groups of people in a meeting situation or display your digital photos on your television at home. In addition to this adapter, you need a standard HDMI cable (sold separately) that's long enough to connect your iPad to your monitor.

CAUTION   The Apple Digital Video Adapter enables you to display whatever appears on your tablet's screen simultaneously on an HD monitor or television set that has an HDMI input.

Keep in mind, however, that certain apps that play copyrighted video content, such as television episodes or movies downloaded from iTunes, or content streamed using the Netflix or HBO Go apps, cannot be displayed on a monitor using this adapter.

CONNECTING TO A VGA MONITOR

The Apple VGA Adapter ($29.00) connects from your iPad's 30-pin Dock Connector port to a monitor cable (sold separately) that then attaches to a standard VGA computer monitor. This enables you to display content from your tablet on a computer monitor as you give presentations or demonstrations using content, data, drawings, or animations from your iPad, for example. This type of connection works with most LCD projectors as well.

CONNECTING TO A SOUND SYSTEM OR HOME THEATER SYSTEM

There are several ways to give your iPad a louder voice. The method that gives you the most flexibility to wirelessly stream audio and video content, as well as photos between your tablet and television set, is to connect an Apple TV device ($99.00) to your home theater system and to have a Wi-Fi hotspot set up in your home. With this equipment, you can fully use your iPad's AirPlay feature.

Keep in mind, however, that Apple TV and other home theater equipment can just as easily be used in a work environment, office, conference room, or auditorium, enabling you to stream content from your tablet and share it with others on large-screen TVs and monitors that are connected to high-end audio systems.

You can also connect your iPad directly to your home theater system using the Apple Composite AV Cable ($39.00 USD), which enables you to watch iPad video on a big screen with stereo sound. Depending on the input connections available as part of your system, the Apple Component AV cable (which serves the same purpose as the Apple Composite AV cable but offers different connectors) is also available.

> TIP The Apple Digital AV Adapter, Apple VGA Adapter, Apple Composite AV Cable, Apple Component AV Cable, and Apple TV device are all sold separately and available wherever Apple products are sold, including Apple Stores and Apple.com.

If you want to give a presentation or transform a blank wall in your home or office into a 60" diagonal screen, the Cinemin Swivel Video Project ($299.99, www.wowwee.com/en/products/tech/projection/cinemin/swivel) or the Cinemin Slice Projector ($429.99, www.wowwee.com/en/products/tech/projection/cinemin/slice) are extremely portable, battery-powered projectors that connect directly to your iPad. Both devices enable you to give presentations, watch video media, or project digital photos on any wall or screen without needing a television, speaker system, or cables.

You can set up either projector in minutes, and you can use them virtually anywhere with your iPad. These projectors offer WVGA resolution and project an image up to 60" diagonal from about 8' away from a wall or screen.

ACCESSORIES FOR TRAVELING ABROAD

When you travel overseas with your iPad, being able to access the 3G or 4G network and recharge your tablet are relatively straightforward processes regardless of whether you travel with a laptop computer.

USING INTERNATIONAL POWER ADAPTERS

When traveling abroad, you need to be able to recharge your iPad's battery. If you want to recharge your tablet using an electric outlet overseas, you must attach a special adapter to the end of the white USB cable that came with your iPad.

Available from Apple Stores and Apple.com, the Apple World Travel Adapter Kit ($39.00) comes with six international power adapters that connect to the USB cable that came with your iPad. This kit enables you to plug in your tablet just about any-where in the world.

REPLACING YOUR iPAD'S MICRO SIM CARD FOR WIRELESS WEB ACCESS

If you have an iPad Wi-Fi Only model, your tablet is able to connect to the Internet via a Wi-Fi connection anywhere in the world you travel that has a public Wi-Fi hotspot available (this includes many hotels, cafés, and airports).

iPAD 2 WI-FI + 3G OR NEW iPAD WI-FI + 4G (AT&T WIRELESS)

When you leave the United States, your 3G/4G wireless service through AT&T Wireless is not available. However, you can visit any Apple Store or Apple Authorized Reseller while you're overseas (or many cellular service providers) to obtain a micro SIM chip that temporarily replaces your AT&T micro SIM chip while you're traveling.

Because you can purchase 3G or 4G wireless data service on a month-to-month basis or, in some cases, acquire a predetermined amount of wireless data usage, you can easily obtain a new micro SIM chip that works in the country or countries you're visiting, insert it into your iPad, and be able to access 3G or 4G wireless data service in almost any country.

> **NOTE** 4G wireless data service is available for the new iPad Wi-Fi + 4G models when the appropriate micro SIM chip is installed into the tablet while you're travel-ing abroad.

If there's an Apple Store where you're going, an Apple Genius can offer you a micro SIM chip from a local 3G/4G data service provider, help you swap the chip in your iPad, and activate the 3G/4G wireless data account using a major credit card within 10 minutes. Alternatively, you can visit a retail location for a wireless service pro-vider and swap out the micro SIM chips yourself.

After you set up 3G/4G data service in a specific country, any time you return to that country, you can use the same micro SIM chip and purchase additional access. However, when you replace your AT&T Wireless micro SIM chip with the micro SIM chip for the local 3G/4G wireless data provider in the country you're visiting, make sure you do not misplace the tiny AT&T micro SIM chip that you need when you return home.

While traveling, the price for 3G/4G wireless data access varies based on the country you're visiting and the wireless data service provider you need to use. You will probably find the prices to be reasonable in most countries.

Throughout Europe, one of the leading wireless 3G/4G data service providers that supports the iPad 2 and new iPad is O2 (www.o2.co.uk). Upon arriving in any European country, you can visit an O2 retail location (which are as commonplace as AT&T Wireless locations in the U.S.) or visit any Apple Store and obtain a free O2 micro SIM chip.

With the O2 micro SIM chip installed in your iPad, you can sign up for 3G/4G wireless data service for a low flat-fee per day for up to 200MB of data usage, or you can sign up for 1GB of wireless data usage, which you can use within a 30-day period. There's also a plan that offers 2GB of wireless data usage over a 30-day period.

These last two O2 wireless data plans are recurring, meaning you are automatically billed for the plan every 30 days until you cancel. However, you can easily cancel the plan at the conclusion of your trip with no penalties or extra fees. When you install the O2 micro SIM chip, you can activate (or cancel) it and choose a wireless data plan directly from your tablet.

> **TIP** If you know you need to swap micro SIM chips in and out of your iPad while traveling abroad, make sure you bring along the small metal SIM chip ejector tool that came with your tablet. For information about what this tool actually looks like and how to use it properly, visit this page of Apple's website (http://support.apple.com/kb/HT4577).

iPAD 2 WI-FI + 3G OR NEW iPAD WI-FI + 4G (VERIZON WIRELESS)

Because your iPad 2 Wi-Fi + 3G or new iPad Wi-Fi + 4G that's registered with Verizon uses CDMA technology to access the wireless web, before leaving for your trip overseas, contact Verizon Wireless and activate a CDMA Global Data Roaming plan. Or, you can insert a prepaid micro SIM card into the new iPad after you arrive at your overseas destination.

Wireless data roaming is available in many countries for a flat fee of $30.00 for 75MB or $100.00 for 200MB. For more information, contact Verizon directly at (800) 922-0204.

19

DIGITAL PHOTOGRAPHY ON YOUR iPAD

The new iPad has two powerful, high-resolution cameras built in that, when used with the Camera app, make snapping detailed, clear, and vibrant photos as easy as tapping on the device's screen.

When it comes to viewing, organizing, enhancing, printing, and sharing digital photos on your iOS device, you have a multitude of options. The Photos app that comes preinstalled on the iPad offers decent photo organizing and basic photo-editing features. However, available from the App Store is Apple's iPhoto app ($4.99). It dramatically enhances your ability to view, organize, edit, enhance, share, and print images on the iPad 2 or new iPad, but it works particularly well with the new iPad's Retina display.

When using your iPad as a business tool, there are many situations in which being able to snap photos of people, places, or things can be beneficial. The photos you take, edit, or store on your iPad can then be imported into various apps, such as Contacts, Pages, Numbers, or Keynote, as well as database apps, such as FileMaker Go or Bento.

Many other apps also enable you to import or somehow utilize digital photos. For example, the Square app that's used for credit-card processing allows photos to be imported as part of its virtual cash register functionality, so you can tap an item's photo that someone is about to purchase to create a detailed receipt.

Of course, if you're active on Facebook or Twitter and use your iPad for online social networking to promote yourself, your product(s), services, or a business, you can easily share photos taken with or stored on your tablet with others via these and many other online services.

LOADING DIGITAL IMAGES INTO YOUR iPAD

Before you can view, edit, print, and share your favorite digital images, you'll first need to shoot them using the Camera or Photo Booth app that comes preinstalled on your iPad, or transfer images into your tablet.

Aside from shooting images using one of your iPad's built-in cameras, there are several ways to import photos into your iOS device and then store them in the Photos app:

- Use the iTunes sync process to transfer photos to your device. Set up iTunes to sync the image folders or albums you want, and then initiate an iTunes sync or wireless iTunes sync from your primary computer.

- Load photos from a Photo Stream (via iCloud).

- Receive and save photos sent via email. When a photo is embedded in an email, as shown in Figure 19.1, hold your finger on it for a second or two until a menu appears giving you the option to Save Image or Copy the image to your device's virtual clipboard (after which you can paste it into another app).

- Receive and save photos sent via text message. Tap the image you receive using the Messages app, and then tap the Copy command to copy the image to your device's virtual clipboard (after which you can paste it into another app).

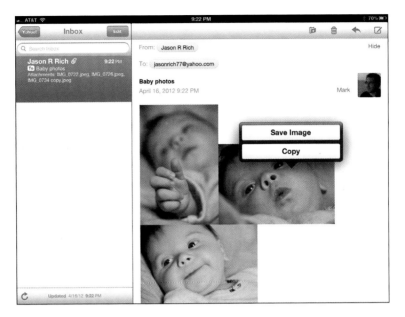

FIGURE 19.1

If you receive a digital photo attached to an incoming email, you can save that image in the Photos app by holding your finger on the image thumbnail (within the email), and then tapping the Save Image option when it appears.

- Save images directly from a website as you're surfing the Web. Hold your finger on the image you're viewing in a website. If it's not copy-protected, after a second or two, a menu appears enabling you to Save Image or Copy it to your device's virtual clipboard (after which you can paste it into another app).

- Use the optional Camera Connection Kit ($29.00, available from Apple Stores or Apple.com) to load images from your digital camera's memory card directly into your iPad.

NOTE When you use the Save Image command, the image is stored in the Camera Roll album of Photos. You can then view, edit, enhance, print, or share it using the Photos app or another app, such as iPhoto or PSTouch.

TAKING PICTURES WITH THE CAMERA APP

The Camera app that comes preinstalled with iOS 5.1 is easy to use for shooting digital images or video clips. To begin using the Camera app, launch it from your iPad's Home screen.

The main camera viewfinder screen (shown in Figure 19.2) appears as soon as you launch the Camera app. The main area of the screen serves as your camera's view-finder. In other words, what you see on the iPad's screen is what you'll photograph or capture on video.

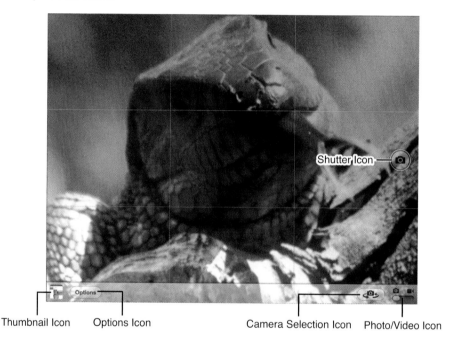

Thumbnail Icon   Options Icon   Camera Selection Icon   Photo/Video Icon

FIGURE 19.2

From the Camera app's main screen, you can snap digital photos or shoot video.

Along the bottom of the screen are several icons. In the lower-left corner, you'll see a thumbnail image of the last photo or video clip you've shot. Tap it to view that image or video clip by automatically launching the Photos app.

Next to the thumbnail image is the Options icon. Tap it to turn on or off the virtual Rule of Thirds grid that can be superimposed on the screen to help you frame or compose your images. The grid, however, does not appear in your actual photos.

As you know, the iPad 2 or new iPad has two built-in cameras—one on the front of the device and one on the back. Tap the icon located near the lower-right corner of the screen to switch between cameras.

Also near the lower-right corner of the Camera screen is the Camera/Video virtual switch. Tap it to move the switch to the left and place the Camera app into Camera Mode for shooting digital photos, or move the virtual switch to the right to shoot video.

Located on the right side of the screen is the camera's shutter button. Tap it to snap a photo or start and stop the video camera. In Camera Mode, tap this camera-shaped shutter button to snap a photo. You hear a sound effect, and a single photo is saved in your iPad. In Video Mode, the camera-shaped icon transforms into a circle with a dim red dot inside it. The dot gets brighter when you tap it to begin shooting a video clip.

HOW TO SNAP A PHOTO

Snapping a single digital photo using the Camera app is simple. Follow these steps:

1. Launch the Camera app from the Home screen.

2. Make sure the Camera app is set to Camera mode.

3. Tap Options to turn on or off the grid feature as you see fit.

4. Choose which of your device's two built-in cameras you want to use by tapping the camera selection icon.

5. Compose or frame your image by holding up your iPad and pointing it at your subjects.

6. Select what the main subject of your photo will be, such as a person or object. Tap your finger on the screen where your subject appears in the view-finder, and an autofocus sensor box appears on the screen at that location. The camera focuses in on where this box is positioned (as opposed to focus-ing on something in the foreground, background, or next to your intended subject). If you're photographing multiple people, the Camera app displays several autofocus sensor boxes, one over each subject's face.

7. If you want to use the Camera app's zoom feature, use a pinch motion on the screen. A zoom slider (shown in Figure 19.3) appears near the bottom of the screen. Use your finger to move the dot in the slider to the right to zoom in or to the left to zoom out on your subject.

8. When you have your image framed in the viewfinder, tap the shutter button (the camera-shaped icon) to snap a photo. You see an animation of a virtual shutter closing and then reopening on the screen, indicating the photo is being taken. At the same time, you hear an audio effect.

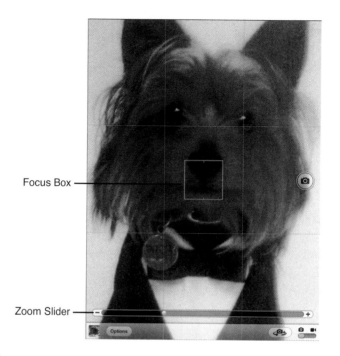

Focus Box

Zoom Slider

FIGURE 19.3

As you're framing an image, you can zoom in (or out) on your subject using the onscreen zoom slider. Use a pinch finger gesture on the screen to make this slider appear, and then move the slider to the right or left to increase or decrease the zoom level. A pinch or reverse-pinch finger motion can also be used for zooming in or out.

9. In a few seconds, the photo is saved on your device in the Camera Roll album of Photos. You can now shoot another photo or view the photo using the Photos app (or another photography-related app).

HOW TO SHOOT VIDEO

You also can easily shoot video from the Camera app. Follow these steps to shoot video on your iPad:

1. Launch the Camera app from the Home screen.

2. Make sure the Camera app is set to Video Mode. (Check the virtual switch displayed in the lower-right corner of the screen, and make sure the shutter button icon is circular and the screen shows a dim red dot.)

3. Choose which camera you want to use by tapping the camera selection icon. You can switch between the front- or rear-facing camera at any time.

4. Hold your iPad up to the subjects you want to capture on video. You can set up your shot by looking at what's displayed on the tablet's screen.

5. When you're ready to start shooting video, tap the shutter button icon (the red dot–shaped icon). The red dot gets brighter, which indicates you're now filming. Your iPad will capture whatever images you see on the screen as well as any sound in the area.

6. As you're filming video, you'll notice a timer displayed in the upper-right corner of the screen. Your only limit to how much video you can shoot is based on the amount of available memory in your iPad and how long the battery lasts. However, this app is designed more for shooting short video clips, not full-length home movies.

7. Also as you're filming, tap anywhere on the screen to focus in on your subject using the app's built-in autofocus sensor.

8. To stop filming, tap again on the red dot shutter icon. Your video footage will be saved. You can now view, edit, and share it from within the Photos app.

NOTE   The Photos app enables you to trim your video clips, as well as view and share the videos. If you want to edit your videos, plus add titles and special effects, you'll definitely want to purchase and use Apple's feature-packed iMovie app, which is available from the App Store ($4.99). For more information about iMovie, visit www.apple.com/ipad/from-the-app-store/imovie.html.

TIPS FOR SHOOTING EYE-CATCHING PHOTOS USING YOUR iPAD

Even though you're using a tablet to shoot photos, as opposed to a full-featured digital SLR or point-and-shoot digital camera from a company like Nikon or Canon, you can still use basic photo composition and framing techniques to snap professional-quality images.

To generate the best possible, in-focus, well-lit, and nicely framed images when shooting with your iPad, follow these basic shooting strategies (many of which also apply when shooting video):

■ Pay attention to your light source. As a general rule, the light source (such as the sun) should be behind you (the photographer) and shining onto your subject. When light from your primary light source shines directly into your camera's lens (in this case your iPad), you'll wind up with unwanted glare or an overexposed image.

■ As you look at the viewfinder screen, pay attention to shadows. Unwanted shadows can be caused by the sun or by an artificial light source. When shadows show up in your images, they can be distracting, so make sure they aren't covering your subjects.

■ Candid photos of people are great for showing emotion, spontaneity, or true life. The key to taking great candid photos is to have your camera ready to shoot and to be unobtrusive, so your subjects don't become self-conscious when they have a camera (your iPad) pointed at them. Try to anticipate when something interesting, surprising, funny, or that will generate a strong emotion will happen, and be ready to snap a photo. Also, don't get too close to your subject. You're better off being several feet away and using the zoom, so you as the photographer don't become a distraction.

■ As you get ready to tap the shutter icon and snap a photo, hold your iPad perfectly still. Even the slightest movement could result in a blurry image, especially in low-light situations.

■ Get to know the lag time of the Camera app. *Lag time* refers to the time between when you tap the shutter icon and when the image is taken and saved on your tablet. If you get used to this lag time, you can compensate for it and not miss time-sensitive shots (like your child shooting a basket or making a goal). Try to anticipate what's about to happen, especially if your subject is moving, and snap photos accordingly, knowing that perfect timing is essential.

■ When shooting portraits of people or specific objects, make sure you use the Camera app's autofocus sensor box to focus in on your subject. As you look through the viewfinder, tap the main subject's face, for example. This will ensure that the Camera app focuses in on the person and not something in the foreground, background, or to the side of your subject.

■ Your subject does not have to be looking directly into the camera to capture an interesting shot. Sometimes, a more thought-provoking image is created when your subject is looking slightly away from the camera. When shooting animals, however, you'll typically get the best shots by specifically focusing in on their eyes.

■ As you're framing your subjects in the viewfinder, pay attention to what's in the foreground, background, and to the sides of the subject. These objects can often be used to frame your subject and add a sense of multidimensionality to a photo. Just make sure the autofocus sensor of the Camera app focuses in on your intended subject, and not on something else in the photo, to ensure clarity.

> **TIP** When shooting a digital photo, hold the iPad as still as possible. This is also important when shooting video. However, when shooting video, if you choose to pan up, down, left or right, for example, use slow, fluid motions.

HOW TO USE THE RULE OF THIRDS WHEN SHOOTING

It's a common mistake for amateur photographers to hold their camera directly up to their subject, point it at the subject head-on, center the subject in the frame, and snap a photo. The result is always a generic-looking image, even if it's well lit and in perfect focus. Instead, as you look at the viewfinder screen to compose or frame your image, utilize the Rule of Thirds. This is a shooting strategy used by professional photographers, but it's very easy to take advantage of, and the results are impressive.

Imagine a tic-tac-toe grid being superimposed on your camera's viewfinder. Or, tap the Options icon when shooting with the Camera app and turn on the Grid feature. The center box in the tic-tac-toe grid corresponds to the center of the image you're about to shoot as you look at the viewfinder screen. Instead of framing your subject in this center box, reframe the image so your subject is positioned along one of the horizontal or vertical lines of the grid, or so the main focal point of the image is positioned at one of the grid's intersection points.

> **TIP** As you're shooting, instead of holding the camera head-on, directly facing your subject, try shooting from a different perspective, such as from slightly above, below, or to the side of your subject. This enables you to create more visually interesting images.

Using the Rule of Thirds when framing your images takes a bit of practice, but if you use this shooting technique consistently and correctly, you'll discover the quality of your images will vastly improve. Of course, you also want to take into account lighting, as well as what's in the foreground, background, and to the sides of your main subject. And be sure to tap your creativity when choosing your shooting angle or perspective for each shot.

> **TIP** When you're shooting a subject in motion, capture the subject moving into the frame, as opposed to moving out of it, while also taking into account the Rule of Thirds.

USING THE PHOTOS APP TO VIEW, EDIT, ENHANCE, PRINT, AND SHARE YOUR PHOTOS AND VIDEOS

After you shoot photos or import them into your iPad, to view, edit, enhance, print, or share those images, launch the Photos app from your iPad's Home screen. Alternatively, from the Camera app, tap the image thumbnail icon displayed in the lower-left corner of the main Camera app's screen.

VIEWING PHOTOS AND VIDEOS

The View Images screen on the iPad (shown in Figure 19.4) displays several viewing tabs at the top center of the screen labeled Photos, Photo Stream (if applicable), Albums, and Places.

FIGURE 19.4

When the Albums tab is selected, this screen of the Photos app displays thumbnails that represent each album that's stored on your tablet.

Tap the Photos tab to see thumbnails of all images currently stored on your tablet (shown in Figure 19.5), regardless of which album they're stored in. Use your finger to move up or down and scroll through your images.

When the Photos tab is active, the Slideshow and Share icons appear in the upper-right corner of the screen. Tap Slideshow to create a slideshow of your images and adjust specific settings, such as transition effects and what music will be played.

When viewing your image thumbnails by tapping the Photos tab, tap the Share icon in the upper-right corner of the screen to share, copy, move, or delete any of the images being displayed.

Photo Stream   Places

Photos   Albums

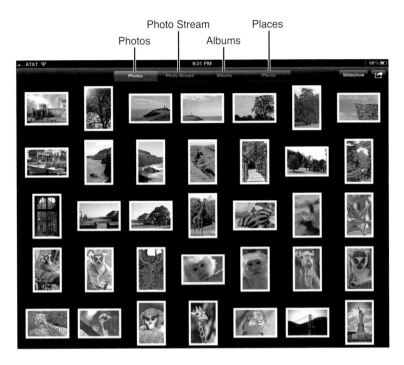

FIGURE 19.5

From the View Images screen, tap the Photos tab to view thumbnails of all images stored on your tablet in the Photos app.

When you tap the Share icon, the Select Items screen displays, again showing thumbnails of all images stored on your tablet. At this point, tap one or more image thumbnails to select them. Once selected, a thumbnail displays a checkmark icon near its lower-right corner.

In the upper-left corner of this screen, the other Share icon (this one displays the word Share) and a Copy icon are visible. Depending on the type of album, you might also see a red Delete icon here. In the upper-right corner of the screen, an Add To and Cancel icon appear.

Tap the Share icon to email or print the selected photos. Tap the Copy icon to move the selected images to another album, or tap the Delete icon (if applicable) to erase the selected images from your iPad altogether.

Tap the Add To icon to copy the selected images into a new album that you can create when prompted. Tapping the Cancel icon exits you out of this screen.

From the main View Images screen, tap the Albums tab (displayed at the top-center of the screen) to view thumbnails representing the individual albums that contain your photos. By default, all photos and videos shot using the Camera app are saved in the Camera Roll album. From this screen, tap any album thumbnail to reveal individual thumbnails of all images stored in that album.

> **TIP** To create a new album, from the main Album screen, tap the Edit icon that's displayed near the upper-right corner of the screen. Then, tap the New Album icon that appears near the top-left corner of the screen. When prompted, enter the album name when the New Album pop-up window appears. You can then copy or move photos into that new album using the Copy or Add To commands.

From the main View Images screen, tap the Places icon to see a map showcasing where images were shot. This geotagging feature works with all photos taken using your iPad (or another iOS device), or with images shot with a digital camera that has a geotagging feature. If none of the images stored on your iPad have geotagging associated with them, this Places feature is not displayed.

> **NOTE** In the Photos app, the thumbnails for video clips shot using the Camera app are also displayed. However, in the lower-left corner of a video clip's thumbnail is a movie camera icon, and the length of the video is displayed in the lower-right corner of the thumbnail, as shown in Figure 19.6.

Video Camera Icon   Video Time

FIGURE 19.6

The thumbnails for video clips stored in the Photos app look a bit different than those for photos. Video clips have a video camera icon in the lower-left corner and the length of the video displayed in the lower-right corner of its thumbnail.

VIEWING AN IMAGE IN FULL-SCREEN MODE

When viewing thumbnails of your images from the main View Images screen, tap any single image thumbnail to view a full-screen version of that image. As you're then viewing an image, tap it to make the various command icons for editing and sharing the image also appear on the screen (as shown in Figure 19.7).

FIGURE 19.7

When viewing an image in full-screen mode, tap anywhere on that image to reveal the command icons you'll use to edit, enhance, and share that image.

To exit out of the single-image view and return to the multi-image thumbnail view offered by the main View Images screen, tap the left-pointing arrow-shaped icon displayed in the upper-left corner of the screen. The word displayed in this icon is the album name in which the photo is stored, such as Camera Roll. If you were previously looking at the main View Images' Albums screen with the Albums tab selected, this icon will have the word Albums displayed in it.

As you're viewing a single image in full-screen mode, along the bottom of the screen will be a filmstrip depiction of all images stored in the current album, or all images stored on your iPad if you were previously using the Photos viewing mode. In the upper-right corner are command icons used for editing photos, viewing slideshows, sharing images, or deleting the image you're looking at in full-screen mode.

EDITING PHOTOS AND VIDEOS

After selecting a single image to view in full-screen mode, tap the Edit icon (displayed in the upper-right corner of the screen) to access the editing commands for photos.

TIP When you tap the thumbnail for a video clip, you'll have the option to play that clip in the Photos app. You also can tap anywhere on the screen (except for the Play icon) to access the video trimming (editing) feature, as well as the Share icon and the trash can icon (used to delete the video clip from your iPad).

To trim a video clip, look at the filmstrip display of the clip located at the top of the screen, and move the left or right editing tabs accordingly to define the portion of the clip you want to edit. The box around the filmstrip display turns yellow, and the Trim command icon appears on the right side of the screen. Before tapping on Trim, tap the Play icon to preview your newly edited video clip. If it's okay, tap the Trim icon to save your changes. Two additional command icons appear: Trim Original and Save As New Clip. Trim Original alters the original video clip and replaces the file, and Save As New Clip creates a separate file and keeps a copy of the original clip.

THE EDIT COMMANDS FOR PHOTOS

When you tap the Edit command icon when viewing a single image in full-screen mode, the following command icons appear near the bottom center of the screen. These icons provide the tools for quickly editing and enhancing your image.

- **Rotate:** Tap this icon once to rotate the image counterclockwise by 90 degrees. You can tap the Rotate icon up to three times before the image returns to its original orientation.

- **Enhance:** Tap the Enhance feature to instantly sharpen the photo and make the colors in it more vibrant. You should notice a dramatic improvement to the visual quality, lighting, detail, and sharpness of your image. This command impacts your entire photo. Using the Photos app, it is not possible to enhance just part of an image.

- **Red-Eye:** If the human subjects in your photo are exhibiting signs of red-eye as a result of using a flash, tap the Red-Eye icon to digitally remove this unwanted discoloration in your subjects' pupils.

- **Crop:** Tap this icon to crop the image and reposition your subject in the frame. If you forgot to incorporate the Rule of Thirds while shooting a photo, you can sometimes compensate by cropping a photo. You also can cut away unwanted background or zoom in on your subject based on how you crop it. When the crop grid appears, position your finger in any corner or side of the grid to determine how you'll crop the image. When you're finished, tap the Crop icon to confirm your changes.

TIP As you're cropping an image and moving around the cropping grid using your finger, first tap the Constrain tab to force you to keep the basic dimensions of your image intact but still use the crop feature. This enables you to make perfectly sized prints later, without throwing off the image dimensions.

- **Revert To Original:** Tapping this icon displayed near the top-left corner of the screen instantly removes your edits and returns the photo to its original appearance.

- **Undo:** The last edit you made to the image is undone, but any other edits remain intact.

- **Save:** After you've used the various editing commands to edit or enhance your image, tap the Save command to save your changes. It's located near the upper-right corner of the screen.

- **Cancel:** Exit out of the photo editing mode of the Photos app without making any changes to the photo you're viewing. You can find this icon near the top-left corner of the screen.

PRINTING PHOTOS

iOS 5.1 is fully compatible with Apple's AirPrint feature. So, if you have a photo printer set up to work wirelessly with your iPad, you can create photo prints from your digital images using the Print command in the Photos app. Follow these steps to print an image:

1. Launch the Photos app from the Home screen or by tapping the photo thumbnail in the Camera app.

2. From the main View Images screen, tap any thumbnail to view an image in full-screen mode. (You might need to open an album first by tapping the album's thumbnail if you have the Albums viewing option selected.)

3. Tap the full-screen version of the image to make the various command icons appear.

4. Tap the Share icon that's displayed in the upper-right corner of the screen.

5. From the Share menu, select the Print option.

6. When the Printer Options submenu appears, select your printer, determine how many copies of the print you'd like to create, and then tap the Print icon.

> **TIP** To print wirelessly from your iPad using the AirPrint feature, you must have a compatible printer. To learn more about AirPrint, and to configure your printer for wireless printing from your iPad, refer to Chapter 8, "Wireless Printing and Scanning via Your iPad," or visit http://support.apple.com/kb/HT4356.

SHARING PHOTOS AND VIDEOS

The Photos app offers several ways to show off and share your favorite digital images. As you're looking at a photo in full-screen mode on the iPad, tap the Slideshow icon to create a slideshow of your images and view it on your iPad screen. Using optional cables, you also can connect your tablet to an HD television set or monitor to display your slideshow, or connect it to your home theatre system wirelessly via Apple TV.

EMAILING PHOTOS

Tap the Email Photo option to send one to five images to one or more recipients via email from within the Photos app. When viewing a single image, tap the Share button, followed by the Email Photo option. A compose email screen appears with that photo already attached to the body of the email. Use the virtual keyboard to fill in the To and Subject fields, as shown in Figure 19.8, and then tap the Send icon.

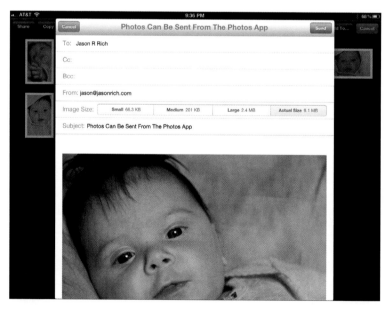

FIGURE 19.8

You can send an email with one to five photos attached to it from within the Photos app.

To send one to five photos in a single email message, follow these steps:

1. Launch the Photos app.

2. From the main View Images screen, tap the Photos tab.

3. Tap the Share icon that's displayed in the upper-right corner of the screen.

4. Using your finger, tap one to five image thumbnails to select the images you want to include in an email. As you select each image from the Select Items screen, a checkmark icon appears in the lower-right corner of each thumbnail.

5. After you've selected the images, tap the other Share icon. It displays the word Share in it and can be found near the upper-left corner of the screen. If the Share icon is not active, you might have inadvertently selected more than five images to include in the email.

6. Tap the Email option that appears.

7. When the compose email screen is displayed, your selected photos are already attached (embedded within) the outgoing email message. Simply fill in the To field with the email addresses for your intended recipients, and then fill in the Subject field using the virtual keyboard.

8. Tap the Send icon to send the email containing your images.

ASSIGNING A PHOTO TO A CONTACT

Follow these steps to link an image stored in the Photos app to a specific contact in the Contacts app:

1. From within the Photos app, select a single photo and view it in full-screen mode.

2. Tap the image to make the various command icons appear.

3. Tap the Share icon.

4. Tap the Assign To Contact option.

5. An All Contacts window, displaying the names associated with all of your contacts, appears. Scroll through the listing, or use the Search field to find the specific entry with which you want to associate the photo.

6. Tap on that person or company's name from the All Contacts listing.

7. When the Choose Photo window opens, use your finger to move or scale the image. What you see in the box is what will be saved.

8. Tap the Use icon in the upper-right corner of the Choose Photo window to save the photo and link it to the selected contact.

9. When you launch Contacts and access that person's entry (shown in Figure 19.9), you will see the photo you selected appear in that entry.

FIGURE 19.9

If you use the Contacts app to manage your contacts database, you can attach a photo to each contact entry.

TWEETING A PHOTO

As you know, Twitter functionality has been integrated into several popular iPad apps, enabling you to compose and send tweets from within those apps. Photos is one of the apps that integrates with Twitter, enabling you to select a photo and tweet it to your followers, along with an accompanying text-based message.

After tapping the Share icon while viewing a single photo in full-screen mode, select the Tweet option. Compose your tweet message (which will already have the selected image attached), and then tap the Send icon.

COPYING A PHOTO

From within the Photos app, you can store a photo in your iPad's virtual clipboard, and then paste that photo into another compatible app, such as Pages, Numbers, or Keynote. Follow these steps to copy a photo into your device's virtual clipboard:

1. From within the Photos app, select a single photo and view it in full-screen mode.

2. Tap the image while in full-screen mode to make the various command icons appear.

3. Tap the Share icon.

4. Tap the Copy Photo option. It is now stored in the virtual clipboard.

5. Launch a compatible app, such as Pages, and hold your finger down on the screen to use the Paste option and paste your photo from the clipboard into the active app.

DELETING PHOTOS STORED ON YOUR iPAD

To delete photos stored in the Photos app on the iPad, access the main View Images screen, and tap the Photos tab. Next, tap the Share icon. When the Select Items screen appears (shown in Figure 19.10), tap your finger to select one or more images. After the images are selected, tap the red-and-white Remove button that's displayed in the upper-left corner of the Select Items screen.

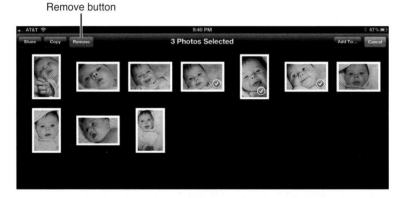

FIGURE 19.10

From the Select Items screen, you can select image thumbnails and then tap the Remove button to erase those images from your iOS device.

NOTE Although you can delete entire albums from your iPad, you cannot delete individual photos from the Photos app unless they were actually taken using the tablet. If you transferred (synced) images from your computer, for example, those images must be deselected during the syncing process.

WORKING WITH iCLOUD'S PHOTO STREAM IN THE PHOTOS APP

If you have your iPad set up to work with iCloud, the Photo Stream feature is turned on, and your tablet is connected to a Wi-Fi Internet connection, you'll discover the Photo Stream tab displayed along the top center of the main Photos screen. The iCloud Photo Stream feature automatically stores, syncs, and displays up to 1,000 of the most recently shot or imported digital photos from iPhoto '11 on your primary computer, your iPhone, and your iPad.

> **NOTE** A Photo Stream can include up to 1,000 images and store them for up to 30 days online. By default, this is the most recent 1,000 you shoot or transfer to your Photo Stream. However, you can manually edit the collection of images that are part of your Photo Stream. Beyond the 1,000 images stored on iCloud (or after the 30 days), all your digital images are automatically backed up and stored on your primary computer's hard drive (or on a hard drive connected to your primary computer).

When viewing the Photo Stream on your iPad from within the Photos app, thumbnails representing the images are displayed. To view these images as a slideshow, tap the Slideshow icon. To share, copy, or delete any of the Photo Stream images, tap the Share icon. After you tap the Share icon, a new Share icon, along with Copy and Delete icons, appear near the upper-left corner of the screen. Tap one or more image thumbnails to select them, and then choose which Share command you'd like to utilize.

> **NOTE** When you delete photos from your Photo Stream, not only are the images deleted from your iPad, they also are erased from the Photo Stream stored on iCloud and on the Photo Stream you can view from your primary computer and/or iPhone that's linked to the same iCloud account.

Unlike other images stored in albums, photos viewable from your Photo Stream are not permanently stored on your iPad. To move one or more images from the Photo Stream to an album, tap the Share icon, tap the thumbnails for the images you want to store on your tablet, and then tap the Save icon that's displayed near the upper-right corner of the screen.

To create and use the Photo Stream feature of iCloud, you must set up a free iCloud account, have the latest version of OS X Lion or OS X Mountain Lion installed on your Mac, and have the most current version of iTunes. In addition, you must update your iPhoto '11 software on your Mac with the latest version (iPhoto '11 version 9.2 or later).

TIP   To utilize iCloud's Photo Stream feature, from the Settings app on your iPad, tap the Photos option listed under the main Settings menu. Then, turn on the Photo Stream option from the Photos menu screen. To utilize this feature and be able to upload and download photos to and from your iOS devices, a Wi-Fi Internet connection is required.

NOTE   If you're a Windows PC user, you can install the iCloud Control Panel on your computer and use it to transfer photos to and from your Photo Stream. To download this free Windows software from Apple's website, visit http://support.apple.com/kb/DL1455.

UPGRADING TO APPLE'S iPHOTO APP

If you want photo organization, editing, viewing, and sharing options that are beyond what the free Photos app is capable of, visit the App Store and purchase a copy of Apple's iPhoto app ($4.99). Not only does the iOS version of iPhoto offer similar functionality to iPhoto '11 for the Mac, it includes a handful of new features, such as Journals and Smart Browsing, plus it makes syncing or transferring images between iOS devices, Macs, and iCloud's Photo Stream a straightforward process.

ORGANIZING YOUR IMAGES FROM THE iPHOTO ALBUMS SCREEN

When you launch iPhoto, the first thing you see is the Albums screen. Displayed at the top center of this screen (shown in Figure 19.11) are multiple command tabs that enable you to decide how you want to view your images. Tap Albums to view thumbnails for each album stored within iPhoto, and then tap on any album thumbnail to view the images within that album and start working with them.

Tapping the Photos option from the Album screen displays a complete collection of thumbnails representing all images stored on your tablet on a single (scrollable) screen. From this screen, tap any thumbnail to begin working with an image.

FIGURE 19.11

The Albums screen of iPhoto automatically sorts your images into albums.

Any time you import new photos from your PC or Mac using iTunes, or use the iPad Camera Connection Kit, new events are created and viewable by tapping the Events tab. Or, you can organize your edited photos into visually stunning journals, and then view and share those journals by tapping the Journals command tab.

VIEWING INDIVIDUAL PHOTOS USING iPHOTO

From the Albums, Photos, or Events screens, tap any image thumbnail to view that image and start working with it using the photo editing and enhancement tools built in to iPhoto, as shown in Figure 19.12.

Along the top of iPhoto's Editing screen are a series of command icons and menu options. The main area of the Editing screen is where you'll view one image at a time. At any time, press the question mark icon to get onscreen help using the applicable features or functions within iPhoto.

As you're editing a photo, you can zoom in on a specific area of the image using a reverse-pinch motion with your thumb and index finger, or double-tap the area of the photo that you want to zoom in on.

Whenever you're viewing a selected image, by tapping the Edit icon that's displayed in the upper-right corner of the screen you can access an extensive collection of photo editing and enhancement tools, each of which is represented by an icon that's displayed along the bottom of the screen.

FIGURE 19.12

View an image, and then use iPhoto's editing tools to edit and enhance it.

The Effects icon (displayed to the right of the paintbrush icon), for example, gives you instant access to a handful of special effects sorted by categories, such as Artistic, Vintage, Aura, Black & White, Duotone, and Warm & Cool. Tap any of the effects bars to reveal a collection of special effects that you can add to an entire photo with a single tap on the screen. You can easily mix and match special effects to create a truly artistic or visually stunning image.

Located near the bottom center of the Editing screen are five additional command icons that give you easy access to a handful of other photo enhancement and editing tools. Tap the magic wand icon to auto-enhance an entire image with a single tap, or tap the Rotate icon to rotate an image clockwise by 90 degrees. You can tap this icon multiple times, as needed.

> **TIP** Another way to rotate an image is to use your thumb and index finger on the touch screen to perform a circular gesture.

One other way you can gather your favorite images for easy viewing, sharing, and editing, for example, is to separate them by tapping the Favorites icon (which looks like an award ribbon) for each of them. This stores those images in a separate Event.

When you're finished editing a single image, tap the Edit icon again to automatically save your changes and view the image in its newly edited form. While in single image viewing mode, swipe your finger from right to left or left to right to scroll through the images stored in the same album or event folder.

PRINTING AND SHARING IMAGES USING iPHOTO

From the photo viewing screen, tap the Share icon (displayed near the upper-right corner of the screen) to reveal the app's extensive Share menu. From here, you can transfer an image to a journal, the Camera Roll, or iTunes, or you can post the photo online via Twitter, Facebook, or Flickr. If your iPad is connected to the same wireless network as another Mac or iOS device, you can wirelessly beam the image to that computer or device, or email photos from within the app.

CREATING AND SHOWING OFF JOURNALS

Think of a journal as a digital collage feature with a personalized theme. After selecting a collection of photos to be included in a journal, select the Journal option. Start by adding an original title to your journal, and then choose a theme.

iPhoto offers six different journal themes: Cotton, Border, Denim, Light, Dark, and Mosaic. After choosing your theme, tap the Create Journal command icon. The app automatically creates the journal, which takes anywhere from a few seconds to several minutes, depending on how many photos are being included.

When the basic journal has been formatted (see Figure 19.13), you can personalize it by moving around photos, resizing images, adding captions, including maps, displaying dates, or even showing the current weather when the image was taken (if it was shot using an iPhone or iPad).

Just like individual photos, journals can be viewed on the iPad's screen, published online, or shared via email. As you're viewing a journal, tap a single image to view it in full-screen mode, and then you can switch back to the Journal view.

FIGURE 19.13
The Journals feature of iPhoto offers a new and fun way to showcase and share a handful of images.

iPHOTO OFFERS MANY PHOTO-RELATED TOOLS IN A SINGLE APP

The iPhoto app is truly a one-stop shop for handling all your digital photography needs from virtually anywhere. The app works flawlessly with images shot on your iPhone or iPad using the Camera app (or a compatible app), as well as with images imported into your iPad from other sources, including your digital camera. What's great about iPhoto is that it offers an extremely powerful collection of tools, yet the app itself is very intuitive. (However, onscreen help is always just a screen tap away.) Even if you don't think of yourself as a skilled photographer, using this app, you can easily enhance all your digital images to dramatically improve their visual appeal.

UTILIZE POWERFUL PHOTO EDITING CAPABILITIES WITH THIRD-PARTY PHOTOGRAPHY APPS

If you want even more powerful photo editing tools available to you from your iPad, check out one or more of the third-party photography apps available from the App Store. The following is a small sampling of some iPad photography apps that offer some really useful editing features.

CAMERABAG

CameraBag ($1.99) enables you to bypass the Camera app and shoot digital images from directly within this app. You can then preview your images and add any of 14 special effects or filters to them. It's also possible to load images into the CameraBag app that were shot using the Camera app or transferred into your iPad.

Each effect available from CameraBag dramatically alters the appearance of your image in seconds. For example, you can quickly make a photo look like it was shot using a 35mm camera in 1962 or 1972, or add an effect that automatically enhances or alters the colors of an image.

After you shoot an image and add your favorite effects, it is saved to the Camera Roll album. You also can email it from within the app. CameraBag is easy to use and is great for adding effects to photos before sharing them on Facebook or Twitter, for example.

PHOTOGENE

This app offers some of the same functionality offered by Photoshop Elements for the Mac or PC, for example, but enables you to do professional-level editing on your tablet's screen. Priced at just $2.99, this app is a bargain considering the photo editing and enhancement features it offers. In addition to serving as a photo editing tool, Photogene can replace the Photos app for viewing and organizing your images and albums. In addition to cropping, rotating, adjusting, retouching, and enhancing images, you can add text-based captions, frames, border effects, and other visual enhancements to your photos.

> **NOTE** Photogene is for photo editing, but it also enables you to add special effects or filters to your images before you share them.

For example, this app offers 11 different image filters that you can use to alter an image with a single tap on the screen: Dream, Painting, Comics, Posterize, Charcoal, Night Vision, Rainbow, Sepia, Smooth, Pixelate, and Pencil.

Using the Retouches tool, you can fix blemishes on the face of someone in a portrait or remove an unwanted object from a photo. You also can adjust the colors and white balance of a shot using a series of finger-controlled sliders.

SNAPSEED

This advanced photo editing tool is easy to use but enables you to quickly incorporate a handful of professional-quality visual effects to your digital photos. You can also crop images, transform them into black and white, add frames and borders, or manually adjust the focus of an image after it has been shot.

The majority of effects can be controlled by sliding your finger around on the screen using an intuitive proprietary interface. The visual effects you can create, however, go from subtle enhancements to extremely dramatic alterations to an image. One set of filters and effects tools in this app enable you to transform a modern-day, full-color image into one that looks like it was shot using an old-fashioned camera. Or, you can bring out the natural colors in an image using what Snapseed refers to as "Drama" enhancement tools.

PHOTOSHOP TOUCH (PSTOUCH)

Developed by Adobe, which is a pioneer in creating digital photo–editing software for Macs and PCs, including Photoshop and Photoshop Elements, this iPad-specific version of Photoshop, called PSTouch ($9.99), offers advanced photo-editing capabilities on the tablet's screen. Unlike many photo-editing apps, this one enables you to edit or enhance parts of an image, as opposed to an entire image. Plus, you can perform advanced editing tasks, such as adding special effects, replacing colors, adding digital frames to images, adding text to photos, or cleaning up backgrounds.

Using PSTouch requires a bit of a learning curve, but you can create professional-quality results using the powerful and unique editing tools built in to this cutting-edge app.

Index

D

E

F

I

U

V

W

X

Y

Z

Try Safari Books Online FREE for 15 days

Get online access to Thousands of Books and Videos

Feed your brain

Gain unlimited access to thousands of books and videos about technology, digital media and professional development from O'Reilly Media, Addison-Wesley, Microsoft Press, Cisco Press, McGraw Hill, Wiley, WROX, Prentice Hall, Que, Sams, Apress, Adobe Press and other top publishers.

See it, believe it

Watch hundreds of expert-led instructional videos on today's hottest topics.

WAIT, THERE'S MORE!

Gain a competitive edge

Be first to learn about the newest technologies and subjects with Rough Cuts pre-published manuscripts and new technology overviews in Short Cuts.

Accelerate your project

Copy and paste code, create smart searches that let you know when new books about your favorite topics are available, and customize your library with favorites, highlights, tags, notes, mash-ups and more.

Addison-Wesley · Adobe Press · ALPHA · Cisco Press · FT Press · IBM Press · Microsoft · New Riders · O'REILLY

Peachpit Press · PRENTICE HALL · Que · Redbooks · SAMS · SAS Publishing · WILEY · WROX

FREE
Online Edition

Safari Books Online

Your purchase of *Your iPad at Work* includes access to a free online edition for 45 days through the **Safari Books Online** subscription service. Nearly every Que book is available online through **Safari Books Online**, along with thousands of books and videos from publishers such as Addison-Wesley Professional, Cisco Press, Exam Cram, IBM Press, O'Reilly Media, Prentice Hall, Sams, and VMware Press.

Safari Books Online is a digital library providing searchable, on-demand access to thousands of technology, digital media, and professional development books and videos from leading publishers. With one monthly or yearly subscription price, you get unlimited access to learning tools and information on topics including mobile app and software development, tips and tricks on using your favorite gadgets, networking, project management, graphic design, and much more.

Activate your FREE Online Edition at
informit.com/safarifree

STEP 1: Enter the coupon code: RXEIEBI.

STEP 2: New Safari users, complete the brief registration form. Safari subscribers, just log in.

If you have difficulty registering on Safari or accessing the online edition, please e-mail customer-service@safaribooksonline.com